To My Father
For giving me his time, his help and his wisdom
To My Mother
For giving me my health and my education
And to Anne
My wife and my best friend

NOW PITCHING
BOB FELLER

by Bob Feller
with Bill Gilbert

CITADEL PRESS
Kensington Publishing Corp.
www.kensingtonbooks.com

CITADEL PRESS BOOKS are published by

Kensington Publishing Corp.
850 Third Avenue
New York, NY 10022

All Kensington titles, imprints, and distributed lines are available at special
quantity discounts for bulk purchases for sales promotions, premiums,
fund-raising, educational, or institutional use. Special book excerpts or
customized printings can also be created to fit specific needs. For details,
write or phone the office of the Kensington special sales manager:
Kensington Publishing Corp., 850 Third Avenue, New York, NY 10022,
attn: Special Sales Department, phone 1-800-221-2647.

First Citadel printing: May 2002

10   9   8   7   6   5   4   3   2

Printed in the United States of America

Library of Congress Control Number: 2001099897

ISBN 0-8065-2362-X

Contents

THE REST OF THE TEAM

Playing baseball takes a team effort, and so does writing a book. That's why we want to devote this space to expressing our gratitude to the other members of our team.

We are grateful to our editor at Birch Lane Press, Sandy Richardson, and to our agent at the Scott Meredith Literary Agency, Russell Galen, who was promoted to Vice President while we were writing this book, which may or may not be related.

The friendly and cooperative professional staff of the National Baseball Library in Cooperstown, New York, was a great help on this book, as always, especially Bill Deane, the Library's Senior Research Associate, and Pat Kelly, the Photo Collection Manager.

Special thanks are also due to Anne Feller, Dave Gilbert and Lillian Gilbert for their editorial assistance, and to Ed Liberatore, who never stopped encouraging us to write this book.

Bob Feller and Bill Gilbert

Introduction

In the 1930s Van Meter, Iowa had about 300 residents and no traffic lights and was a good place to grow up listening to a Des Moines sportscaster named Dutch Reagan and watching trains rumble west carrying beams from Indiana steel mills, the beams bearing banners proclaiming their destination: "The Golden Gate Bridge, San Francisco." One Van Meter boy was bound for glory and got a fistful of it on Chicago's south side.

Correct thinkers think that "baseball trivia" is an oxymoron: Nothing about baseball is trivial. But connoisseurs of, shall we say, arcana adore this question: Name the occasion when every player on a major league team had precisely the same batting average before and after a game. It was April 14, 1940, when Bob Feller of the Cleveland Indians pitched a no-hitter against the White Sox on opening day. All the White Sox were batting .000 before and after the game.

Feller, a baseball prodigy, was a major leaguer before he was old enough to shave, the only major leaguer who returned to his hotel to do high school homework. On July 6, 1936, after his junior year and four months before his 18th birthday, he pitched for the Indians in an exhibition against the St. Louis Cardinals. His first pitch was a called strike. The batter turned to the catcher and said, "Let me out of here in one piece." The batter had just seen—sort of—the fastball that later would cause a batter (Hall of Fame wit and pitcher Lefty Gómez) to say, after taking a called third strike with his bat on his shoulder. "That one sounded a little low."

In September of 1936, before returning to high school for his senior year, the 17-year-old "phenom" broke the American league single-game record and tied Dizzy Dean's major league record by striking out 17 Philadelphia Athletics, thereby becoming the only pitcher ever to achieve as many strikeouts in a game as he was years old. This and the rest of Feller's career, recounted in this memoir, illustrate the axiom, "As the twig is bent . . ."

In the movie, *Field of Dreams* (and the novel on which it is based, W. P. Kinsella's *Shoeless Joe*), an Iowa farmer and baseball fanatic hears a voice from the sky say, "Build it and they will come." The farmer inexplicably but correctly intuits this message to mean that if he builds a ballpark, Shoeless Joe Jackson will return from the dead.

The farmer does, and Joe does, saying, "This must be heaven." The farmer says, "No. It's Iowa."

No, *this* is Iowa: Bob Feller's father, a farmer, built his son a ballpark—felled treed, leveled a pasture, erected bleachers. He even switched other fields from corn to wheat because wheat took less time to harvest, leaving more time for baseball.

(Fathers. In Commerce, Oklahoma, at dusk after days in the zinc mines, a father makes a switch-hitter of the boy he named after his hero, Tigers catcher Mickey Cochrane. The father is Mutt Mantle.)

Feller, with Ted Williams and Joe DiMaggio (they were 20, 21, and 24 respectively in 1939) were baseball's golden trio on the eve of the war that was to consume what could have been their most productive years. After Pearl Harbor, Feller immediately enlisted in the navy, chafed under a stateside assignment with a physical fitness program, then became chief of an antiaircraft gun crew on the battleship USS *Alabama,* which had a population about ten times that of Van Meter. In two years, the *Alabama* steamed 175,000 miles and won eight battle stars for participating in eight Pacific landings.

Feller won 100 games at a younger age than anyone else ever has. He had 108 wins when he enlisted, at an age when Cy Young, baseball's winningest pitcher (511) had won none, and Walter Johnson, the second-winningest (417) had just 57. The war probably cost Feller at least 100 wins. Even so, he had more "low hit" games than anyone until passed by the Rangers' Nolan Ryan (16—five no-hitters and 11 one-hitters). Ryan has had 192 more starts than Feller had.

What is he proudest of? Probably having been on his ship off Saipan when U.S. forces shot down 400 enemy aircraft. And he has something else to treasure. Ted Williams, baseball's best pure hitter, ever, said of Feller:

"That was the test. Three days before he pitched, I would start thinking about Robert Feller, Bob Feller. I would sit in my room thinking and seeing him, thinking about him all the time. . . . Allie Reynolds of the Yankees was tough, and I might think of him for about two hours before a game, but Robert Feller, I'd think about him for three days."

That is a compliment as elegant as Williams' swing.

—George Will

AUTHOR'S NOTE

This book tells the story of one of the greatest pitchers in the history of baseball. It talks about the life he has led both on the field and off—as a sports hero to millions and as a hero in World War II, though he prefers not be thought of as a war hero. It is his own salute to the sport he loves and all that it means to him.

The book delves into some of the issues in baseball over the years, subjects that Bob became involved in during his career. He was one of the leaders in the second half of the 1940s in building support for a players' association, along with Johnny Murphy, Allie Reynolds, Dom DiMaggio, and others. He was one of the founders of the Major League Baseball Players Association in 1954, along with such others as Stan Musial, Robin Roberts, Ralph Kiner, Eddie Yost, and players from all the teams.

Since this book was published in hardcover in 1990, the issues Bob Feller discussed have not changed. As Sandy Koufax once said, "Baseball hasn't changed—only the money has." Relations between labor and management still result in disputes and even strikes, salaries continue to escalate, and questions about moving teams or even eliminating them cause other problems between players and the owners of their teams. Thus, while readers may be surprised at the dollar figures that existed when this book was written, so low they seem like amounts from the distant past, they will understand that the issues involved remain the same.

Likewise, Bob's love of baseball and Bob Feller himself haven't changed, and for that we—and baseball—can be grateful.

—Bill Gilbert,
Christmas, 2001

NOW PITCHING
BOB FELLER

Thank you for your support.
With best wishes,

Bob Feller

CHAPTER ONE
The Iowa Farm Boy vs.
"The Gas House Gang"

It has always seemed such a natural marriage—baseball and me. I've been pitching at every age, as a major league rookie who broke in when Joe DiMaggio did, 1936, when I was 17, to today as a 71-year-old still pitching in Old Timers Games. From the day Dad gave me a real baseball uniform from a mail order house in Chicago back in 1928, I've never wanted to do anything else, whether I was seven or 70 or in between.

You have to love baseball to play as much of it as I always have. Imagine pitching over 300 innings a year for the Cleveland Indians and then between three and seven innings every day on a barnstorming tour of 35 cities in 30 days after the major league season ended, plus 25 or 30 innings in spring training. Imagine logging over 500 innings a year that way.

Imagine yourself in your 71st year of life and your 54th year of baseball, pitching almost 100 innings that summer, more than 50 years after some baseball people and writers said you would ruin your arm because you're pitching too much.

Through all those balls and strikes, imagine pitching against your boyhood heroes like Lou Gehrig and Rogers Hornsby and having Babe Ruth hold your bat in that classic picture as he says farewell at Yankee Stadium in 1948.

Imagine yourself embroiled in one of the most controversial plays in the history of the World Series, or being called a hero in 1941 because you joined the Navy two days after the United States entered World War II and a villain in 1947 because you were injured and had to pass up the All-Star Game. Imagine being blessed enough to have a Hall of Fame career, but never realizing your lifelong dream of winning a game in the World Series.

Imagine being lucky enough to win 266 games and pitch three no-hitters and 12 one-hitters while playing with and against the greatest stars of your time—DiMag, Ted Williams, Hank Greenberg, Joe Cronin, Jimmie Foxx, Larry Doby, Lou Boudreau, and so many others whose names will be showing up on these pages. And imagine playing with the real characters of the game—Satchel Paige with his warnings never to look back because there's a man back there and he might be gaining on you, Rollickin' Rollie Hemsley and his alcohol-inspired Superman feats like tip-toeing along hotel ledges ten floors above downtown streets, Bill Veeck and his Barnum-like genius for attracting people to his show, and the first major league hitter I ever struck out, Leo "The Lip" Durocher.

If you can't imagine being lucky enough to be a starting pitcher in the majors while on high school vacation and being allowed to live a life that had all this and much more, I can't either. But I have. And before I forget too much of it or the computers do all of our remembering for us, I want to share all of this with you and preserve it for some baseball historian somewhere—the memories of what baseball was like in the 1930s, '40s and '50s and what we were like too—the men who played the game and the people who watched us.

Maybe a pitcher's first strikeout is like your first kiss—they say you never forget it. My first strikeout as a major league pitcher was in an exhibition game against the St. Louis Cardinals on July 6, 1936, four months before my 18th birthday and less than one month after finishing my junior year at Van Meter High School in Iowa.

Over 12,000 fans came to Cleveland's old League Park, even though it was an exhibition game. The score was 1–1 when our manager, Steve O'Neill, waved me in from the bullpen to start the fourth inning. As a quiet kid who wasn't even shaving yet, I was facing a bunch of grizzly, hell-raising veterans on the famous "Gas House Gang" team that included Dizzy Dean, Pepper Martin, Ducky Medwick, Johnny Mize, Rip Collins and their fiery manager, Frankie Frisch, "The Fordham Flash."

The Cardinals in those years, in fact the Cardinals in most years, were one of the best examples of the greater emphasis on team play compared to today. The Brooklyn Dodgers of the 1940s and '50s and our own Indians of that same period were two other excellent examples of the "team attitude" which you and your teammates displayed and which management encouraged.

The Cardinals had some great talent, and they also had players who were completely willing to give themselves up by bunting their teammate from second to third, even though they knew they'd get charged with a time at bat without a hit. They were willing to hit the ball on the ground to the right side to advance their teammate to third, again knowing they would be thrown out and charged with another time at bat without a hit—but their teammate would be on third with only one out and able to score after a fly ball and get the Cards another run.

They had hitters willing to punch the ball to the opposite field for a hit to start a rally in the late innings, instead of trying to knock it out of the park just because "singles hitters drive Fords—home run hitters drive Cadillacs." They had base runners willing to make it difficult for the opposing second baseman to turn a forceout at second into a double play, and starting pitchers willing to come into a game in relief if their team needed them.

You have individual players today with those same team values, but how many teams as a whole play the game that way? Some of them claim to have "a good team attitude," but you have to wonder. The 1979 Pittsburgh Pirates talked a lot about "family." When they won the National League pennant and then defeated the Baltimore Orioles in the World Series, there was so much talk along those lines that the Pirates became the most famous "family" since the Kennedys. But when they took the annual team picture that year, their two biggest stars refused to be included because it might represent a conflict between the sponsor of the photo and some of the sponsors they represented. So much for that "family."

The St. Louis Cardinals of 1936 never talked about "family"—they just played like one. I knew all about them. Dad and I saw them in the 1934 World Series, and we could pull in the Cubs games on our radio back home on the farm, especially if we put the headsets in a metal dishpan on the living room table to amplify the sound. We strung copper wiring in the trees and the barn to pick up the signal. We couldn't listen to any of the games during the week—this was before night baseball—because I was either in school or doing my chores, but on Sunday, Dad and I would sit in the living room in the afternoon if we weren't playing catch, and listen to the Cubs and their announcer, Bob Elson. Later, a sportscaster came to WHO in Des Moines and did re-creations of the Cubs games. His name was Ronald Reagan.

Since the Cards were a National League team, I knew about them from those Cubs broadcasts and from one of my biggest treats as a kid, a trip to the 1934 World Series in St. Louis when the Cardinals defeated the Detroit Tigers in seven games. I was only 15, but I remember thinking to myself while I sat there in Sportsman's Park, "I can do that." I told Dad the same thing on our drive back home, and he didn't jump on me for sounding cocky. He said he agreed with me, that I had the ability to make it in the big leagues.

I remember something else from that Series—the sight of Dizzy Dean getting hit right between the eyes going into second base to break up a double play. He made the mistake of going in standing up, and Bill Rogell wasn't going to use valuable time to get out of his way. He did exactly what the pivot man should do in that case. He stood his ground and made his throw.

Dizzy was examined at the hospital, and the announcement was made: "X-rays of Dizzy Dean's head showed nothing." This was 25 years before the same story went around about Yogi Berra.

Now it was less than two years later, and I was pitching against those same stars I saw in the World Series. Scared? Never. Not in my entire pitching career was I ever scared of any hitter or any situation. That's a luxury you can't afford if you're going to make it as a pitcher. Challenges and crises are what pitching is. If that's a problem for you, then you'd better take up another line of work.

It also doesn't hurt for a pitcher to have a mean streak in him or at least an attitude that sometimes borders on defiance. It may sound melodramatic, like a line from a B movie, but it's true that the hitter is up there trying to take bread out of your mouth so he'll have some for his. You simply can't let him do that to you, and to your teammates.

That doesn't mean you have to be dirty about it. You don't have to hit batters intentionally and otherwise be a dirty player, but you sure as heck have to be tough out there or the hitter will have you right where he wants you. Pitching is like hitting in that respect—you have to believe you can do it. You have to have the talent, but if you're out there with any question in your mind at all about your ability to win and your ability to defeat every single hitter who stands up there as a threat against you, then you're going to be a failure.

I wasn't about to let that happen to me. As I stood out there on the mound, I knew I was on the verge of achieving something that dreams are made of, and I was determined in my own high school student's mind not to let the St. Louis Cardinals or anybody else keep me from becoming a successful major league pitcher.

That was my attitude as I prepared to pitch to the first major league hitter of my life, Brusie Ogrodowski, the Cards' backup catcher, in the fourth inning. You've never heard of him because he couldn't hit much, so he played only that year and the next. But there he was, the first man I faced in the majors, even if it was an exhibition game.

O'Neill did a smart thing. Frankie Pytlak, Joe Becker and Billy Sullivan were our catchers that year, but O'Neill put himself behind the plate when I came into the game. He wanted to handle me himself, with his 17 years of experience as a big league catcher. He hadn't played in eight seasons, but he wanted to give me his personal treatment because he thought I had the potential to make it big.

I knew my fast ball always had an intimidating effect on hitters, but that was in amateur ball. I was about to find out what the major leaguers thought of it, and of me.

My first pitch to Ogrodowski was a called strike, and it made that smacking sound as it hit O'Neill's mitt, the sound that is so sweet to a pitcher and his catcher. Ogrodowski turned to O'Neill and said, "Let me out of here in one piece."

He was serious. He laid the next pitch down, bunting down the third base line to Sammy Hale. He was an easy out, but he achieved his purpose—he got out of there in one piece.

That brought up Durocher. He was a shortstop in the majors for 17 years and he was having an excellent season. He led the National League in fielding that year and hit a respectable .286. In addition to his ability, he was an intimidator. He broke in with the Yankees in 1925, and the stories started going around both leagues in a hurry about this brash kid who quickly took on Babe Ruth and Ty Cobb in separate confrontations. He never backed down from anybody, and he wasn't above starting a nice little riot every now and then if it helped his cause. Leo and I are close friends today, but in 1936, we were strangers and opponents.

I was still throwing nothing but fast balls, and each one seemed faster than the one before. One of them sailed over Durocher's head, one went behind his back, and Cal Hubbard, the umpire, called two others strikes. I was wild, which was frequently the case in my early years, and I had a big windmill windup and a habit of glancing into left field and then flashing my eyes past third base as I turned toward the plate. It scared the hitters even more.

I had Leo's attention. I was the intimida*tor*, and he was the intimida*tee*. After one of my pitches, he stepped out of the batter's box, turned toward Hubbard and said, "I feel like a clay pigeon in a shooting gallery."

After the second strike, with the count two and two, Durocher bolted into the Cardinals' dugout and pretended to hide behind the water cooler. Hubbard, a giant of a man who had starred in pro football before becoming an umpire, lumbered over toward the dugout and ordered Leo to get back up there. He said, "You've got another strike coming, Leo."

He went back, but only long enough to take a feeble swing, just going through the motions of swinging while not getting within shouting distance of home plate. He didn't want to have anything at all to do with those fast balls. Strike three swinging, sort of. I had my first strikeout as a major league pitcher.

Cleveland isn't that far from Iowa, but it seemed like a long way from those times back on the farm and the Norman Rockwell life we led, where every day could have been one of his *Saturday Evening Post* covers.

Still, baseball was a big part of everything I did there, so much that folks on the other farms and around town in Van Meter used to shake their heads and chuckle about Bill Feller wasting all that time with his boy Bob when he could be planting more corn. When he switched from corn to wheat because that requires less time to harvest and leaves more time for baseball, they were sure he'd lost his mind completely.

One of my favorite baseball memories, in fact, came not in the big leagues but back in Iowa in 1928, when I was nine years old. *Both* Babe Ruth and Lou Gehrig were coming to town. Well, they weren't exactly coming to my town because Van Meter had only a few hundred people, but they were coming to Des Moines, and that was less than 25 miles away, to play an exhibition game. The major league season was over, so Ruth and Gehrig had put together two barnstorming teams—the Bustin' Babes and the Larrupin' Lous—and they were touring minor league cities by train and car all during October.

They were going to play at the Des Moines Demons' park, and each of them would come to bat every inning. The thought of a nine-year-old farm boy named Bob Feller getting to see Babe Ruth and Lou Gehrig—and nine times at bat for each of them, plus a pre-game batting show and Babe pitching one inning—was making me jump out of my skin. But there was even more exciting news than that. A hospital in Des Moines was selling baseballs autographed by the Babe and Lou for five dollars, and I came up with my own plan for being able to buy one of those balls.

Our county had a serious problem with gophers in those days, so the county government had a program which gave you a bounty of ten cents a pair for the front claws of any gopher you killed. The little varmints were more than just pests—they were damaging the crops, and the farmers wanted to get rid of them.

So I recruited my pal and neighbor, Paul Atkins, and gave him a gunny sack and told him to hold it over the gopher holes in our alfalfa field. Then I ran a hose from the gopher's mound to the exhaust of Dad's 1922 Dodge truck, turned the engine on and pulled the choke knob out all the way. I was careful not to use up all the gas. After all, it cost Dad six cents a gallon—nine cents minus a three-cent tax rebate if you used if for agricultural purposes.

Paul and I smoked out 50 gophers from those holes in two hours, all of them the victims of smoke inhalation and asphyxiation. Dad drove me to the Dallas county courthouse the next day in Adel. We went straight to the treasurer's office and I proudly presented my 50 sets of gopher claws and collected my $5.00. Later that week we drove down to the Demons' ballpark on Sixth Avenue at the Des Moines River in Dad's '27 four-door Rickenbacker Brougham sedan, and I bought myself one of those baseballs autographed by Babe Ruth and Lou Gehrig themselves—my first gopher ball.

I still have that ball.

I would have been crazy even to dream that I would meet up with both Ruth and Gehrig later, but that's what happened. I pitched against Lou several times—we'll get into that in another chapter—and I was able to be of some help to Babe on his last day in his Yankees uniform.

It happened 20 years later, in June 1948. It was Babe Ruth Day at Yankee Stadium, a chance for all of us to pay one final salute to the Babe for all he had done in bringing so much enjoyment to all of us, and for rescuing baseball after the Chicago "Black Sox" scandal in 1920. The Babe was wasted away by this point, losing a long struggle against cancer. He was dying, and all of us knew it.

I was the starting pitcher against the Yankees that day, and as I warmed up before the game with our bullpen catcher, Bill Lobe, Ruth walked through the Cleveland dugout on the third base side of Yankee Stadium—"the house that Ruth built"—on his way to home plate for pre-game ceremonies. Because of his drained condition, he was unsteady on his feet, so Eddie Robinson, our first baseman, alertly reached into the bat rack and pulled out the first bat he could put his hands on so the Babe would have something to lean on as he strolled onto the field and stood at home plate during the ceremonies. Ruth took the bat into his hands and said to Eddie, "It feels good." Robinson told him, "It's a Babe Ruth model that Bob Feller uses." My name was on the bat.

The contrast between the two baseball players must have been a stunning one. There was our muscular first baseman, the very picture of health and strength, six feet three inches, 210 pounds, with black wavy hair and a real Ladies Day favorite, who hit 172 home runs of his own, next to the emaciated, once robust home run king.

As the Babe stood at home plate—head bowed, in those familiar pin stripes and his immortal Number 3 on his back, cap in one hand, bat in the other—a photographer snapped the emotional sight from behind. The picture became a classic overnight.

When my first turn at bat came in the second or third inning, I couldn't find my bat. I sent the bat boy into the clubhouse to get another one. It wasn't until 34 years later, in 1982, that I found out what happened to my bat. It was the one Eddie Robinson gave to the Babe that day. After the ceremonies, Ruth brought my bat back to the dugout. Then Eddie did something understandable: He kept the bat. He couldn't bear giving up something so precious. I've never blamed him. I would have done the same thing.

The only time since 1948 that I've seen my Babe Ruth model bat is in Babe Ruth's hands in that picture.

But at this moment in 1936, I couldn't be thinking about the past or the future, even if they involved Babe Ruth. The only thing I could be thinking about were the St. Louis Cardinals.

Leo Durocher had some company that day. I pitched three innings and struck out eight batters. Dizzy Dean, who spoke in an Arkansas twang and baseball clichés, told me after the game, "You sure poured that ol' pea through there today, fellows." The Cleveland papers called me "Master Feller." I signed a contract with the Indians the next day.

Steve O'Neill must have liked what he saw. Despite my wildness, or maybe because of it, he began working me into action whenever he could, usually in games already decided, to test me in real competition, not just an exhibition game like the one against the Cardinals. These were real games and the results counted.

It was a dazzling, dizzying life—cities I'd read about, players I'd heard about, thrills I'd dreamed about:

WASHINGTON, July 19—My first big league game, not an exhibition, against the Senators. One inning in relief, no runs, no hits, no strikeouts, two walks. A mop-up appearance in a 9–5 loss at Griffith Stadium. That's what the record showed. But Buddy Lewis says the record is wrong. He told me a couple of years ago that I struck him out in this inning. I've always known that too, but for some reason the official scorer never wrote it down. But Buddy Lewis, an outfielder and an excellent hitter, says he remembers that he was my first official strikeout.

CLEVELAND, July 24 & 26—Two innings of relief in a 16–3 romp over the Philadelphia A's and one inning in a 13–0 clobbering by the A's. Not exactly prime time appearances even for a kid. In the combined three innings, a total of three runs, six hits, two strikeouts and—good news—only one walk.

DETROIT, August 3—Two innings, one run, two hits, two strikeouts, two walks. We still lost, 9–4, to the Tigers in what was then called Navin Field, now Tiger Stadium.

ST. LOUIS, August 14 & 16—Another total of two innings, one run, three hits, two strikeouts, three walks. We won the game in the 14th inning, 12–10, over the Browns, but lost in my next appearance two days later, 9–2. It was another mop-up job. I did not figure in the decision.

One month after my debut, my personal stats added up to six appearances, eight innings, five runs, eleven hits, six strikeouts, eight walks, no wins, but no losses either. I was doing all right, and some people had trouble believing that a kid could hold his own as a major league pitcher in the same year he was playing for his high school team.

I was sure of one thing: When I went back to school in September and the teacher asked us how we spent our summer vacations, I was going to have the best answer in the whole school.

CHAPTER TWO
A Country Boy Grows Up Fast

The year 1936 was an eventful one for a lot of people, not just me. The King of England, George V, died and was succeeded by the Prince of Wales, who became Edward VIII in January and abdicated in December so he could marry a divorceé. Franklin Roosevelt buried Alf Landon under the biggest political landslide in American history. Joe Louis was knocked out by the German boxing star, Max Schmeling, and Adolph Hitler pointed to the black man's defeat as proof that the German's were becoming a "super race." But Jesse Owens shattered that argument before Hitler's eyes by winning four gold medals in track as the star of the 1936 Olympics in Berlin.

Back home, the Depression still had a strong grip on the lives of a lot of people, and the Dust Bowl was causing severe hardships among farmers throughout the Midwest and Southwest.

Baseball was one source of relief from all that. Americans went out to the ball game and thrilled to the play of the rookie for the Yankees, Joe DiMaggio, who began his career in left field—Jake Powell was still their center fielder—and led the American League's outfielders by throwing out 22 runners, in addition to hitting .323 with 29 home runs and 125 runs batted in. "Joe D.," as most players still call him, was on his way. The Yankees, well, they were just the Yankees. They ran away from the rest of the league and won the pennant by 19½ games, then beat their city rivals, the Giants, in six games in a "nickel series," when that was all it cost to take the subway to the games.

The Indians weren't winning any pennant. We finished fifth behind the Yankees, Tigers, White Sox and Senators, but every day seemed to bring a new thrill and a new excitement for this kid right off the farm. Earl Averill was hitting .378 for us, but he still missed the batting championship by ten points. Luke Appling was that much better. Hal Trosky, my fellow Iowan from the town of Norway, hit 42 home runs for us, second only to Gehrig's 49, and Hal drove in 162 runs to lead the league.

While I was watching all this and realizing I wasn't nearly the hitter I used to think I was, Steve O'Neill was gaining enough confidence in me to think about giving me a chance as a starting pitcher. He made the big decision on August 23, when he handed me a new white American League ball with the signature of the league's president, Will Harridge, on it and told me I was his starter against the St. Louis Browns, managed by my boyhood hero, Rogers Hornsby. O'Neill was throwing an all-kids battery against the Browns. My catcher that day was Charlie George, a 22-year-old rookie who was making his first start too.

If I had any doubts about how I might do once I got the chance—and I didn't—they evaporated with the first hitter, Lyn Lary. Lary was the St. Louis shortstop and a tough out. He hit .289 that year and led the league with 37 stolen bases. Managers warn you not to walk a hitter who has that much speed, because he'll steal second and the result is the same as if you had given up a double, and with my wildness, a walk was always a definite possibility.

But I struck him out, on three pitches. Harlond Clift singled to right, but I got the next two hitters on strikeouts too, Julie Solters and Beau Bell. After six innings, I had 12 Ks—the scorekeeper's symbol for a strikeout—and the American League record of 16 by Rube Waddell with the Philadelphia A's way back in '08 was within reach. So was the major league record of 17 by Dizzy Dean. I'm sure the guys in the press box were thumbing through their record books and making note of all this, but down on that field at League Park, not far from Lake Erie, I wasn't thinking records. I was just thinking win. I wanted to beat the Browns, to look good doing it and go the full nine innings. I wanted to impress O'Neill and everybody else so much that I would be immediately established as a starting pitcher.

It's a good thing I didn't have my heart set on that strikeout record, because I didn't get it. I missed Waddell's American League mark by one, but I got everything I had hoped for. I struck out the side in the ninth, ending the game by getting Lary again. I finished with 15 strikeouts. We won the game, 4-1, and I gave up only six hits, walked four and went the distance. It was my first major league victory. I found out later I had become the youngest pitcher to do all of the following on the same day: start, win, and complete a major league game.

After the game, some kids were waiting for me at the dressing room door and asked me for my autograph. The funny thing was that some of those kids were older than I was.

I was being rushed by events into celebrity status, something I didn't care about one way or the other. The only thing I cared about was becoming a good pitcher, good enough to win consistently in the big leagues. But the treatment that a successful athlete receives, including requests for autographs and personal appearances, was not long in coming.

One of my earliest requests to make an appearance came on my first trip to New York with the Indians. Tom Meany, one of the New York writers, asked me to attend a father-son evening program in Bronxville with Ruth, Gehrig and himself. The four of us rode up together. Meany was voted into the writers' section of the Baseball Hall of Fame in 1974, so there were four future members of the Hall of Fame riding in the same car.

We had to make a stop on the way up. Meany and Ruth wanted to enjoy some liquid refreshment to fortify themselves for the drive, so we stopped in a bar while Tom and the Babe threw down a couple of belts. Gehrig had a glass of water and I didn't have anything, just a chat with Lou as Ruth and Meany proceeded with the business at hand.

One of my first requests for an autograph was when I was invited to throw out the first ball at the final game of the Illinois State Amateur Baseball Championship in Springfield at the end of my summer vacation with the Indians in '36. We played a day game in St. Louis, and a member of the sheriff's office picked me up and drove me a hundred miles to Springfield for the game that night.

Governor Horner, Grover Cleveland Alexander and I were on the mound for the pre-game ceremonies when a local boy, ten years old, dashed out of the stands, ran to the mound and asked me to autograph his baseball. Thirty years later, a fellow retired pitcher told me he was that kid—Robin Roberts.

The wheel of fortune was going to come around to my spot again, much sooner than anyone, especially me, had a right to expect. O'Neill came right back with me against the Red Sox the following week, but I let "the Green Monster" in Fenway Park psyche me out and I lost to the Red Sox, 5–1. That left field wall, so much closer than others, can shake up a kid pitcher, and O'Neill told me after the game that's what he thought happened to me.

Frankly, I thought Jimmie Foxx had more to do with it. He roughed me up for three hits and three runs batted in. Whatever the reason was, now I had my first major league defeat to go with my first win.

O'Neill did say one other thing that made sense to me. With the wisdom of his 25 years as a player, coach and manager, Steve told me, "You were pressing. A great player can relax in pressure situations. But if you press, you tighten up your muscles and lose your speed and power. You want to be loose out there. Take charge. Be in command."

Steve's advice stuck with me. It didn't produce any immediate improvement, because I got roughed up even worse in New York and lasted only one inning against the Yankees. But I bounced back to win my next start, going the full nine innings and beating the Browns, 7–1, in Cleveland on Labor Day. I pitched a seven-hitter and struck out ten.

O'Neill started me again six days later against the Tigers in Detroit, and that's when the wheel of fortune came up with my number again.

I was always younger than my opponent, but on this day, September 13, it was close. The A's 74-year-old Connie Mack, in his 39th year of managing, was starting Randy Gumpert. I was 17. He was 18.

The A's were a weak team that year—they finished last—but they had some respected hitters like Lou Finney, Pinky Higgins, Wally Moses and Bob Johnson. It would be another test for me, but I knew that if I were going to make it, I'd keep having tests handed to me to see if I could cut it as a major leaguer. I wanted all the tests they could throw at me, including this one.

I was all too aware that this wasn't Iowa and the American Legion baseball program. It wasn't even the major leagues of later years, when the batting averages dropped after World War II. In 1936, Luke Appling hit .388 to win the American League batting title, and Paul Waner's average leading the National League was .373. The fifth best hitter in the National League, Arky Vaughan, hit .335, enough to win the championship in many years today.

Those three became some of the greatest hitters I faced in my career, and some of the toughest outs for me to get, along with DiMaggio and Williams. You can include some others in there too, like Hank

Greenberg, Al Simmons, Cecil Travis, Jimmie Foxx and Charlie Gehringer.

I'd include several other all-time greats in that list, but they were ending their careers when I came up, which may have been a blessing for me. Hornsby was in his next-to-last season, Bill Terry was in his last, and Lou Gehrig, who hit .354 that year and .351 the next, was finished after that, hitting only .295 in 1938 and retiring early in 1939. Babe Ruth retired the year before I started. I have mixed feelings about that. I would have enjoyed the challenge of facing the Babe, but who knows how I would have done against him?

Some National Leaguers would be on my personal list of the best hitters I ever faced, except that I didn't get to face them that much. Great hitters like Stan Musial and Willie Mays certainly belong on any such list, but I never had the fun of competing against them that often, which shows you how silly it is that baseball's executives have never gotten around to inter-league play, making our sport the only one without it. It's the worst kind of injustice to the fans, to deny them that opportunity to see the stars.in both leagues, but it becomes downright absurd when you play in the majors for 18 years without the chance to play against half of the players in your sport except in All-Star Games and the World Series.

I felt strong that day against the A's, and my pitching showed it. I was blowing my fast ball right by those hitters, but I was so strong that I was also wild, which is frequently the case when a pitcher feels unusually strong. By the end of the sixth, I had 12 strikeouts, the same pace I set three weeks before when I struck out 15 Browns. Unlike that game, though, I didn't go through the seventh and eighth innings without a strikeout this time. I got two in the seventh and two more in the eighth. I had tied Rube Waddell's American League record with 16 strikeouts.

The Cleveland fans were letting me know with all their yelling that they were rooting hard for me to break the record, but I wondered if they'd break my neck instead if I missed. That was looking more likely, too, because I didn't strike out either of the first two hitters, getting them on a pop-up and a ground ball. Then Connie Mack sent up Charlie Moss to pinch hit for Gumpert, and I walked him. That 5–2 lead looked like money in the bank at the start of the inning, but a walk can change the complexion of things in a hurry. In this case, if the A's got another man on base, that would bring the potentially tying run to the plate, something you never want to do. That's when the manager comes out to the mound and threatens to commit murder and mayhem, with you as his victim.

Now my challenge was to get the next hitter, George Puccinelli, any way I could. That's when a pitcher tells himself, "Forget the strike-outs—just get this guy out so we can get out of here with the win." George was an outfielder and a big right-handed hitter who had a .278 average that year. He was almost 6'2" and he weighed close to 200 pounds, so he was no easy out.

I was going to my curve ball more now than in the early innings because I was getting tired and losing a little of the zip off my fast ball. I always had confidence in my curve because I had been throwing it since I was eight. I've never agreed with those who say kids shouldn't throw curves until their teens. I taught it to myself in throwing the ball back to Dad in our homemade batting cage. I threw it from then on, but I wasn't hurting my arm because I was throwing 12 months a year. That's the difference. How many kids throw year-round? But for those who do, curve balls are harmless—because the muscles in the kid's arm are strong and in condition and can therefore take the strain of a curve ball.

Puccinelli and I battled each other to a full count. Charlie George was my catcher again, and he asked for time out and then trotted out toward the mound. I met him a few steps in front of the mound and we decided I might have enough gas left in the tank to throw one more good fast ball. That's what I would throw, even though it was also what Puccinelli would be expecting.

I cut loose with everything I had left and Puccinelli took it. Strike three—called. I had broken the American League strikeout record for a single game, with a strikeout for every one of my years, the only pitcher to equal his *age* with strikeouts in a game. I gave up only two hits, but I also gave up nine walks and nine stolen bases—count 'em, nine—because of my high kick when I threw my fast ball. The runners were getting a big jump on me and stealing second with regularity.

So it wasn't exactly a textbook game, but I was establishing myself as a major league pitcher and breaking strikeout records set by such greats of the game as Waddell and Dizzy Dean.

By the end of the season, I had posted some numbers that were continuing to support my self-confidence. I lost in Detroit my next time out after setting the strikeout record, but my teammates gave me first-class hitting support in my last two games, scoring 26 runs as we beat the White Sox, 17–2, and the Tigers, 9–1. My final stats showed five wins, three losses and 76 strikeouts in 62 innings.

That was a lot of pluses, but there were some minuses, too—two big ones. There were some rumblings about whether my contract with the Indians was valid, and Dad, who paid a surprise visit to Cleveland to help me over my first rough spots, my best friend, best teacher and the most important person in my young life, was developing some health problems.

Any teenage kid would be upset to hear that his father's health was becoming a source of concern to his doctors, but in my case that concern might have been even greater than normal. Athletes are frequently closer than other boys to their fathers because they have spent so much time together over the years. Dad helped son become an athlete, and in some cases even coached him.

Some great baseball players are quick to credit their fathers; Mickey Mantle and Duke Snider make it clear that their dads had a great deal to do with their early success, and their happiness. Mickey's father was the one who convinced him to become a switch hitter, and Duke's did him not one big favor but two—converting his son into a left-handed hitter because he knew it would be to his advantage in many of the ball parks, and nicknaming him "Duke."

I knew even in my teens that any success to come my way would be due in large measure to the time, advice and instruction from my father, and the love and patience that he included with it. To learn after my dream summer that Dad might be sick—really sick—was something for me to worry about in the midst of all the happiness.

All of these things were part of the overall picture when I returned to Van Meter to start my senior year in high school. It was October now, and my classmates—all 16 of them—had a five-week head start on me, but I didn't mind that. I was just glad to be back home.

There was a big welcome for me, and the mayor, John Jungman, and the governor himself, Clyde Herring, showed up. There was a baseball exhibition game, and I pitched two innings for each team. Of the 12 putouts, I got 11 on strikeouts.

Then I started school. The first thing that happened was I was elected class president, an honor I didn't seek and one that probably was related in some small way to how I spent my summer vacation. I think my classmates knew that our valedictorian, Florence Wishmeyer, would do most of the work anyhow. I started riding the bus back and forth every day with my sister Marguerite, ten years younger.

Going back to my Iowa roots after a season in the big leagues and all the fuss about my speed and my strikeouts was what any kid would want to do. I was going to be 18 in another month, but I still wanted to enjoy the farm life and my last year in school. As important as baseball always has been to me, I knew even then that there are other things in life, too.

Besides, what kid wouldn't enjoy the life I led in Iowa? Baseball and farming, and I had the best of both worlds. I helped Mom and Dad by doing the usual farm chores and some of the planting in the spring and harvesting in the fall. Mom and Dad, in turn, enjoyed my love for playing ball and encouraged it. And they never got after me for things like painting a batter's box on the sidewalk in front of the house so I could practice different batting stances and grow up to hit .400 like my idol, Rogers Hornsby.

They first noticed my enthusiasm for throwing a ball when I was five and Dad would roll a rubber ball to me and I would fire it back to him—or into the wall. He used to position himself on the davenport in the living room and equip himself with a pillow which he threw toward my wild pitches from the kitchen before they hit something. It worked most of the time, but there were still some throws that missed the doorway and loosened the plaster on the wall. My grandmother, who lived with us, was afraid I might knock the house down.

Mom and Dad weren't surprised at all when they read one of my first school compositions at age seven:

> When I was a tree, and my brothers and sisters, there were many of us there but there is not many of us now. Many of us have been cut down and made into lumber and it came my turn and they cut me down and made me into a big board. And Mister Stucke's manual training boys got me and made me into a home plate for the baseball diamond. And that's the end.

With such enthusiasm for baseball, imagine my elation at age ten when Dad gave me my first baseball uniform. It didn't have a number on the back of the shirt, much less a name, but it was a real flannel uniform, complete with a hat and stirrups to wear over my socks, just like Rogers Hornsby's, who was not only my hero but Dad's too. Before that I also had a bat, a green one, and two gloves. One was a

Rogers Hornsby fielder's model and the other a Ray Schalk catcher's mitt. Who could have blamed me, with all that excitement, if I dreamed that night that some day I would pitch against Rogers Hornsby's team, and against Hornsby himself? He pinch hit against me, and I got him out.

Abner Doubleday could have related to my life in those years, and Tom Sawyer could have too. It was a life without electricity or indoor plumbing, a typically simple, enjoyable life on an American farm in the Midwest in the 1920s and '30s.

Dad solved the power problem by buying a "Delco electric plant" with a generator, 32 batteries and a wind charger, a system that gave us three days of use at a time. With his ability we had enough juice to provide heating and lighting for our house and "out buildings"—the smokehouse, barn, icehouse, chicken house, corncrib, hoghouse and the machine shed. All of those buildings got their electricity by wire from a big pole in the middle of the livestock yard behind our house.

Inside the white frame farmhouse, we read by the light from kerosene lamps and communicated by a battery-powered telephone that we cranked up by a handle on the side and rang a certain number of times for a specific family. The Feller ring was one long ring and four shorts. That's how you got us. It worked, but there were 17 families on our "party line" and a couple of gossipy ladies could tie it up. It was cause for rejoicing in any family when you could move up in class with a real luxury—a private line. Indoor plumbing didn't come until much later, in 1940, when I built a new house on the farm for Mom and Dad and my kid sister, Marguerite.

Our family life revolved around that farmhouse with its big kitchen, pantry, living room, dining room and three bedrooms upstairs. We even had a trap door from the kitchen to the fruit cellar that came in handy in case of a tornado. We were living in history—the first two rooms were built in the 1870s, about the same time that my grandfather on my mother's side was known as one of the best pitchers in the area.

There were days every winter when we had to walk the three miles to school in the snow and temperatures in the teens or lower, but if you knew your way you could take a shortcut across the neighbors' pastures. I wanted to get to school so I could play basketball and do my exercises on the gym equipment. And Mom, who was a teacher in a one-room country schoolhouse a mile from our farm before she married Dad, wouldn't entertain any notion about staying home from school just because there was a foot of snow on the ground.

Even the Great Depression and the Dust Bowl couldn't spoil the fun of a boy on an Iowa farm in those years. The Dust Bowl crisis was worse in the western part of the state, but we had our share of the dust and the other problems—the invasions by grasshoppers and locusts and the severe crop losses caused by all of this. The books and movies reflected the hard times, *Grapes of Wrath* and *Tobacco Road*. Things were much worse than anything else before or since, including the awful drought of 1988. The '30s were worse.

I'm sure my parents and everyone else's worried about money and the crops, but we were lucky—or smart. Mom and Dad always planted plenty of alfalfa, clover and short grass so the animals had enough to eat—the cows and horses and pigs and chickens. And we humans had enough, too, thanks to our vegetable garden of eggplant, cabbage, peas, corn, carrots, beans, horseradish and rhubarb. We even had an apple orchard and a grape vineyard, plus peaches and pears. Nobody at our house was going to starve, and if things got really bad, Mom could always go back to teaching or to her other profession as a registered nurse. Fortunately, things never came close to that.

In the winters, we had another source of income. The shortcut for drivers traveling from Van Meter to Des Moines ran past our farm and those of our neighbors. In those days of mostly dirt roads, the drivers would get stuck in the mudholes during the spring thaw and be faced with having to stay there until spring. Then the farmers and their sons would come to the rescue. We'd ride to the scene with a team of horses and chains and pull those 1920 cars out of the mud. Each farmer charged $2.00 to deliver you out of the local mudhole. We were providing the horses, chains and manpower, and every driver we pulled out thought that $2.00 was an extremely reasonable price.

To battle against drought, we would dig a hole in the bed of the Raccoon River near our farm and fill our five-gallon buckets, carry them to a tank on a truck or wagon and haul the tank of water a mile back to the farm for our livestock. I was always accompanied by my dog. His name was "Tagalong," because that's what he did.

Winter or summer, baseball was always high on my list of things to do. I played every chance I got, on teams, with Dad and by myself. If I didn't have a game, I'd play catch with Dad and practice my pitching, fielding and hitting. If Dad wasn't around, I'd do simulations as if I were really pitching so I could keep my arm muscles in shape and sharpen my reflexes at the same time. If it was winter, Dad and I would put jackets on and head for the barn to play catch.

I don't think Dad ever intended to coach any of my teams, but he had the same experience other fathers have. When he saw what his son's coach was teaching, he decided maybe he should get into coaching himself. In my case, all it took was a visit to vacation Bible school when I was nine. When Dad arrived, the preacher was teaching me how to play shortstop. He was showing me his recommended way of fielding ground balls—down on one knee. That was all Dad needed. He must have decided to become a coach before we even got home.

One of the best gifts parents can give to any child who shows an interest in athletics is simply a chance to play, but my parents gave me even more than that. They gave me a *place* to play. Dad decided the best thing he could do for me after he became convinced I had some potential was to build a diamond and form his own team. As incredible as it may sound, I had my own ballpark, complete with bleachers, scoreboard and refreshments, right there on the farm.

We leveled part of the pasture land and cut down some trees for poles to support a chicken wire fence from first to third base to protect the fans. We had a temporary fence to protect the infield from the livestock between games. Dad bought all the equipment including uniforms and named the team Oakview because of the oak timber between our ballpark on the top of the hill and the Raccoon River a mile away. Together we built the bleachers and put up the scoreboard so everything would look first-class. We charged 25 cents to get in—35 cents for a doubleheader—and Dad formed a team and scheduled games for every Sunday all summer long. On most Sundays, two or three hundred people came to watch our team of players in their late teens and their 20s, and one 13-year-old play baseball against good teams from Des Moines and other cities and towns.

It was a real-life "field of dreams," with a father in Iowa clearing a farm field to build a baseball park—more than 50 years before the movie on the same subject.

I was a shortstop at the beginning, when I was 12 years old and playing for the sixth grade team. I wasn't fielding ground balls on one knee despite what the preacher had suggested in vacation Bible school. I thought I was a fairly good shortstop, and I loved the hitting part. But the more Dad saw of me in our first two seasons, the more he thought I should be a pitcher.

I resisted, knowing that pitchers don't get to play every day—therefore they don't get to hit every day either. But Dad won out, and in my last two years with him I became a pitcher for our Oakview team. In those same seasons, I was playing the infield and pitching for an American Legion team in Adel.

My catcher was Nile Kinnick, who became an All-American quarterback at the University of Iowa and a Rhodes Scholar before being killed in World War II. Today there's a beautiful recreation park in Adel, Feller-Kinnick Park. Nile would like that.

No coach ever has enough pitchers, or admits it, and Dad had even more reason to feel that way. He had to go out and recruit some to make our team competitive with those he was scheduling, and in some cases he had to pay them. He also had to pay the umpires and some of the costs for the other team, so he lost money every year that he operated Oak View Park. Another pitcher, especially one who would pitch for free, would be a big help. I hit .322 in 1933 as the Oakview shortstop, but Dad was more impressed with my throws from short than he was with my hitting. So in the spring of 1934, when I was 15, I became a pitcher and the world lost a player who I thought was a promising shortstop and hitter.

We were playing Winterset, the home town of John Wayne and Baseball Hall of Famer Fred Clark. Dad waved me to the mound from short when our starter got into trouble. I took the ball with a man on third and no outs, struck out the first two batters I ever pitched to, and then threw the runner from third out at the plate when he tried to steal. It was fun, but it wasn't as much fun as playing every day at shortstop and getting to hit three and four times every game.

But I never did win my argument. Dad started me a few games later after a couple of other relief jobs, and much to everyone's surprise, especially my own, I struck out 15 batters and pitched a two-hitter against a team from Waukee.

The word flashed around that part of Iowa so fast that the manager of our next opponent, Valley Junction—now West Des Moines—asked Dad to use me as his starting pitcher because it would help attract a larger crowd to his park. He was right. Dad said okay, and when the word got around, 2,000 people showed up. I pitched a one-hitter and struck out 20 hitters. We won, 9–1, with Valley Junction's only run coming on an error and a passed ball.

Next came De Soto. I struck out the first batter and had a no-hitter until the ninth inning. I ended up allowing only one single, won the game on a 2–0 shutout and finished with 15 strikeouts. I won my next game with 18 strikeouts and then beat a team with four semi-pro players and struck out 17.

I was on my way to somewhere. I wasn't sure where all this was leading me, but in my 15-year-old mind I realized that, for better or for worse, a pitcher was being born.

I'm sure folks were waiting to see if this kid was just a flash in the pan, doing things at 15 that he'd never do again. I was aware of the talk when the 1935 season started. I was still playing for Dad, who had agreed to co-manage the Farmers Union team of Des Moines, which always played the best amateur teams in Iowa. After practicing with Dad during the off-season, I was ready for the new year. In my first start, I pitched a three-hitter and had 17 strikeouts as we beat the team from Slater, Iowa, 2–1. Then I faced the team from Yale (Iowa, not the university) and pitched the first no-hitter of my career. The three I pitched for the Cleveland Indians were great thrills, but this first one was just as big a kick. To make it even more exciting, I struck out 22 men. Then I pitched another shutout and beat St. Mary's on another three-hitter, 1–0, with 19 more strikeouts.

The whole season went like that. We won the state championship and even though I was still competing against older players, almost all of them adults. I was still achieving success, with help from Dad and my teammates, playing in the American Amateur Baseball Congress. I won 25 games for the Farmers Union team and lost only four. I averaged 19.4 strikeouts per game.

Dad was even hearing talk about his son being "the next Walter Johnson." All of this could have been hard to handle if I hadn't been so determined to make the grade in baseball. I wasn't going to allow myself to get too high or too low because of what people might be saying at any time in my career. I was going to make it to the big leagues and it wouldn't be because of what people were saying, it would be because of what I was doing.

One day when Dad and I were working in the wheat field, a man in a white shirt and tie with his coat slung over his arm came walking toward us from the house. Dad was running the combine and I was sitting on our caterpillar tractor. It was Cy Slapnicka, a former major league pitcher and then a scout for the Indians. As he walked into the field, he was walking into my life. Slap and I became close friends as soon as I joined the Indians and we remained close until he died at 93 in Cedar Rapids, the town where he was born. Slapnicka became the Indians' general manager in the fall of 1935 when Billy Evans moved to Detroit as the Tigers' GM.

Slap engaged Dad in small talk and said only a few words to me, but we knew what he was doing. He wanted to see me close-up and find out when I would be pitching in Des Moines again. I found out later that he wasn't really in those parts to see me anyhow. His first target was a pitcher named Claude Passeau, who signed with the Pirates that year and won 162 games in 13 years in the National League, mostly with the Cubs.

Eventually Slap signed me to a contract, making sure to get Dad's signature as my legal guardian. But we wanted to keep the signing a secret so I could play high school basketball and baseball. I wasn't getting any money from the Indians contract, but we didn't want to take any chances with my eligibility, so we declared the matter top secret.

My contract with Slap was for $1.00. Dad made sure everything was legally binding and notarized. As a bonus I got a ball autographed by the Cleveland team.

That turned out to be a stroke of genius. A year later, a bit of trouble flared up, caused by some people who saw me continue to progress and wanted to break my connection with the Indians. It became a big news story, even involving the Commissioner of Baseball, Kenesaw Mountain Landis, but we knew that we held all the cards, thanks to that $1.00 contract.

I went on another streak right after signing with the Indians, or right after Dad signed for me. I struck out 22 hitters against Bondurant, then got another 23 against an All-Star team of the best players from eastern Iowa. There were 5,000 fans at the game, and they were going crazy that this kid could strike out 23 All-Stars.

After that there was the tournament for the state championship, played at the Iowa State Fair. We won the title, and I had 18 strikeouts in the opening game. Then it was on to Dayton, Ohio—playing in another state for the first time in my life—to see if Farmers Union was good enough to win the national semi-pro championship. That's where my first serious problem arose.

Scouts from every Major League team were after me in Dayton. We lost our opening game, 1–0, to Battle Creek, Michigan, when our center fielder dropped a routine fly ball. I pitched a two-hitter and struck out 19, but at the moment that didn't matter as much to me as our loss. My disappointment became complete when we lost our next game and were bounced from the double elimination tournament. I didn't even get into that game because of pitching the first one, so I suffered on the bench.

Maybe I was disappointed, but the scouts weren't. They swarmed all over the Van Cleve Hotel and came after Dad and me from every direction and at every opportunity. It was pretty flattering stuff for a kid of 16, but it was a crazy scene too. A fist fight even broke out in the lobby between a Cleveland scout, Buzz Wetzel, and a scout for the Detroit Tigers, Steve O'Rourke.

Word started to leak out that I had already signed with the Indians, and O'Rourke was sure that Wetzel had known this all along, so O'Rourke felt used and insulted. He accused Wetzel of making a fool of his fellow scouts. The only hitch in O'Rourke's logic was that Wetzel didn't know about my signing any more than anyone else did. Slapnicka had kept such a tight lid on it that even his own scout didn't know.

None of this had any particular effect on me, at least not right away. I had already signed a contract with Slapnicka to go to the Fargo-Moorhead Twins in the Class D Northern League, so those guys could have all the fist fights they wanted to. I put my disappointment at not winning the national championship behind me, and went home to start my junior year in high school.

I was back in my routine as a teenage kid in those years—school, hunting and chores on the farm. Dad was feeling sick from time to time, so I had to be able to pick up the slack. If I wanted to have fun after working on the farm, I went with some of the guys from school to watch the University of Iowa play football 150 miles away, or to the movies in Des Moines.

And there was always Van Meter. We had our good times at the drugstore owned by Dorothy Kramme's father. Dorothy was one of my classmates, and her brother—Walter—later became the business manager for Roger Williams, the pianist. We'd go to the drugstore and sit at the soda fountain and have a chocolate sundae for a dime or get our hair cut at Fritz's barbershop for a quarter. We'd splurge once in a while for a meal at Landers Restaurant and buy our groceries at England's or Maylander's stores or at Booneville.

There was a hardware store and a tile factory that provided jobs after the local coal mine gave out. And we had a justice of the peace to help maintain law and order and perform marriage ceremonies.

That was Van Meter, Iowa, 50 years ago, population 300, and it's

Van Meter today. The population is still under 1,000. You still don't have to worry about getting stuck at a traffic light in my home town. There isn't one.

When any of us drove our family car, we were the most experienced teenage drivers you could imagine. Farm kids, especially the boys, start driving at an early age, handling the vehicles around the farm. I had been driving since I was nine, behind the wheel of the family Star two-door coupe, our Caterpillar tractor and Dodge truck.

We knew all the tricks of those years too, including going up a hill backward if you were running low on gas in a Ford Model T. Cars in those days had "gravity-feed" tanks, meaning the gas had to flow downhill to get from the tank to the engine. So if you were low on gas and had to go up a hill, you turned the car around and went up the hill backward. And if you really wanted to have fun, you could drive over to a spot near Des Moines in Polk County where the road was concrete for five miles, the longest stretch of concrete road in the state.

There was a sign along that stretch that said:

SPEED LIMIT 60 MILES PER HOUR—MODEL TS DO YOUR BEST

Midway through my junior year in high school, my contract with the Indians became a news item all over again. Word had drifted down to Iowa from Dayton that I was under contract with Cleveland, which prompted some people to claim that I was a professional athlete as a result. This was exactly the wrong time for such a claim to be made, because the Van Meter basketball team, with me as the center, had just won the Dallas County championship plus the sectional and regional championships. Now the question was whether I would be ruled a professional and, if so, whether Van Meter would be made to forfeit all of our victories and our three championship trophies.

A hearing was scheduled in Des Moines. Our coach, Leland McCosh, and our Superintendent of Schools, O. E. Lester, were ordered to appear, and so was I. Dad came along for support.

The hearing resulted in a ruling in our favor, based on the conclusion that I was not a professional because I had not received any money for signing with the Indians and had not played with them yet. Those three championship trophies which our superintendent and coach had brought with them in the car, just in case we had to give them back, stayed in the trunk and made the trip back to Van Meter with us.

Then came 1936, the end of my junior year and the beginning of a dream come true, when I spent my summer vacation pitching for the Cleveland Indians instead of the Farmers Union, in stadiums instead of in front of bleachers, with 40,000 and 50,000 people watching, against hitters like DiMaggio, Gehrig, Hank Greenberg and Rudy York and Cecil Travis and Luke Appling instead of semi-pro players whose names I didn't even know.

When I came home to that welcome from the mayor and the governor after winning five games for the Indians and breaking the American League record for strikeouts in a single game, the dream went on, but not for long.

You'd think that a kid in my position couldn't have a worry in the world, but I did. I had two. The first one was originated by a fellow Iowan, Lee Keyser, the owner of the Des Moines team in the Western League. After I got off to such an exciting start with the Indians and the press—what we call "the media" today—started writing all those stories about this 17-year-old "phee-nom," Keyser sent a complaint to Judge Landis that I really didn't belong to the Indians at all because they had signed me improperly.

Keyser said I had been signed by the Indians directly off the sandlots, in violation of major league rules which prohibited big league clubs from signing amateurs. All minor league teams had territorial rights. Minor leagues were supposed to be signing the amateurs. Slapnicka's defense was that I had been signed to pitch for a minor league team, Fargo-Moorhead. But I had never pitched for Fargo-Moorhead or for the New Orleans Pelicans, who technically "bought" my contract from Fargo-Moorhead when Slap transferred me to New Orleans on paper. When I got off to such a sensational start, Slap had my contract transferred to the Indians.

The Cleveland management maintained that the charge by Keyser was strictly a technicality, which Dad said was true, but the question was whether Landis would rule against the Indians and I would be a free agent, able to sign with any team I chose. That was a tempting situation. After such a start, other teams would have been delighted to bid high to get me, and it was common knowledge that I could pick up a huge bonus if Landis declared me a free agent. You can imagine how much money would have been involved in such a situation today.

In addition to the realization by everyone that this was a technicality, the Indians had another strong argument in their favor. It was also common knowledge that many other big league players—30, 40, 50, who knows?—had been signed under circumstances a lot more deceiving than mine. They were players who had been playing college ball and playing in the minor leagues under assumed names to protect their college eligibility. Landis eventually lowered the boom, declaring almost 200 players as free agents, able to sign with any team. Most of the freed players were Tigers and Cardinals.

There was a lot worse going on than what Slap had done with me. Landis, who had gained a reputation for toughness during a term as a Federal judge, wanted to be sure. He ordered Dad and me to come to Chicago, where he had his offices as commissioner, and answer some questions.

He was an impressive sight to a kid, but not an intimidating one to me. He asked what I thought were reasonable questions, and I gave him straight-from-the-shoulder answers. No, I told him, I didn't want to play for any other team, and yes, the Indians were treating me very well.

Landis, who had thick, wavy, snow-white hair, steely eyes that pierced your thoughts, and the air of a man who had presided over the court proceedings connected with the Teapot Dome Scandal, wasn't going to be convinced easily or render his decision quickly. The man named for Kenesaw Mountain in North Carolina, the scene of a Civil War battle, made no promises as we left his office, not even on when he would make a decision.

The whole episode flared up during the season, and it wasn't until December 10 that Landis handed down his ruling in New York at the major league winter meetings. Scouts from the Yankees, Red Sox and other teams were waiting in the lobby of the Chamberlain Hotel in Des Moines, ready to offer me up to $200,000 as a bonus for signing with them if Landis declared me a free agent. What they never seemed to understand through the whole episode was that it didn't make any difference what Landis declared—I was going to stay with the Indians. I liked the organization and the people in it, and they had outhustled all the other teams by signing me first. All of that was important to me. Even if Landis said I was a free agent, I was ready to turn down every offer but Cleveland's.

Then there was the matter of that $1.00 contract. If Landis had gone one step beyond free agency and also said the Indians couldn't sign me, Dad was prepared to take him to court on the basis of our contract, and he had told Landis so in our meeting.

The press was having a field day with all the speculation, and the scouts were flashing their check books all over the lobby, but Dad and I knew the outcome before Landis announced his decision. I wasn't going to be pitching for anybody but the Cleveland Indians.

Landis ordered the Indians to pay $7,500 to the Des Moines team for allegedly signing a player off the sandlots in its area. But the important decision, the one the press had been speculating about in so many stories it surprised Dad and me, was that the Indians would be allowed to keep me. When the word reached the Feller farm, there was rejoicing all around. It was what all of us wanted, especially me.

My rookie season in the majors was going to have a happy ending after all. And only a month later, in January 1937, I signed a contract for my first full season with the Indians. It was for $10,000, the most baseball money ever paid to a kid so young at the time.

I like to think that today's young players would make the same decision, in consultation with their parents, that I did in 1936, but I'm not so sure. Players leave college a year early to start playing professional basketball, they sign with agents while they're still in college even knowing it's illegal, and they set forth some of the same demands for high salaries, bonuses and incentive clauses that the older, more established professionals do.

Money is important, but other things are too, including loyalty and a sense of values and priorities. I wonder how many more future examples we'll see of professional athletes who spend their entire careers in one city, with the fan loyalty and closeness that goes with such an association. You look at players who spent their entire careers with one team and remember how good it was for everybody, especially the fans.

Kids grow up today wondering if their hero will still be playing for the home team next year. That was unimaginable until free agency became a fact of life in professional sports. Joe DiMaggio playing for somebody else? Ted Williams leaving Tom Yawkey's Red Sox? I played my entire 18 years with the Cleveland Indians. Brooks Robinson spent his whole 23 years with the Baltimore Orioles. Stan Musial was never anything but a St. Louis Cardinal, and he played for 22 years. And Carl Yastrzemski followed Williams with the Red Sox.

I remember a comment by Jim Palmer, who spent his entire 19-year career with the Orioles as one of baseball's greatest pitchers. When free agency opened up everything and players started jumping from team to team, Palmer remained in Baltimore, and the word was that he was agreeing to contracts that were definitely less than he could have made by moving to another team.

Some of his teammates saw things differently and moved on, including Reggie Jackson, who made a one-year rest stop with the Orioles and let it be known early that year, 1976, that he would be signing with the Yankees and moving to New York for 1977. He added, "The trouble with Baltimore is it's in Baltimore."

In later years, when Palmer heard and read criticism that he was paying too much attention to proper care for his pitching arm and missing too many games because of nagging arm injuries, he asked a question that is food for thought these days: "What about me? I'm the one who stayed."

But on matters far more important than baseball, 1936 wasn't ending on a happy note at all. It was a tragic one instead.

I had to take Dad to the Mayo Clinic in Rochester, Minnesota that fall. He was looking bad and feeling worse. The diagnosis was the worst, just what you dread to hear: Cancer of the brain. Inoperable. Terminal.

Dad was going to die.

CHAPTER THREE
"The Higher We Rise, the Better the View"

That senior year in high school may qualify me for the shortest one on record—under five months. Having arrived in early October at Van Meter High, I left in February for spring training. I was headed for my first full season as a major leaguer.

What I didn't know was that I was also headed for other problems, on top of Dad's illness. I was about to face what every pitcher dreads—a serious arm problem and the possibility that my career was ending almost before it began.

There was a lot of talk around baseball that I was a flash in the pan, a hard-throwing kid who would never again have the half-season that I had in '36. The hitters would catch up with me, some of the talk went, especially my second or third time around the league. They'd learn to see the ball sooner through my windup and my high kick with my left leg. They'd "sit on" my fast ball, waiting for me to throw it and ignoring the possibility of a curve ball. More than one player was quoted in the papers as saying those things, and some managers were, too. The Indians wanted me to be as prepared as possible, because the American League was just waiting to take its best shots against me.

And then there was always the matter of finishing my high school education. The Indians hired a New Orleans teacher to serve as a tutor so I could complete the studies necessary for me to graduate on time. When I wasn't working on my fast ball, curve and change of pace, I was working on my English, history and math—the only pitcher in baseball who had to do homework in the evening at the hotel.

The Indians traveled north with the New York Giants aboard their private train, steam engine and all, in those years before jet planes. Baseball teams would come north from spring training with another team and play each other in various towns along the way to help pay for the expenses of spring training, places like Jonesboro, Spartanburg, Pine Bluff, Hattiesburg and Hickory. The Giants decided to send their ace, Carl Hubbell, against me in several games on the trip, not to prove anything about Hubbell, the great Hall of Famer, or any of their other players, but to put as many people as possible in the ballparks along the way. Bill Terry was their manager, his first year after retiring as a player.

In our first duel, I pitched three innings in New Orleans, didn't allow a hit and struck out six batters, four of them in a row. By the end of the trip, we drew 37,000 in the Polo Grounds in New York, the largest crowd until then ever to see an exhibition game, and we went seven innings each. When I left, the Indians were leading, 2–0. My stats for the trip showed I pitched 27 innings against the Giants, struck out 37, gave up seven runs and didn't lose a game. As good as those numbers were, what mattered even more to me was the assurance that 1936 had not been a freak year. I was going to make it. I was sure of it.

One guy who wasn't sure of it was Dick Bartell, the Giants' shortstop. Bartell was a real firebrand, enough so that he was called "Rowdy Richard" by some. He was a good hitter who enjoyed 18 years in the major leagues with six years over .300 and a career batting average of .284. He even reached the magic mark of more than 2,000 hits in his career.

Whatever the reason, he wasn't going to give me any credit that he didn't have to. After facing me a couple of times, Bartell told someone that I wasn't as fast as people were saying, that they had a dozen pitchers in the National League who were faster. As an example he mentioned Van Lingle Mungo of the Brooklyn Dodgers. In addition to having one of the great names of all time, Mungo had excellent pitching credentials. He had led the National League in strikeouts the year before with 238. He was a hard thrower all right, but most people thought I was faster.

Most of the Giants, including Mel Ott and their manager, Bill Terry, were complimentary during that trip, saying they thought I was extremely fast and was going to experience a successful major league career. But not Bartell. Naturally his comments leaked back to me, so I bore down even harder. I faced him 19 times on that trip—and struck him out 16.

I had a scare in spring training. I hit a batter in the head—"beaned" him, something I never wanted to do in all the years I played baseball. I never hit a batter on purpose, and if any manager had ever ordered me to do it—and no one ever did—I would have disobeyed. There are some orders in life that you simply don't have to obey because they are so outrageously criminal or immoral. And deliberately hitting a man in the head with a baseball coming at 90 miles an hour or more, from only 60 feet, six inches away is one of those acts. If any manager had ordered me to stick a ball in a batter's ear, I would have told him to stick it in his own ear.

The player I hit was Hank Leiber of the Giants. He was an outfielder who played in the National League for ten years. When I hit him, I prayed I hadn't hurt him or his career. I guess it was a little of both, because he was forced to miss the first half of the season—but when he came back he was able to pick right up and have a good season and an excellent World Series when the Giants lost to the Yankees in five games. He hit .293 in 51 games in the second half and then had the second highest average on the Giants, .364, in the Series.

At least I was spared any further anguish. A Cleveland player had already been involved in what still is the only fatality in major league history resulting from being beaned by a pitch. I didn't want to be the second. Ray Chapman, the Indians shortstop, was hit in the head by a pitch from Carl Mays of the Yankees in a game in New York in 1920. It was Chapman's ninth year in the majors, all with Cleveland, and he was in his prime. He had hit .300 and .302 in two of his previous seasons, and he was .303 when the Mays pitch hit him accidentally in August. He was 29.

I didn't want to have anything at all to do with the possibility that history might repeat itself. I'm not the only fastballer who ever felt that way. I think most of us have, and I know that Walter Johnson did. He lived in fear that he would do what Carl Mays did.

The hitters knew it, too, and they weren't afraid of taking advantage of Johnson's concern and compassion. Shirley Povich of the *Washington Post*, one of the best baseball writers in history and a member of the writers' section of the Hall of Fame, remembers that Eddie Collins even made Johnson pay for it once, when Walter hit him in the ankle with one of his fast balls.

Collins was a second baseman with the A's and the White Sox for 25 years, a man who got more than 3,000 hits, finished with a lifetime average of .333 and was an early selection for the Hall of Fame. They didn't call him "Cocky Collins" without good reason, either.

Povich remembers that after Johnson cracked him on the ankle with his fast ball, Walter dashed in from the mound to Collins, in a heap at home plate, to make sure he hadn't shattered the ankle into a million pieces.

Johnson quickly asked, "Are you all right, Eddie?"

"I don't know," Collins told him.

So Johnson stood around while the trainer worked on Collins at the plate. Then, after Collins was helped to his feet and started limping toward first, Johnson said, "Here, Eddie, let me help you."

So he helped this opposing player down to first base, Collins limping along as well as possible in all that pain.

On Johnson's next pitch, Collins stole second.

While Hank Leiber was recovering from his beaning, some people began suggesting that batters should be required to wear helmets instead of just caps. Football players wore helmets, so why shouldn't baseball players, at least while they're at bat?

After his recovery, Leiber told a reporter, "There's talk about wearing helmets, but I can't see that they'd do any good. They would make the batter more conscious of what little danger exists. Better and quicker medical attention would prevent serious injuries."

Today, it's unthinkable that any player from little league to the majors would ever bat without a helmet. It was another 20 years after I hit Leiber before batting helmets became mandatory.

All the preparation—all the extra work with O'Neill and Schang in spring training and all the games against the Giants on the road north— were behind me now as I stood on the mound back home in Cleveland, ready to face the St. Louis Browns in our first home series of the 1937 season. The first man up in the game was our teammate of last year, Bill Knickerbocker, the Browns' shortstop, who had been traded to St. Louis over the winter and was now their leadoff hitter.

My third pitch of the game, on a 1–1 count, was a curve ball. It was raining and the mound was slippery and greasy. I slipped and lost my balance just as I was releasing the pitch. My arm popped. You could hear it all over the infield. I felt a severe pain in my throwing arm before the ball even reached the plate. My right elbow was killing me.

Now I was throwing hurt, not the brightest thing a pitcher can do, but when you're a kid trying to make it, you don't want to miss any chance you get, and this was a big chance for me. I kept on pitching, but the result was predictable: Four runs by the Browns in the first inning, with the help of four walks. This was no way to establish myself, so I couldn't leave with that as my performance. I decided not to tell anybody about my arm. I was going to keep on pitching, pain or no pain. I could scream my guts out after the game.

Things did not get better immediately. With one out in the second inning, I walked three straight batters. Now the game is only four outs old as far as my pitching is concerned, and I've walked seven men already. I kept my fingers crossed that O'Neill wouldn't yank me, and I certainly wasn't going to glance toward the dugout and give him a chance to catch my eye. I was looking elsewhere—wherever O'Neill wasn't.

The plot thickened when who should step up to the plate but my boyhood hero, Rogers Hornsby. As if I didn't have enough awe for him already, he had clobbered a 450-foot home run the day before off Johnny Allen, our best pitcher. But I was able to put the pain out of my mind just long enough to strike him out and then do the same with Harlond Clift. I was out of the inning without any more runs by the Browns.

I still kept my injury, if that's what it was, a secret on the bench. The only thing pitchers fear as much as arm trouble is a reputation for it, and I didn't want either one. People were saying and writing that I was on the verge of a sparkling baseball career, and I wasn't going to give anyone any reason to start whispering about arm trouble.

After six innings, though, the pain was unbearable. I finally told Steve my depressing news. O'Neill, of course, got me out of the game immediately for my own good.

There was one consolation for me: Even while throwing in pain to every batter I faced in the whole game, I gave up only four hits and got 11 of the 18 outs by strikeouts. If a teenager pitching in severe pain can do that, surely there must be a future in the sport for him.

I wasn't really that worried at first, although the Indians certainly were, especially management. But when days stretched into weeks and weeks into two months, I began to worry too, and everyone else was in a state of panic. Was fate being cruel and snatching everything from me just after putting it within my grasp? Two months of X-rays, massages, secret trips to doctors, daily bulletins in the Cleveland papers, various experiments—each a failure—were causing everyone to worry more, including me. My story was a real-life soap opera. Through the crash of the Hindenburg and the coronation of King George VI, the medical reports about my right elbow remained on page one daily in the Cleveland papers.

In the middle of it all, I had to leave the team to go home to graduate from high school. Florence Wishmeyer had done a lot of the work that I had to do as class president. The *Des Moines Register-Tribune* sent its private plane, *Good News II*, a single-engine bi-wing, up to Cleveland to fly me home. Charlie Gatchett, the paper's pilot, and Sec Taylor, its sportswriter and a college football referee, brought me home in style. Gatchett was killed flying in the China-Burma-India theater in World War II.

The principal had a huge baseball made out of paper mache and all 17 diplomas were put in it for the ceremony. I gave the school a trophy case as an expression of my appreciation for all the understanding and support everyone had given me—the school administration, the teachers and my classmates and their parents. Three of the first trophies to go into that case were the ones we won in basketball that year—the ones we didn't have to give up after the fuss about my eligibility.

NBC covered the ceremonies "live" coast-to-coast on its "Blue" radio network. They told me it was a first, the only high school graduation carried live on nationwide radio. I was beginning to get used to "the press," and my interviews included two on Station WHO in Des Moines with the local sportscaster, Ronald Reagan—we called him "Dutch." But having NBC cover my graduation was pretty heady stuff even in my new worldly existence.

As our diplomas were being pulled one by one from that giant baseball, I thought about our class motto:

THE HIGHER WE RISE, THE BETTER THE VIEW

I wondered if I had already had my view.

After I flew back to Cleveland, we tried other cures for my ailing elbow, all with the same discouraging results. Concern continued to grow, both in Cleveland and down on the farm. Mom and Dad already had enough to worry about because of Dad's illness, and now this. The Indians were becoming gravely concerned. After this long, the question arose as to whether my career was in jeopardy. A pitcher needs a sound elbow on his throwing arm as much as a piano player needs all of his fingers. The Indians, and others, were saying privately that I was what today we call "a franchise player." They had an enormous amount at stake in my health. They were saying that not only was I an important part of their future—I *was* their future.

Cy Slapnicka had moved up the ladder from scout to general manager in the fall of 1935. Having discovered me, he felt a personal involvement. He was determined that he was going to find somebody, somewhere, who could solve this problem. He found him almost under his nose, in an office at 6007 Euclid Avenue, a few blocks from the ballpark. He was one A.L. Austin, a small, powerful man with bulging eyes and strong, stubby hands, who practiced something called mechano-therapy—bone and muscle manipulation. He was an apprentice to the world renowned "Bonesetter" Reese of Youngstown, who specialized in such things. Slap had visited Austin's office the day before to see and hear what Austin could do for me.

Austin ran his strong fingers up and down my right arm as I sat on his examining table. Then the specialist in this strange new field turned to Slap and said, "This boy has adhesions in his elbow. Hold on, son."

Then he grabbed my right wrist with his left hand and my elbow with his right. He gave a sudden twist—and darn near pulled my arm apart. The pain was blinding, but only for a moment. Then, magically, the pain was gone.

Austin said to me, "There, that ought to do it. Now you take a rest for 24 hours and then go right out and pitch. Don't worry about it."

"Will it be all right if I throw curves?"

"Throw anything you want."

It would have been impossible to tell who was more elated—Slap or me. We just about danced our way out of that office. And the next day, when the elbow still felt great, we were ready to jump out of our skin all over again.

Austin's bill to the Indians was $10.00.

The acid test came a few days later. Steve O'Neill started me against the Detroit Tigers in the first game of a Fourth of July doubleheader in Cleveland. I hadn't pitched since April—only six innings all year—but

30,000 fans showed up to cheer, and maybe to satisfy their curiosity, too.

It was no Cinderella story. No, I didn't pitch a no-hitter. I didn't even pitch a complete game. But I did pitch four strong innings and struck out three hitters in a row at one point. Then O'Neill took me out as a precaution and ordered me to go to the clubhouse for still another examination by the team physician, Dr. Ed Castle.

Dr. Castle looked my arm over thoroughly, over and over. Then he patted me on the shoulder and said, "It's as good as the day you were born."

There wasn't any dancing on Euclid Avenue that night, but as far as I was concerned, there should have been. I had weathered my first baseball storm. Even at 18 I was realistic enough to know that others were to follow—and they did—but I was willing to face them all. And the first one was right in front of me—the challenge to be a consistent pitcher, to help my team every time O'Neill gave me the baseball.

The Indians not only found the man who could cure me, but also saved my career by resisting the temptation to order me to pitch with the pain in the hope that it might work itself out. That sounds insane, but I'm sure some teams and some managers would have done just that.

The scrap heap is piled high with the bones of players forced into playing when they were injured, or who did it because nobody on their team advised them against it. There's a difference between playing when you're injured and playing when you're hurt. There's nothing wrong with taping up a sprained ankle if you can perform on it, but if you have a broken bone in your leg and play anyway, as some football players have done, you're flirting with an early end to your career, and a limp for the rest of your life. And you're not going to help your team. You're going to hurt it because you won't be able to perform up to your capacity. That do-or-die stuff may be great for the movies, but in real life an athlete who isn't smart about his injuries may not even be an athlete too long.

The Indians had the right attitude about my injury. They could have ordered me to pitch and picked up some nice paydays. People were curious about this kid who was striking out so many batters, and the Indians had every right to expect many big paydays in 1937, especially if I kept winning, but they resisted that temptation for as long as it took me to get over my elbow problems.

They passed up three months of possible starting assignments for me, maybe 18 games. But when I came back, they knew definitely that I was 100 percent healthy. I was able to pitch for the Cleveland Indians through 1956, thanks in part to the enlightened way they handled my injury in 1937.

Seven days later, I went the distance against the Tigers in Detroit. We lost, 3–2, and it was my fault. I walked six men and I made a wild throw in the ninth that let in the winning run. But I did get to pitch a complete game with no pain in my elbow. I had only four strikeouts but I also pitched a two-hitter. After that two-month scare, things could have been a lot worse.

New York came to town, and I got my first chance to start against the Yankees, the best team in baseball. It was the kind of challenge that always had me straining a bit, at any age. I pitched against them only once in '36, for one inning. They roughed me up for five runs in the first inning, with some help from three walks by me and three hits. When you allow six base runners in the first inning, you're going to lose—and I did.

But that was last year, and this was 1937. I was a year older now, and at that age, a year can make a major difference. There were 59,000 people in Cleveland Stadium including Mom, Dad and Marguerite to see the latest edition of New York's "Murderers' Row." Gehrig was having his last season, DiMaggio was leading both leagues in home runs, and Red Ruffing and Lefty Gomez were two of the best pitchers in baseball.

By the ninth inning, we were locked in a 1–1 tie and the biggest crowd of the season was being treated to a tense battle between the champions and the home team, between the kid and the mighty Ruffing, a 20-game winner that year and three other times and the winner of 273 games in a career that lasted 22 years, even with two years out for wartime service.

I was pitching a five-hitter with seven strikeouts, but I also had given up eight walks. In the ninth, a dramatic confrontation occurred, the first involving the two of us. It was Bob Feller against Joe DiMaggio, with the ball game on the line.

Ruffing, in those days before designated hitters in the American League, led off the ninth with a single. Frankie Crosetti laid down a bunt to move the runner into scoring position, and I pounced on it. But my throw to first hit Crosetti in the back. Then, in my frustration, I walked Red Rolfe to load the bases. That set the stage for Joe D. and me.

I got two quick strikes on Joe. Then my catcher, Frankie Pytlak, signalled for another fast ball, but I had a different idea. I checked the runner off third as I went into my windup. I threw my change of pace, and DiMag sent it deep into the dusk along Lake Erie. A grand slam. Final score: Yankees 5, Indians 1. A headline the next day would tell the whole story:

DIMAGGIO BEATS FELLER IN DUEL OF ACE YOUNGSTERS
BEFORE 60,000 AT STADIUM

After the game, many of the Yankees told reporters they agreed with a statement made earlier in the season by the president of the National League, Ford Frick, that I belonged in the minor leagues so I could get more experience. Frick was a former sportswriter who'd become head of the league and later would be Commissioner of Baseball, but Cy Slapnicka disputed the logic, league president or not.

Slap told the press after Frick popped off, "If that's true then the Cardinals and the Giants and some American League teams should be sent to the minors, too."

But after DiMaggio's grand slam, the Yankee players brought up the Frick quote again and said he was right. They didn't mention that I had a five-hitter for eight innings and held them to one run over that time. Gehrig, who was one of my strikeouts, said Ruffing was faster, even though he didn't hit against Ruffing. DiMaggio said he thought Tommy Bridges of Detroit was faster. Bill Dickey said that comparing me to Lefty Grove, which some people were doing, was silly. There wasn't a compliment in the whole Yankee dressing about a teenager who had just held the best team in baseball to one run in eight innings.

A feud was born. It became one of baseball's best, and it lasted throughout my 18 years in the majors.

A more constructive comment after the game came from Dad. At dinner with Marguerite and my parents, Dad, allowing me a proper amount of time to get over my disappointment and disgust, asked me, "What did you throw to DiMaggio?"

"A changeup."

"A change? Throwing changeups in the dark? You know better than that. He couldn't have seen your fast ball."

Dad was right. I swore to myself I'd never make that mistake again.

I thought about that pitch 41 years later, when Kirk Gibson limped out of the dugout in the first game of the 1988 World Series and hit one of the most dramatic home runs in Series history, starting the Los

Angeles Dodgers toward their upset championship over the Oakland A's.

Dennis Eckersley had no business throwing a flat, sidearm curve ball in that spot, but he did. Gibson was hurt and was having trouble swinging the bat. He missed most of the Series because of a badly pulled hamstring muscle in one leg, and ligament problems in the other. After he dragged himself and his bat to the plate on two bad legs in that first game, he showed he couldn't keep up with Eckersley's fast ball. He was fouling off pitches that he would normally put into orbit.

When the count reached three balls and two stikes, every ball player watching knew what was coming—the fast ball again. Gibson would never be able to catch up with it. He'd strike out, and the A's would win game one of the World Series. Only it never happened.

Eckersley went with his curve, hung it out over the plate and up around the letters and Gibson became a hero. I couldn't believe my eyes when I saw the curve coming, and other players have told me the same thing. It was the wrong pitch at the wrong time in the wrong place, but I could relate to it. The only difference was that I was lucky enough not to make my mistake in the World Series.

After the family went back to Van Meter with DiMaggio's grand slam still vivid in everybody's memory, I returned to my usual Cleveland routine. It always bothered Mom that I never was homesick, not even in my first weeks away from home. I was doing what I wanted to do, getting a start in the profession I loved, and as long as I was making satisfactory progress I wasn't going to get homesick. As much as I loved home, that wasn't where I wanted to be any more. I wanted to be exactly where I was, pitching in the major leagues, so there wasn't any reason to be homesick.

Besides, Slap and our trainer, Lefty Weisman, made me feel at home. Slap and Abigail didn't have any children, so they had me over at every opportunity and treated me like their own teenage son. They lived on Scarborough Road in East Cleveland and they'd take me out to the country in Slap's Packard—he always drove Packards—and we'd have dinner in the farm houses, especially on weekends when the dinners were family-style affairs.

At Lefty's, it wasn't dinner out, it was chicken livers at home on Meadowbrook Road. They had kids, and trainers don't make the salaries that general managers do, so they couldn't afford to eat out as often as the Salpnickas. But Sally Weisman's chicken livers were good enough to keep any man at home.

In 1936, I was living in a rooming house for the elderly at 1910 East 89th Street with Lloyd Russell, alias Buzz Burton. He played minor league ball in the Northern League as Buzz Burton and college ball at Baylor University using his real name. Under either name, he was still playing for the Indians. He was a football star at Baylor University and later became its coach and athletic director. Slapnicka knew what he was doing—I wasn't going to get into any trouble at the rooming house. The most fun I had was listening to the tales of a Civil War veteran who lived there.

Not long after that, Slap moved me to Devon Hall, a dormitory-style hotel, for late 1936 and all of 1937, rooming me with another rookie, Roy Weatherly—"Stormy." He was a little guy, only 5'6", but he could hit a baseball. The Indians had their choice of signing Tommy Henrich or Stormy when Judge Landis ruled that the major league teams were stockpiling minor leaguers to such an extreme that many players were being deprived of the opportunity to advance. Landis declared about 90 players to be free agents and two years later he again did the same thing. When the Indians were faced with a choice of Weatherly or Henrich, an Ohio boy born in Massilon, they picked Roy.

It worked out fine for both of them. Roy, a left-handed-hitting outfielder, broke in with me in '36, and Tommy, who was also a left-handed-hitting outfielder, sold himself to the Yankees the next year, played 11 seasons—with three years out for World War II—had a good lifetime batting average of .282 and was so dependable in pressure situations that he became known as "Old Reliable."

Roy did almost the same thing. He played ten years, missed two others for the war, hit .286 lifetime and even was Tommy's teammate on the Yankees in 1946 and 1950.

When Stormy and I were rooming together at Devon Hall, we ate our dinners at the Forum Cafeteria at Ninth and Euclid with some of our teammates, including Jeff Heath, Soup Campbell and Bill Zuber. We knew the food had to be good at the Forum—the umpires ate there.

We took the electric bus from the ballpark to the Forum, and we'd each load up two cafeteria trays for $1.00. But Stormy eventually developed a strong preference for the food back at Devon Hall—he married the dietician.

We found all the entertainment we wanted at the movies and on the radio. I loved going to see *Snow White, The Wizard of Oz* and *Gone With the Wind* at the Palace, the State and the Hippodrome, all on

Euclid Avenue—especially the Palace. They had vaudeville shows with the feature movies and you could get a whole night's entertainment with comedians like our local boy, Bob Hope, the dog acts, jugglers and even table tennis players from China. It was vaudeville at its best, and I loved it—all that and a full-length movie, too. And if you really wanted to go first-class, you could go to see the big bands at the Hollenden House, or the Cleveland and Statler Hotels. Me? I stayed in my room, lifted my dumbbells and went to bed early.

Radio was still king in those days before television. America's idea of a good time was to turn on the radio on Sunday nights and listen to Jack Benny, Edgar Bergen and Charlie McCarthy, Fred Allen, and Amos 'n Andy. During the week there were the quiz shows, where you could win $5.00 on Dr. I.Q., where one of the announcers out in the audience would tell the emcee on stage that he had a contestant, saying "I have a lady in the balcony, Doctor." And if you were lucky enough to get picked to go on Phil Baker's show, "Take It Or Leave It," you could work your way all the way up to the $64 question.

Life in another city was different for a young professional athlete in those years. No compact discs or TV sets or VCRs to pass the time away. A long-distance phone call home was a big thing, and riding the electric bus or the streetcar was the only way to go because young ballplayers had to wait to buy that first car. Most new cars cost between $600 and $1,200, and some were even more than that.

After DiMaggio's grand slam, I promised myself I'd settle my score with the Yankees, but in the meantime I had to get back into the winning groove. I did it my next time out, a one-inning relief job in Philadelphia when we beat the A's, 9–8. I didn't allow a run or a hit, got a strikeout and didn't walk anybody. It was my first win of 1937. I won again in Washington with a nine-inning performance when we beat the Senators, 11–2. I pitched a seven-hitter with nine strikeouts and then found myself with another shot at the Yankees, in Yankee Stadium.

It still was not to be. I went the full nine again, and had 12 strikeouts, but I gave up nine hits and ten walks. Gehrig homered with two out in the ninth to tie it, 5–5, and we lost in the tenth. I didn't get the loss, but I knew I was the reason for our defeat. No wonder we lost. I was disappointed again, but there was one improvement this time. The papers didn't have any quotes from the Yankees putting me down. I didn't need any. I remembered all the ones from the first time.

There was something more than my new rivalry with the Yanks to worry about. The Indians were struggling. By the time we got back to Cleveland from that road trip, we had lost 11 out of 13 games and had dropped to fifth place. What made it even worse was the talk we were beginning to hear and the stories we were beginning to read—Steve O'Neill was in trouble. If we didn't start winning soon and finish strong, he might be fired. It wasn't his fault, but the old saying is true—it's easier to fire the manager than to fire the whole team.

Fortunately, we hit a hot streak as soon as we got back to Cleveland. As baseball players say, it must have been the home cookin'. We started to win again, and I contributed with a 5–2 victory over the Browns. It wasn't anything to write home about, a seven-hitter with seven strikeouts, but at this point—August 11—the team needed every win it could get to salvage the season, and so did I, for the same reason.

Over the next two weeks, we continued at a respectable pace. We didn't have a long winning streak, but we were winning often enough to keep the talk about firing O'Neill to a minimum. I didn't welcome the idea of a new manager. What the heck—I was still only in my second year of professional baseball, and Steve was the only manager I'd had. As far as I could tell at my tender age, he was a good manager, and he was like a third father to me, behind Dad and Slap. I didn't look forward to adjusting to a new manager. I had enough things to worry about, like continuing to come back from my elbow injury—not to mention having a father with cancer.

I hit my stride in late August. The Red Sox came to town and I beat them, 8–1, on a four-hitter that included 16 strikeouts. I struck out Joe Cronin, Boston's All-Star shortstop and now a member of the Hall of Fame, twice in that game. Getting Cronin on strikes twice in one game was an achievement. He didn't strike out often and was a consistent hitter, with a .307 average that year and a .301 career average over 20 seasons.

On Cronin's second strikeout, I caught him looking at a fast ball, and the umpire, Lou Kolls, called him out. Cronin just stood there in the batter's box and glared out at me, the veteran All-Star staring down the 18-year-old.

Then he turned back and glared at Kolls behind the plate. Finally, he said to the umpire, "If I didn't see, how did you?"

The Senators came in after that, and I lost a 6–2 game to them. I didn't pitch that badly—six hits in seven innings and only three runs— but any loss would be a disappointment after my big win over the Red

Sox. I didn't have the time, or the inclination, to lick my wounds though. The Yankees were coming to town.

It was 85 degrees that day, September 2, plus all the humidity from Lake Erie, but I wasn't going to worry about pacing myself. I wanted those Yankees in the worst way after they mouthed off about me. I was going to follow that old pitching strategy for a big game—throw as hard as you can as long as you can.

The Indians could see that I was getting swamped with phone calls for interviews and offers for all kinds of deals all the time, so they changed roomates for me. Instead of Roy Weatherly, Wally Schang was my roomie now. He was an Indians coach by then after 19 years as a player, and he was 48 years old, so the Cleveland management thought he would be a steadying influence on me with all the people I had coming at me from so many different directions, and he was.

The night before my game against the Yankees, Wally thought something was wrong. It was only eight o'clock and I was getting ready for bed. He was curious, and concerned too.

He asked me, "Are you sick?"

"No, why?"

"It's only eight o'clock."

"Never felt better. I just want to be ready for those Yankees tomorrow."

I went right at them all day long, from my first pitch of the game to Frankie Crosetti. I shut them down completely for seven innings and beat them on a five-hitter, 4–2, after DiMaggio spoiled my shutout with a two-run homer in the eighth. I struck out 12 Yankee hitters, including Gehrig three times on curve balls. That was 24 strikeouts against the Yankees in my last two starts against them.

Gehrig was battling Charlie Gehringer of the Tigers for the 1937 batting championship and ended second at .351. I'm not sure how often he struck out three times in one game, but it couldn't have been too many. And each time he was swinging. The great Lou Gehrig, one of the top hitters in baseball for more than ten years, couldn't hit my curve ball. I didn't need any more encouragement than that.

As we were leaving the field after the game, Lou went out of his way to come over to me and say, "Just keep pitching, Bob. You're going to do all right in this league."

One of the writers mentioned in his story that I had 99 strikeouts for my brief season now, and more than one-third of them were Yankees.

None of those guys said after the game that I should be in the minor leagues getting more experience.

I was on a real tear for the rest of the season. I won six of my last eight starts. The team stayed hot too, playing at a .750 pace over the last two months, enough to regain some respectability with a fourth-place finish. Johnny Allen led the league's pitchers in won-lost percentage because of his outstanding record of 15 wins and only one defeat. We weren't the first-place team, but we weren't in eighth place either.

My final stats showed that I ended the year with nine wins and seven losses and 150 strikeouts in 143 innings. That was the fourth best strikeout total in the American League and the highest ratio of strikeouts to innings pitched of any pitcher in either league.

The newspaper headlines told the story:

ALLEN, FELLER SHARE AMERICAN LEAGUE PITCHING HONORS

FELLER BOASTS BEST STRIKEOUT AVERAGE

The Indians management and I were excited about how well I had come back from my elbow injury in my first game of the year. Those numbers showed a lot of pitching by me from July 4th to the end of the season. Wes Ferrell led the league with 281 innings and my 143 innings for half a season meant I would have topped Ferrell over a whole year, all of it with no more elbow problems. We were ready, all of us, for a bright new season in 1938.

I received a unique sort of recognition from the Associated Press for my comeback from injury. I was voted its flop of the year. AP took a poll, although taking one to determine the biggest disappointments in something seemed to me to be an exercise in negative thinking, but maybe it was a slow news day.

Whatever the reason was, I was voted this "honor" after being hurt for half the season. AP showed its consistency. Dizzy Dean was voted the biggest flop in the National League, and he was hurt for half the season, too.

Diz was hit on the toe by a line drive off the bat of my teammate, Earl Averill, in the All Star Game in Washington. His toe was broken. By coming back too soon and changing his pitching motion to compensate for the pain in his toe, Dizzy developed a sore arm and ruined his career. Even though he hung around a few more years, he was washed up at age 26, after 120 wins in his previous five seasons.

And you call a star like that a "flop" after he gets hurt? I don't.

Pressure and criticism from the reporters never bothered me to the extent that it caused me any problems. The natural tendency is to lash back at the media when they criticize you, but those same reporters and columnists are the ones who also help to make you famous, give you the opportunity to lead a comfortable life on a nice salary and may someday even vote you into your sport's Hall of Fame.

Besides, it could have been worse for me in 1937. We could have had television. Any athlete of today has a far more difficult burden to carry, and far more pressure to handle, than we did in the 1930s and '40s, and the difference is TV.

Your performance is seen by millions, which gives you the opportunity to gain far more recognition, and riches, than in earlier years, but there's a down side to that too. When you fail, not only does the whole world see it, you fail over and over again. You fail on the instant replay three times after the "live action." You fail again on the evening news, at six and eleven. You fail once more before the next game on the pre-game show.

In my time, there were some advantages to having only radio and newspaper coverage.

Television also compounds an athlete's life today because it has made sports journalism so much more competitive. Newspaper, radio and TV reporters are competing against each other to show something that the others didn't, to get you to say something that the others don't have in their stories, and to get a story from you before anyone else.

In this age of sports enlightenment, you even have women reporters in the dressing room with you after the game. All of this is supposed to be progress, but I'm just as glad I didn't have this kind of progress when I was playing.

I think today's athletes, although they admittedly benefit so much from television exposure, deserve a lot of credit for the way they handle its negative side. When you make a bad pitch and the hitter puts it out of the park and you cost your team the game, it's a real test of your maturity to be able to stand in front of your locker 15 minutes later and admit it to the world. How many people in other professions would be willing to have their job performances evaluated that way, in front of millions, every afternoon at five o'clock?

Gordon Cobbledick came to my defense in his column in the *Plain Dealer*. He wrote, "Feller went into the 1937 season under the greatest pressure ever imposed on a ball player." He said I "made monkeys" of the Giants in spring training and recalled that I struck out 11 Browns in six innings in my first start "with an arm that was injured on the third pitch of the game."

He pointed out that all the talk while I was hurt about my being finished put even more pressure on me when I came back. "But Feller came back," Cobbledick wrote, "and his performance in the last half of the season was phenomenal."

He recited my record over the second half and then finished his column with, "Maybe some of you can tell me what there is in this record to stamp an 18-year-old schoolboy as one of the flops of the year."

Those votes for Diz and me were an education for the three of us, Cobbledick included, on the subject of polls. We learned in 1937 what Harry Truman proved 11 years later.

CHAPTER FOUR

Life With Rollickin' Rollie Hemsley and Other Notables

Rollie Hemsley walked into my life in 1938, the man they called "Rollickin' Rollie"—and for good reason. Every time he'd get too much fire water in him he'd manage to get into a fight. He never won one in his life. The next morning, he'd have two black eyes and show up at the ballpark looking like a tree full of owls.

He quit the habit during the '38 season and never had another drink after that for the remaining 34 years of his life, but at the time the Indians got him from the Browns, his reputation always preceded him. The Cleveland papers carried stories that year during spring training with headlines like:

VITT TO FINE PLAYERS WHO DRINK WITH HEMSLEY

RUN-INS INSTEAD OF RUNS BATTED IN
DOT ROLLICKING ROLLIE'S CAREER

Steve O'Neill had been fired, much to my sorrow, and our new manager was Oscar Vitt, coming off a successful season when he led the Yankees' farm club, the Newark Bears, to the International League championship. Vitt was exactly the opposite of O'Neill. Steve led with a touch that was firm but gentle. Vitt used the same approach to men as a Marine drill sergeant, an attitude that was to cost him—and us—dearly only two years later.

He was a guy who survived the 1906 earthquake in San Francisco as a teenager. He showed his resourcefulness by forming a partnership with an adult and making money by rebuilding the chimneys of private homes, knowing that the law then said a private home couldn't be occupied unless the chimney was in working order.

But Vitt was only one of two newsmakers who joined us that year. Hemsley, the other, made far more news over the course of his career than Vitt did, even including Vitt's problems that began in 1938 and exploded in 1940.

Rollie was an immensely likeable teammate and widely respected as an outstanding catcher. He was a decent hitter, too, with batting averages over .280 five times, but he was his own worst enemy with that bottle.

He broke in with the Pittsburgh Pirates in 1928 but got himself traded to the Cubs in '31 after he played only ten games for the Pirates that year, the result of a prank with water-filled bags being thrown around a hotel room. He managed to stick with the Cubs the rest of '31 and all of '32, when they lost to the Yankees in the World Series.

But the Cubs couldn't endure Rollie's antics any more than that, so he found himself playing for Cincinnati the next year. The Reds put up with him for 49 games and then unloaded him to the Browns, where be became Rogers Hornsby's problem.

Rollie found a home there. He lasted four-and-a-half seasons with the Browns. Hornsby put up with Rollie some of the time, lowered the boom on him at other times, and all in all got more out of him than other managers had while working through and around Rollie's drinking. But even Hornsby had a limit, despite everyone's fondness for Hemsley and the respect for his ability, especially in handling pitchers.

The final straw for the Browns was when Rollie rented a car one night in Philadelphia after the curfew hour for the players set by Hornsby for road trips. Rollie pointed his rented car toward the nearest watering hole, enjoyed a fine evening and topped it off in the usual Hemsley manner—with a fight. He and a sailor tangled after Rollie took offense to something the guy said, so Rollie ended up as a guest of the city in jail.

Hornsby was the one who got the call from the cops. He had to go downtown and bail out his catcher, but "The Rajah" didn't let it end there. He fined Hemsley $500, a far stiffer fine in 1938 than today, and

Young Bob Feller on his way to greatness. (National Baseball Library, Cooperstown, NY)

Nine-year-old Bob Feller in his
first baseball uniform

As a high school senior in spring
training, 1937.

Graduation day, Van Meter High
School, 1937.

The first picture ever of Bob Feller and Joe DiMaggio, taken in 1937.

Bob Feller at 18, with his frequent mound opponent during the 1937 spring training exhibitions, New York Giants great Carl Hubbell. (Associated Press).

Bob on the cover of Time Magazine on April 19, 1937...

...and on Newsweek's cover ten years later.

The Feller fast ball outraces a Harley-Davidson motorcycle going at 83 MPH. Bottom photo shows Feller's pitch, calculated at 104 MPH, already through the bull's eye while the cyclist approaches his own. Demonstration took place in Chicago in 1940.

Pitcher Bob Feller at the start of a sensational career.

In the Cleveland dressing room after his 1940 Opening Day no-hitter, the only one ever pitched.

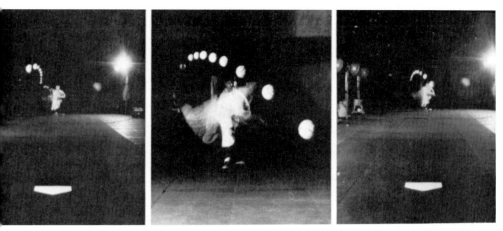

The trajectory of the Bob Feller fast ball, the path of his curve, and the slider that he popularized after World War II. (Look Magazine)

With his dad, who built Bob's real-life field of dreams on their Iowa farm. (Associated Press)

In the 1940s with (left) Clark Gable during the war; (right) two other baseball men, Bing Crosby of the Pirates and Bob Hope of the Indians; and (below) the legendary Cy Young, for whom the award for Best Pitcher of the Year is named. (United Press International)

ordered him to return to St. Louis immediately while the rest of the team finished the road trip without him.

The Browns started shopping Rollie around, and the Detroit Tigers expressed an interest in him. Birdie Tebbetts and Rudy York were doing their catching, and even their future Hall of Famer, Mickey Cochrane, was putting himself behind the plate occasionally even though he was now their manager. They had some good pitchers, including Eldon Auker, Roxie Lawson, Tommy Bridges and Schoolboy Rowe, and the Tigers wanted to be sure they had a competent staff of receivers to go with their good pitchers.

They offered the Browns $75,000 for Hemsley, and St. Louis agreed. Rollie had become as unhappy with the Browns as they had with him, so when word reached him about the deal, he did what he always did— he went out and celebrated. He overdid it, naturally, and when the Tigers heard that he had gone off the deep end again, they quickly called the Browns and canceled the deal.

Despite his storybook drinking exploits, the Indians were interested in Hemsley, and I was one of the reasons. Cy Slapnicka thought he would be an excellent receiver for me because of his skill and savvy plus the knowledge acquired over his ten years in the Majors. So Slap sent one of our catchers, Billy Sullivan, and two other players, Ed Cole and Roy Hughes, to the Browns in exchange for Hemsley.

Rollie was a great, steadying influence on me in my first years in the big leagues. He was an excellent receiver, running a game alertly from behind the plate and excelling in the playing part of his job too as a good catcher with an outstanding throwing arm.

In later years, Jim Hegan became the best catcher I ever had. He didn't hit as well as some others, but nobody was his equal as a catcher, especially with his arm. As an all-around catcher for both hitting and catching, I'd have to rate Bill Dickey of the Yankess in the 1930s and '40s as the best I ever saw. He was as good as anyone behind the plate, and better with the bat.

There were several others I'd include right behind Dickey—Al Lopez, Mickey Cochrane, Gabby Hartnett, Roy Campanella and Wes Westrum. Yogi Berra? An excellent hitter, especially in the late innings with the game hanging in the balance, and the American League's Most Valuable Player three times, but as a catcher I always thought he was above average.

Gary Carter and Johnny Bench belong on any such list too, but Bill Dickey was the best all-around catcher of them all, past or present.

The Hemsley deal was made on February 10, and he was in hot water the next month. He was kicked out of our spring training camp in New Orleans by Vitt after breaking training three times in ten days. Fortunately for me, the Indians were patient enough not to get rid of him. He stayed with us for four years and became one of our most valuable players, and one of my most valuable friends.

While Dad's cancer was in remission, the Indians did a nice thing and gave Mom, Dad, Marguerite and me a free vacation in Florida as a reward for my loyalty in staying with their team after Commissioner Landis declared me a free agent. They sent us to Delray Beach. They even paid for Marguerite's tuition. I left the family only long enough to fly back to Cleveland to sign my contract for 1938 amid much fanfare surrounding not only me but local radio station WTAM as well.

The station was moving its studios to the new NBC Building at 815 Superior Avenue N.E., so they had a big shindig at the Carter Hotel, in formal dress and the works. They invited me to come up from Florida and sign my contract in a live radio broadcast.

It was a miserable evening for going anywhere. There was a raw wind that night and sleet and rain, but 650 guests showed up in evening gowns and tuxedos. The station's sports announcer, Tom Manning, interviewed me and the papers reported that I signed a contract for $17,500, which was in the right neighborhood—a nice neighborhood in those days for a kid who just turned 19 three months before. Manning went one better than the rest of us. He didn't just wear a tux—he was in white tie and tails. And this was radio.

I could afford big-city prices now, like $168 for a full-length mink-muskrat coat at Halle Brothers, which didn't interest me, or to see shows like *Hellzapoppin*, starring Olsen and Johnson at the Palace, which did. I was flattered by the amount of my contract. Frankie Pytlak, who was going to battle Hemsley for the starting catcher's job, was beginning his eighth season in the major leagues. He signed for $9,000. He told the press it wasn't as much as he'd hoped for, but that he was happy with what he got. There were no multi-year contracts in those days either. You had to negotiate a new contract every year, based on what you did the season before. So you either agreed to the amount in the contract mailed to you over the winter, or you met with the general manager and haggled your way through another one.

Vitt was in charge during our spring training camp in New Orleans, and there wasn't any doubt about that. He was a charmer with the reporters, but he was a taskmaster out on the field, and there's nothing wrong with that. But the drill sergeant in him surfaced from time to time, like the day when he told the writers that he might make us walk from our hotel to the ballpark and back every day during spring training.

He said, "That extra mileage on their legs will do the players good."

He never did it, and for good reason. If he had tried, some of those players would have kept on walking. Still, Vitt remained the biggest news in Cleveland over the winter. The *Cleveland Press* topped everyone else in the news media. It ran a 12-part copyrighted series of articles by Stuart Bell on the life of one Oscar Vitt. Our new manager was getting more ink in Cleveland than Franklin Roosevelt.

Another man who entered my life that year deserves mention. He's Ken Keltner, who will be forever remembered as the third baseman who stopped Joe DiMaggio's hitting streak at 56 consecutive games with two of the greatest stops anyone ever saw. But Kenny did a lot more than that in 13 years as one of the best players in the American League, and one of the best teammates a guy could ask for.

Keltner was a lot like the Yankees' Don Mattingly today. We played a 154-game schedule in those years, and Ken gave you 150 games every year. He didn't hit for average the way Mattingly does, but neither does anybody else except Wade Boggs. Still, he hit .325 one year and in the .280s and .290s three other times, and he was a serious long ball threat. He had years when he hit 23, 26 and 31 home runs, and he had 113 runs batted in one year and 119 in another.

He was an outstanding third baseman, and it has always seemed appropriate to me that he was the one who stopped DiMaggio's streak. With his ability to get runs for you with his bat, and to prevent the other team from doing so with his glove, he was an all-around star but, like Mattingly, he was a devoted team player. Keltner never went around seeking publicity or mouthing off in criticism of his teammates or his manager, and you'd never read anything about his love life in the morning newspaper.

Vitt started working on me right away. He was concerned about my high kick because it left us vulnerable to stolen bases. He wanted me to lower my kick with men on base and speed up my delivery, so base runners wouldn't get such big jumps on me. It was a good suggestion, and it worked.

Today it might not be so much of a problem. There isn't that much stealing anyhow. The only runners a pitcher has to worry about are those who lead the league in stolen bases. They'll be trying to add to their total so they'll be able to renegotiate their contracts next year, and they'll run at any time, not just when it makes sense.

The rest of the time the pitcher has to concentrate on the hitters and their fondness for the home run, safe in the knowledge that the man on first base isn't going to try anything. The players aren't the only ones who think that way. The managers do too. When Earl Weaver was managing the Orioles, he called the bunt "the most overrated play in baseball," and his favorite offensive strategy was playing for a three-run homer.

If I were pitching today and Ossie Vitt were my manager again, he might not even worry about my high kick with men on base.

I wasn't the only object of Vitt's attention. He was everywhere, cracking down on infielders and outfielders for fielding flaws, working with the hitters on their stances and their batting strokes, instructing pitchers in everything that occurred to him. He was an infielder for ten years with the Tigers and Red Sox from 1912 through 1921 and he had only a .238 lifetime batting average, but he injected himself into every phase of the game.

With Vitt's players one thing was certain: You may have been loving him or you may have been hating him, but you weren't ignoring him.

The 1938 season got off to the kind of start every pitcher hopes for, and more. I faced the Browns in Cleveland on April 20, and I had everything working that day. When the game starts, pitchers can never be sure how they're going to do. You can feel great while you're warming up and have a lot of zip and movement on your fast ball and a good, crisp break on your curve ball and then start the game and find you have nothing out there. Or you can come out of the bullpen and start the game with your fingers crossed and all of a sudden everything clicks and you're solidly in business with all your stuff.

On that day, I felt strong during my warmups and seemed to have good stuff. When the game started, things kept getting better. I ended up with my first one-hit game. I had 11 others, but the first of something like a one-hitter is always special, and this was no exception.

We won the game 9–0, the forfeit score in baseball, meaning the Browns could have stayed in their hotel rooms and taken the day off and still lost by no more than they did. The only St. Louis hit was by Billy Sullivan, our teammate of the year before who went to the Browns in the Rollie Hemsley deal. He was my catcher in my first game with the Indians two seasons before, and he became the only player who ever apologized to me for getting a hit against me.

It was a drag bunt, on a sign from the new St. Louis manager, Gabby Street, to the left of the pitcher's mound. I fielded it as quickly as I could and gunned my throw to Hal Trosky at first base, but Eddie Rommel, the first base umpire, called Sullivan safe. It was one of the "bang-bang" plays, where the umpire looks at the bag and listens at the same time for the sound of the throw hitting the first baseman's glove.

The Cleveland fans and some of the writers raised a big fuss after the game, saying Sullivan was out, but Rommel didn't buy it. "He was safe," he said, "And it didn't make any difference to me whether Feller had a no-hitter or what inning it was. If that play had happened in the ninth inning, and Feller still had a no-hitter going, I would have made the same call. He was safe."

Sullivan told the reporters in the Browns dressing room, "I was safe, but I wish I hadn't been."

Later in our clubhouse, he was absolutely apologetic. He told me, "I'm awfully sorry I got that hit. As long as we had to lose anyway, I wish you'd gotten your no-hitter."

The no-hitter would have been great, but I wasn't going to complain. Some people were beginning to ask some questions again, because I had been hit hard in a couple of exhibition games in spring training, and the Giants had roughed me up on the last weekend before the season started. Combined with my elbow problems in the first half of '37, some doubters were beginning to be heard, even though I had held the Giants to three runs in 19 innings on our swing north from spring training.

But the one-hitter not only shut up the doubters, it brought out the superlatives again. I threw 136 pitches, with six strikeouts and six walks, and in the headlines the next day I was being called "Fastball Phenom," "Blaze Ball King" and "4-Star Sensation."

Like any pticher, I was just as proud of my hitting. I got two hits in that game and drove in two runs.

The *Des Moines Register* carried a story about the game the next day telling about how much good the one-hitter did for Mom, who had been in bed for five weeks with a serious case of pneumonia. The *Register*'s headline said:

THAT ONE WAS FOR MOTHER

Dad shocked me by telling the paper, "I wouldn't be surprised if he won 25 games. This season won't be as hard on him as last—Bob has learned how to handle himself."

This was Dad? My quiet, conservative father? Telling the world I'd win 25 games?

Well, the most original question in the mob scene in our clubhouse after the game was from reporter Ed McAuley, who asked me why I didn't just make a wild throw on Sullivan's bunt. He would have been safe, but it would have been an error instead of a hit.

I told McAuley, "I can't think that fast." Besides, I thought I could get Sullivan. Trosky had broken toward the ball and was a little late getting to the bag. I had to hesitate a split second before making my throw to him while he was getting there.

Not only did I silence the critics that day, I silenced the Browns, too. They were heckling me hard from their dugout until the fifth inning. The bench jockeys reached their peak in that inning when I went to three balls and no strikes on George McQuinn. I came back and got him on strikes, and also struck out the next hitter, Red Kress. Then the Browns suddenly went quiet.

You can always find something to keep you humble, though. That day's lesson was in the size of the crowd. Only 4,000 fans showed up, even though it was only the second game of the season, after 31,000 came the day before to watch Johnny Allen open the season for us.

My one-hitter overshadowed some other big news that day. Joe DiMaggio ended his holdout with the Yankees and signed for $25,000. Dizzy Dean was still trying to come back from his toe injury and arm problems of the year before and pitched a 10–4 win over Cincinnati for his new team, the Cubs. Dizzy had made the mistake of rushing himself in trying to recover from his toe injury, and he was still paying the price for it.

DiMaggio's holdout seems a reminder of the way we were when you look back on it now. There used to be several big holdout stories each spring. It was as sure a sign of spring as the first robin. But you don't see holdout stories as much any more, because today players sign multiyear contracts.

In my day, and until free agency in the mid-1970s, players received only a one-year contract. You had to negotiate a whole new deal for yourself every winter. If a player was having a bad year and then got hot in August and September, the fans and writers would say he's "putting on his salary drive."

When the Indians traded Jimmy Piersall to Washington after the 1961 season, he held out for a multiyear contract. Ed Doherty, the Senators' general manager and a good friend of Piersall from their days together with the Boston Red Sox, turned him down flat. Piersall then announced he would hold out.

It gave the Senators a lot of publicity over the winter, and they needed it. They were losing 100 games a year with an expansion team. Piersall continued to insist on a multiyear contract, even though it was unheard of in baseball at that time. It dragged out so long that the fans started to side with him, saying his request seemed reasonable. After all, performers in other professions received multiyear contracts.

The Senators were even accused of dragging the whole thing out on purpose just for the publicity. But the dispute was real. Doherty was not about to give in, and he didn't. When Piersall ended his threat of a holdout and signed his contract, it was for one year, just like every one of the other 499 players in the major leagues in 1962.

There was another reason for the excitement in Cleveland over my one-hitter. My catcher was Rollie Hemsley. The Indians and their fans suddenly had visions of greater things from me with veteran Rollie handling me so well behind the plate. Maybe Dad was going to be right—25 wins might not be so crazy to think about after all.

Ed McAuley asked Rollie if I had been pitching with a wet ball in Cleveland's drizzly weather, and Hemsley's answer should have won a prize for originality:

"How could he? Only the grass was wet. The ball never went anywhere but from Bob to me and back again."

Rollie's next game was also mine. He didn't catch again until I pitched again, against the Tigers in Detroit. Frankie Pytlak had been starting ahead of him. I had an eight-hitter with 11 strikeouts and we won the game, 9–4, but then Rollie drank his way into some new problems.

Vitt spotted him unusually happy in the lobby of our hotel, the Book-Cadillac. This was a Sunday evening, and what infuriated Vitt even more was that he had also seen Rollie drunk in the lobby the Thursday before. So Vitt told our traveling secretary, Frank Kohlbecker, to send Hemsley back to Cleveland.

Only when the team showed up at the train station for our trip to Chicago, there was good ol' Rollie, ready to go. Kohlbecker told him at the station, "Rollie, we're suspending you and we're fining you $250. You're not going to Chicago with the team."

There was nothing new in any of this for Rollie. His escapades had become legendary by this time. The teams he played for used to put detectives on his tail, but he was always able to shake them early in the evening. Then they'd spend the rest of the night running into each other at different bars, like a Mack Sennett movie comedy. With Rollie, the day really didn't begin until the sun went down.

His most famous caper was that night in Philadelphia, and that's one we still talk about. He climbed out of his window in the Ben Franklin Hotel, crawled onto a ledge at least several stories above the street, went around the corner on the ledge and stepped back into the hotel through the open window of a room where some of his teammates were playing poker. A sober man never could have done it.

But that wasn't Rollie's only stunt—just his most daring one. Once our dentist got mad at him for not coming to the office for a checkup during spring training in New Orleans, back in the days when bad teeth seemed to be the explanation for every injury you had. If you had a sore arm or a hang nail or anything else, they'd pull a tooth and tell you that was the problem, so teams put a lot of importance on those dental exams during spring training.

Rollie couldn't be bothered with anything like that, so he just never went. The dentist kept after him about it, and one day in the dressing room he started on Rollie again.

Rollie reached into his mouth, took out a set of false teeth which the dentist obviously didn't know about, and said, "Here—take them to your office and check them. But be sure to bring them back tomorrow."

During one of our road trips, Rollie lost another one of his drunken brawls, and when a newspaper photographer wanted to take a picture of his two black eyes, Rollie invited him to his hotel room.

When the photographer arrived and knocked, Hemsley called out that the door was unlocked. As the photographer opened the door, Rollie was hiding behind it and standing on a chair. He dropped the dresser drawer on him with a direct hit. The bottom broke open when it hit the photographer on the head, and the drawer hung around the poor guy's neck like a picture frame. That's what Rollie thought of the photographer's request for a picture of the Hemsley black eyes.

That escapade on the ledge around the Ben Franklin Hotel in Philadelphia may have been Rollickin' Rollie's boldest feat, but his most dangerous one was something he pulled on a Pullman car between Richmond and Washington when we were coming north from spring training one season. He set the car on fire accidentally because he was careless with matches in an upper berth while smoking a cigarette.

They had to stop the train and call the nearest fire department. By the time they got there, half of that Pullman car was ruined.

But I've always had enormous respect for Rollie Hemsley because he did something that the rest of us might not have been strong enough to do. Cy Slapnicka convinced Rollie to join Alcoholics Anonymous after he got off to such a rocky start with us in 1938. As an incentive, Slap gave a large diamond ring to Rollie's daughter, the person who meant more to him than anyone else in the world. It worked. Rollie took the pledge. He drank about a case of Cokes a day for a while because he needed that sugar that he wasn't getting from booze any more, but he never went back to the hard stuff.

Rollie Hemsley was a big reason for my success in those years and even beyond that. When he died in Washington in 1972, I changed my travel schedule immediately—I was on a tour of minor league cities in California—and flew all night so I could be at his funeral.

I got off the "red eye" flight and took a cab to Rollie's funeral home in Silver Spring, Maryland, and got there ten minutes before the funeral started. When I walked in, I became glad I made the effort. I didn't see another baseball person there.

Jeff Heath was another standout personality on our team, a rookie in the '38 season and my roommate for several years in the 1940s. He was a muscular monster, a 200-pounder whose arms were so thick he had to cut the sleeves out of his uniform like Jimmie Foxx before him and Ted Kluszewski after. He went on to become a star, with 194 home runs and a lifetime average of .293 in 14 seasons. He had that rare combination of power and speed and he showed it by twice leading the American League in triples.

Jeff didn't have the drinking problem that Rollie did, but he had a world-class independence about himself. You couldn't start shoving him around because he shoved back—fast.

We were lounging in our room at the New Yorker Hotel in Manhattan one night when we heard a knock on the door. Jeff answered and saw a lovely young thing standing there. He saw something else too—a man in the shadows, obviously armed with a camera. Professional athletes recognize that setup for hush money when they see it. Heath ordered the young lady to step aside, grabbed her boyfriend by the shirt and decked him with one punch. Then he calmly closed the door and called the house detective.

Jeff was able to use his strong build to defend himself like that and also to express himself. Like the time in Cleveland when a fan behind our dugout started getting on Jeff's case after he struck out. All of us watched as Heath reached across the dugout roof, grabbed the heckler by his hair and flattened him.

The story didn't end there. The police found out that Mr. Loudmouth was on probation from prison. They slapped him right back into the cooler for creating a disturbance.

Buck Newsom, our opponent on opening day the day before my one-hitter in '38, was another character of that era. He was a solid major league pitcher, a 21-game winner in 1940 when he helped to lead Detroit to the pennant. He followed that with a sensational World Series against Cincinnati in which he won two games, held the Reds to four runs in three games and went the full nine innings in every game.

He was a personality too, and he made himself into more of one as his pitching skills diminished with age, changing his nickname to "Bobo" and coming up with a "blooper" pitch. He ended up being traded ten times in a 20-year career in the majors. He played for the Washington Senators three different times. We used to say that the only man who served more terms in Washington than Newsom was FDR.

Newsom had this thing about not pitching if there was a scrap of paper on the mound. He'd stop the game and pick up any little piece of paper he saw, or have the ground crew come out on a windy day and pick up the loose hot dog wrappers.

Ken Keltner and I took advantage of that foible once by stopping by a party store in Detroit and picking up a bag of confetti. The visiting team's dugout in Detroit was on the first base side, and when Keltner came trotting across the infield from third base at the end of an inning, he pulled a couple of fistfuls of the confetti out of his back pocket and sprinkled the stuff all over the mound without breaking stride. It looked like a blizzard out there, plus a rainbow.

Newsom blew his stack immediately, stormed around the mound and refused to pitch. It took 15 minutes for the ground crew to clean up the mound to Bobo's specifications.

Down in Winter Park, Florida, they honored Bobo in the best way they knew how, and a way he appreciated. At Harper's Bar, they poured a square of cement into the wooden floor at the corner of the bar where

Bobo stood and drank beer. Then they had him stick his feet into the wet cement and preserved his feet forever right there on the spot where he always stood.

It wasn't exactly the American League Most Valuable Player Award, but it was an honor as far as Bobo was concerned.

Less than a month after my one-hitter in my first start of 1938, I experienced another first—a win in New York. I had pitched in three games in Yankee Stadium since coming up to the Indians two seasons before, but I had two losses and no wins in three games. In the only game we won, the bullpen got the win in a 5–4 game. My rivalry with the Yankees made me want to do better than that—a whole lot better.

I got my fourth chance on May 12. By this time, I was 3–1 with other wins over the Tigers in Detroit and the Browns in St. Louis. My only loss was a game just about as good as my one-hitter. It was a three-hitter that I lost in ten innings to the Senators in Washington, 1–0, to a knuckleballing rookie named Dutch Leonard. Dutch and I hooked up in many a contest after that, and I guess we finished about even in his years with the Senators, but he beat me in our first duel in a classic pitcher's battle.

The Red Sox got to me for five runs in four innings my next time out, so I had several incentives for beating the Yankees on that day in May: I didn't want to lose two in a row, I always wanted to beat the hated Yankees, and I still wanted that first win at Yankee Stadium.

Rollie was behind the plate for me again, and this time we did it— we broke the Yankee Stadium jinx. The score was 3–2 on a five-hitter with nine strikeouts. Even though it was a weekday afternoon, 19,872 fans turned out to see another big matchup, Feller vs. Lefty Gomez, and Lefty didn't let his hometown fans down. He did better than I did, with a four-hitter—so there were only nine hits in the whole game, with all the runs scored in the sixth inning.

The Yankees got their two on a home run by Gehrig with Tommy Henrich on base, but Gehrig hurt Gomez as much as he helped him that day. He was thrown out at second base in the ninth inning after getting on with a single. Myril Hoag was hitting for New York when he swung at a third strike—only Rollie dropped it. Gehrig hesitated, then broke for second, forgetting that Hoag was automatically out under the rules because there were less than two outs when Hemsley dropped the third strike. Rollie threw him out. Gehrig had been the potential tying run. It was the kind of mental mistake that sends the mildest manager into a rage. "Don't run us out of the inning" is one of the reminders that base runners hear, a reminder not to make any mental mistakes on the bases. Gehrig did worse. He ran the Yankees out of the game.

We scored our winning run when DiMaggio also committed a rare mistake. He bobbled a single to center by Earl Averill, and his error allowed Moose Solters to reach third. Moose scored from there on a ground out by Trosky, and we were able to make the lead stand up for the rest of the game.

The Associated Press quoted me later as saying I was tired of worrying about my change-of-pace pitch and how high I was kicking or how low, with men on base, that from then on I was going to "forget all that scientific stuff and just rear back and blow that ball over."

It was an accurate quote, and Vitt probably didn't like it when he read it, but that was a decision I had made. I was pitching all right, but pitching "all right" wasn't my goal. I wanted to be the very best pitcher I was capable of being, and the only way to achieve that was to go back to being what I always was—a power pitcher. I told AP I was going to stop regarding every runner on first base as another Ty Cobb and instead go back to throwing as hard as I could and as accurately as I could, just like behind the barn on the farm.

There's a lot of truth in one of the simplest pitching formulas of all: "Work fast, throw strikes, and get ahead in the count."

That win at Yankee Stadium was followed immediately by something new back in Van Meter—a postage cancellation stamp that read:

VAN METER, IOWA

Bob Feller's Hometown

It even had my picture and two other lines that said it was "National Air Mail Week, May 15–21, 1938."

In Washington, a reaction of a different kind followed. After a game against the Senators on Kids' Day, an AP reporter named Eddy Gilmore was mistaken for me as he left Griffith Stadium.

I had already showered and left, but the kids missed me, and when Gilmore came by, they were sure he was Feller. He protested a couple of times, but with 500 screaming boys, he decided that the best course of action to guarantee his own safety was to go along with the case of mistaken identity.

So he took out one of his reporter's pencils and started signing autographs—mine. He wrote a column about it in which he admitted his deception but emphasized that it was for his own survival and to keep from breaking the hearts of 500 happy kids.

He was one reporter who found out the hard way what it takes to sign autographs in crowds. His toll: three broken pencils and one cramped wrist.

CHAPTER FIVE
My Strikeout Rivalry
With Dizzy Dean

The first victory in New York got me into another winning groove. We had no way of knowing that serious troubles for the Indians loomed in the near future, our first major problems as a team with our first-year manager. Instead, we knew only that we were winning, and I knew I was enjoying a strong and successful season.

I beat the immortal Lefty Grove on a seven-hitter in Cleveland in late June for my ninth win against only two losses, and on the same day, I was named to the 1938 American League All-Star team, the youngest player ever chosen for "the dream game." I was 19.

I didn't get into the game—I was warming up to relieve Grove if we went into the last of the ninth, but the National League beat us, 4–1, in Cincinnati, so I had to wait and hope I could make the team again in 1939 and then get into the game.

It's a good thing I was named to the All-Star team at the beginning of July. The managers of eight teams in the two leagues elected the All-Stars in those days, and if they had waited until the end of July, I might not have gotten one vote.

I was knocked out five times in six starts in July. Oscar Vitt warned me at one point, "I've seen lots of pitchers with as much stuff as you've got and more, and they never amounted to a damn because they didn't know where the ball was going when they turned it loose. You've

78

got to make up your mind to perfect your control or you'll never be a major league pitcher."

Vitt seemed to be overreacting. I had just lost to the Red Sox, 7–4, in Boston. They ganged up on me with five hits and four runs in three innings, but what Vitt seemed to be forgetting was that my record even after that defeat was still ten wins and only five losses.

The mound at Fenway Park was giving me as much trouble as the Red Sox were. It seemed higher than I was used to, and this can make a big difference to someone who pitches in that ball park only two or three times a year.

But I hadn't looked good in July and I was getting as disgusted with myself as Vitt was. I was talking to Ed McAuley in the dressing room after the loss in Boston and I told him how fed up I was. I said maybe I should just go back to the farm and say the heck with it. Then I applied the clincher—"maybe," I said, "I've lost my fast ball."

After McAuley left, I thought to myself, "I probably shouldn't have said that." When I saw the papers the next morning, I was sure of it.

McAuley, working for the *Cleveland News*, ate some steamed clams and washed them down with beer and developed severe stomach pains. So he asked his pal, Gordon Cobbledick of the *Plain Dealer*, to cover for him by writing McAuley's piece for the *News*.

Cobbledick did just that. Meanwhile, Stuart Bell, the writer for the *Cleveland Press*, laid off the story, satisfied I was blowing off steam, which I was, and that I never believed for one minute that I'd lost my fast ball, which I didn't.

Saturday morning, July 23, dawned with headlines in the Cleveland papers screaming:

"FAST BALL IS GONE," FELLER SAYS

"FAST BALL GONE," BOB FELLER SAYS

"MY OLD FAST BALL IS GONE AND MY CONTROL
ISN'T GOOD ENOUGH TO WORK THE CORNERS"—FELLER

What made the stories amusing to me was that they all said the same thing, yet McAuley's, or at least the one under his byline, said I made the remarks in a one-on-one interview in his hotel room.

An AP story from New York outdid the Cleveland papers. It said DiMaggio and I both needed more "testing" and should be sent back to the minor leagues. AP said DiMag "has been something less than a four-alarm fire this season..."

I don't know how AP felt about me by the end of the season, but presumably it changed its evaluation of Joe, who finished 1938 with a .324 batting average, 32 home runs and 129 runs batted in.

Down on the farm, Dad told Mom and Marguerite that all the crops were in by then, so it might be a good time to drive on up to Cleveland and see Bob. They came out to League Park for my next start, against the A's.

When a reporter asked Dad about the comments attributed to me, he downplayed the whole thing and said, "I think the fans expect too much from him. If any other pitcher lost a couple of games, nobody would get so excited. Bob is taking it too seriously." He said he thought I might have been homesick until the family's arrival. Some of my teammates said they thought I'd lost my confidence.

It was my first experience in a full-blown media flap. The story never was the big crisis it was reported to be. It was as much a case of reporters doing almost too good a job of covering for each other as it was a crisis about my pitching future.

Even in those days before television and today's world of constantly expanding communications capabilities, the media could have a profound influence on an athlete's career, for better or for worse. I've been treated well by the media over the years, and I've been treated shabbily. I don't have any problem with that. Many reporters and broadcasters are friends of mine, and people whose work I respect. But I do have one problem on the subject—the overwhelming effect they can now have on you because of the widespread influence of television.

I never went into a shell and avoided reporters when I might be having problems with them. I always hung in there with them, answering their questions with honest and sometimes blunt answers that got me into even more trouble, but eventually things would straighten themselves out.

But they can make you or break you if they choose. The honest professionals play it straight, but if an announcer or writer wants to, he can tell the world you've lost something off your fast ball and the word flashes around the league. It doesn't make any difference whether you have or not, the whole sports world now thinks you have.

As a matter of fact, I used to enjoy sparring with the reporters covering the Indians. If one of them got out of bed on the wrong side one day and would ask why I was having a bad year, I'd say, "Well, I don't really know—but I've been reading your stories, and I see you're having a bad year too."

All the theories went up in smoke the afternoon that Mom, Dad and Marguerite were there. I beat Philadelphia on a seven-hitter, 4–2, before 8,000 fans. I struck out ten and, just as important, walked only three. I put the icing on my own cake with a line drive single to center in the seventh that scored Pytlak. Bob Johnson was the A's leading hitter, and I punched him out on strikes four times.

Why was Pytlak in the game instead of Hemsley? Because one of my fast balls was in the dirt and hit Rollie on the instep of his right foot. I pitched the last four innings to Frankie, the first time that year I worked with anybody but Rollie.

It was a refreshing reminder to all of us that I was still a young pitcher and consistency is always a problem with the young, whether in baseball or anything else. People, especially the writers and broadcasters, are quick to point that out when a kid is winning, but quick to forget it when he's not.

The only loser in the whole episode was Stuart Bell, who had been chewed out by his editor for not reporting my quotes. Bell stormed into the editor's office after I beat the A's and said emphatically, "There! Don't tell me how to cover my beat any more. *I'm* the baseball writer on this paper." His editor said, calmly, "Well, that may be true, Stuart. But you should have said you *used* to be the baseball writer on this paper. You're fired."

Consistency continued to elude me during August. I lost to the Yankees in Cleveland, beat the White Sox in Chicago and had four no-decision games, then lost three in a row to the Browns, White Sox and Yankees.

The Yankee game was my lowest point of the year, even lower than the talk about my fast ball, missing or not, the month before. I not only got beaten by New York, I got embarrassed. It may be the worst performance of my career. I haven't pitched that badly in the Old Timers games. How bad was it? Twelve runs in only seven innings, off the same pitcher. We were short of pitchers, so I got a good long workout.

Joe D. had a homer and seven runs batted in, and Gehrig hit a home run too. It was the low point for the whole team, not just me. Several of our players were developing problems with Vitt in his rookie year as our manager, and my performance that day didn't help anything except the Yankees' morale.

Even with some burgeoning dissatisfaction with Vitt, we managed to put together an entirely respectable season. We finished 20 games over .500 at 86–66 in third place behind the Yankees and the Red Sox. We had four .300 hitters in our lineup, including Jeff Heath's .343, the second highest in the league. Jeff also had the third highest slugging average and the most triples and was fourth in the league in doubles. Lyn Larry was second in stolen bases.

In pitching, Mel Harder had the third highest won-lost percentage, and he and I tied for the third most wins with 17. I led the league in strikeouts with 240 and tied for the third highest number of complete games and was third in innings pitched. Johnny Allen and I allowed the fewest hits per nine innings, and Johnny Humphries led the league's pitchers in the number of appearances.

That's an entirely respectable showing, but the feeling by some was that we could do even better, that there was a sense of dissension beginning to build. Vitt's leadership wasn't the kind that made for happy ballclubs, so the question was beginning to arise as to whether we were winning because of Vitt's managing or despite it.

When the last game of the season arrived on October 2, there were 27,000 fans in the stands at home, and not just to tell us goodbye for six months. Hank Greenberg, the Tigers' powerful first baseman, was reaching the climax in his chase all year long to break Babe Ruth's record of 60 home runs in one season, the most cherished record in baseball. He had 58 by that Sunday, and only the Indians stood in his way. I had won five out of six starts in September and Vitt gave me the responsibility of stopping Greenberg in the first game of a doubleheader.

There were mixed feelings about Greenberg's attempt, especially on the part of the players themselves. Ruth was a genuine American folk hero, and he meant even more to the players, especially those who had been in the major leagues for a while. They were grateful to him for singlehandedly restoring public confidence in their sport after the "Black Sox" scandal erupted in 1920 with all the charges that the Chicago White Sox threw the 1919 World Series to the Cincinnati Reds in a gambling "fix." Ruth's home runs brought new excitement, Judge

Landis was appointed the first commissioner, and eight Chicago players were banned from baseball for life for their rolls in the fix.

Many of the players in 1938 remembered Ruth fondly, and Hal Trosky told reporters after the game that many players, with no offense to Hank, were hoping he wouldn't break Ruth's record because of the loyalty and sentiment they felt for the Babe.

Greenberg came up eight times in the doubleheader and got a double in four trips against me in the first game and three hits, all singles, in the second game. We weren't pitching around him. We were willing to pitch to him and take our chances. If he broke Ruth's record, then more power to him. And we didn't exactly shut him down—four hits in eight trips including a double wasn't anything to be embarrassed about. But he didn't get the home runs when he needed them. We stopped him at 58. The Babe's record was safe.

There *was* a record broken that day, but it wasn't Ruth's—it was Dizzy Dean's. I broke his major league record of 17 strikeouts in a nine-inning game, the one I tied when I set the record for the American League in 1936.

It was one of those days when everything feels perfect—your arm, your coordination, your concentration, everything. There was drama in the air because of Greenberg's attempt to break Ruth's record, and the excitement became even greater when my strikeouts started to add up. I got Detroit's rookie second baseman, Ben McCoy, on strikes in the first inning, and then I really caught fire. I struck out the side in each of the next three innings.

I got two more in the fifth and two in the sixth, then one in the seventh and another in the eighth. Unfortunately, I was also walking seven men, and Detroit took advantage of my wildness to build a 4–1 lead, but by the time the ninth inning arrived, the crowd was concentrating on Greenberg and me. No home crowd ever gave more cheers to a pitcher who was losing the game by three runs in the ninth inning.

Pete Fox struck out to lead off the ninth, my 17th strikeout. I had caught up with Dizzy. York singled, and the crowd moved to the edge of its seat as Greenberg stepped into the batter's box. Would it be a Feller strike out or a Greenberg home run? Neither. I got him on a fly ball.

I walked Birdie Tebetts, and now the crowd really got excited. Those 27,000 fans knew full well what was going on. They were completely aware that I was on a record-breaking pace. They also knew that the next hitter, Chet Laabs, had already struck out four times in the game. The law of averages was against my striking him out again, but he was a big swinger, and those guys are always vulnerable to strikeouts.

I threw two fast balls past him. Then, instead of making the mistake I did against DiMaggio the year before, I stayed hard on Laabs with another fast ball, this one on the inside corner at the knees. Cal Hubbard called him out. It may not have been Hubbard's most accurate call of the day, but it was sure close enough for Laabs to be swinging with two strikes on him already.

But he let it go by, Hubbard's right arm shot into the air and I owned the strikeout record for both major leagues at age 19.

Ed McAuley wrote something nice in the *News* the next day. He wrote about the pressures on a teenager trying to make it as major leaguer, my elbow troubles the year before, my problems with control, the taunting around the league with the players calling me "junior" and a lot worse. He remembered the day a crowd of school kids booed me—in Cleveland—because I wasn't pitching well, plus my slump in August. Then he described my 18-strikeout game and added, "He deserves much . . . because he has suffered much."

Another who deserved much was my catcher, Frankie Pytlak. Behind every good pitching performance is a good catching performance. A no-hitter or a game with a lot of strikeouts means the catcher did an excellent job of knowing what pitch to call for in a given situation, and of setting up each hitter with a successful sequence of different pitches.

That's what Frankie did. So I bought him a new suit.

Hal Trosky, our first baseman, told me after the game that Bing Miller, Detroit's first base coach, predicted to him in the middle of the game that I would break the record that day. Then, in the ninth, he told Hal, "I hope Feller gets to pitch to Laabs—he's a sure strikeout." Even the Tigers were rooting for me at that point.

I was given my biggest welcome home yet by the good folks of Van Meter. There was an all-day celebration that started at 9:30 in the morning and didn't end until midnight. Governor Nelson Kraschel was there, and so was our congressman, C.C. Dowell.

We even played one more baseball game, against a black all-star team. I pitched five innings and struck out ten. My cousin, Harold Manders, who became a big league pitcher himself with the Tigers and Cubs, threw two innings.

Our right fielder was my old pal Rollie Hemsley. He was staying sober now, but he was still having fun—and was able to remember it the next morning. To be accurate, Rollie was our right fielder for all but one inning.

In the middle of my streak of strikeouts, he went into the stands, gave his glove to a girl, and sat with the fans for a whole inning—while the girl played right field.

When the final statistics came out for the 1938 season, they showed that Mel Harder, Johnny Allen and I had been among the leaders in 10 of the 12 pitching categories listed in the *Baseball Encyclopedia*. I led the league in strikeouts with 240, but I also led the league in walks with 208. I had to do better than that.

The writers discovered something else in all those numbers. I had the highest strikeout ratio—the number of strikeouts per nine innings—in 35 years, 7.79 strikeouts for every nine innings. Only Rube Waddell did better, back in '03. I noticed that some of those writers weren't calling me "Master Feller" any more. They were starting to call me "Rapid Robert."

I missed those 25 wins Dad predicted by eight, but a record of 17–11 and leading the league in strikeouts isn't anything to apologize for, especially in the case of a young pitcher who is still learning.

Speed didn't always help me. Sometimes it even hurt me, and that fall was one of the times. I was nailed for doing 87 miles an hour on the road to Des Moines in the maroon '39 Cadillac I'd just bought for Mom and Dad. The ticket cost me $100—which was more than five percent of what the car itself cost.

That ticket was a case of "like father, like son." I had seen Dad get nabbed for doing the same thing, when the family drove me to Cleveland to report to the Indians during my high school vacation in the summer of 1936. A cop pulled us over in Indiana for breaking the speed limit.

He walked up to the car and asked Dad, "Would you like to buy a couple of tickets to the Policeman's Ball?" Dad said sure. He knew what he was doing. He'd rather have them instead of a speeding ticket.

Dad bought the tickets and we headed to Cleveland, hundreds of miles from the site of the Policeman's Ball.

CHAPTER SIX
The Way We Were

Any kid my age would have loved the life I was leading. It amounted to being force-fed in my major league education, but I was loving every minute of it while remaining dead serious about what I had to do to be a successful major league pitcher.

I was traveling by every mode of transportation imaginable. In an age when most 19-year-olds didn't own a car, I had my '37 Buick. I paid $960 for it, but you could get a new Nash for $755 and a Hudson for only $695, about what the air conditioner costs today.

On my first train trip, the Indians helped me with special education. My family had driven me to Cleveland—when Dad got "invited" to the Policeman's Ball in Indiana, so I still had never been on a train when Cy Slapnicka decided I was ready to join the team in the East. Slap never overlooked anything. He made sure his secretary, Bob Gill, went with me to the Pennsylvania Station on Euclid Avenue and 55th Street to catch "The Pennsylvanian" to Philadelphia. Bob's assignment was to go on board with me until we were ready to pull out and show me the finer points of train travel. He made sure to show me how to climb into the berth on a Pullman car. He also pointed out that the net next to the bed was not to rest my arm in—it was for my underwear. I probably would have figured that out by myself.

That first train ride was an extra special one because it also brought back memories of the times I watched the freight trains on the Rock Island Line as they lumbered through Van Meter, especially the ones carrying long steel beams from the US Steel mills in Gary, Indiana. I used to dream of far away places as I gazed at the banners on the cars that proudly told America the destination for those beams:

THE GOLDEN GATE BRIDGE, SAN FRANCISCO

I was seeing cities I'd read about back on the farm—the skyscrapers of New York and its World's Fair in 1939, the white monuments and shrines of Washington, the history in Boston and Philadelphia, the excitement of Chicago, the automobile factories in Detroit and the Mississippi at St. Louis, so majestic compared to the Raccoon back home. I was riding in taxi cabs for the first time, and taking streetcars to Shibe Park in Philadelphia and Sportsman's Park in St. Louis for a nickel or a dime.

Even a veteran traveler like Ed McAuley still appreciated all of the sights and experiences and people. He wrote a column in the *News* one day giving his capsule impressions of the American League cities. He said New York had the fairest fans in the league, Washington was the most beautiful city, and Chicago had the friendliest writers "but the weather changes too suddenly."

McAuley mentioned what all of us knew—that Philadelphia had the most expensive hotel-to-stadium ride in the league, a whopping 95 cents. He didn't like St. Louis because of the heat and low attendance. He rated Boston as "the most attractive spot in the majors" but for two reasons you'd never think of: The personality of the Red Sox owner, Tom Yawkey, and the bar in the press room.

I took another step in 1939 to widen my horizons. I became a pilot. Flying excited a kid like me in the 1930s. Airplanes were flying passengers and not just carrying air mail. Howard Hughes flew around the world in only three and three-quarters days in 1938. Amelia Earhart was achieving all sorts of firsts until she vanished over the Pacific in '37 while trying to become the first woman, an "aviatrix," to circle the earth. I've always thought that if her crew had not left her trailing antenna on the ground just to save two pounds, she would have completed her mission because that antenna would have helped to keep her from getting lost. It was an excellent low-frequency navigation system. All of the excitement about flying created by Earhart, Charles Lindbergh and others fired up my imagination and attracted me to Cleveland Hopkins Airport, where I made my first solo.

After World War II, I bought my own plane, a Beechcraft Bonanza, and flew it so much that it had four major engine overhauls before I sold it 20 years later and started renting planes after that. Today, in my 70s, I still fly enough to keep my pilot's license active. I've logged almost 7,000 hours as a pilot, almost a million miles. As a passenger the figure is close to ten million.

In the late 1940s, I hit on what must be the ultimate arrangement for commuting. I'd fly my Bonanza to the airport from my home in Gates Mills, a Cleveland suburb. The airport was right next to the stadium, so I bought a collapsible motor scooter made for pilots and occasionally treated myself to the ideal trip to work.

I'd fly my plane in from the suburbs, land at the airport, unfold the scooter, fasten its butterfly clips to keep it upright and then putt-putt the half mile over to the ballpark next door. I used to chug all the way into the dressing room, right up to my locker. It's hard to imagine a better trip to work. I didn't need somebody else's friendly skies. I had my own.

The Indians were still playing winning baseball in 1939, but we weren't catching the Yankees, and we weren't even the second best team in the American League. We finished 16 games behind the Yankees and three behind the Tigers in 1937 under Steve O'Neill, and under Oscar Vitt in '38, we were 13 behind the Yanks and three and a half behind the Tigers.

Resentment against Vitt was getting worse. Oscar knew baseball, but he didn't know human beings. Jeff Heath was openly feuding with him. Frankie Pytlak got so mad in spring training that he left the team and went home to Buffalo. There were rumors—Vitt was about to be fired, so-and-so was going to be traded. A hard-driving man by nature, Vitt was constantly getting on his players and even criticizing them publicly to some reporters. The effect on him was even worse than it was on us. He became moody and grim. It was not a happy situation.

But you have to play under all conditions, and dissension is one of them.

We opened our home season on April 21 against Detroit. I'm sure the Tigers were gunning for us after we stopped Greenberg on that last day of the previous season when I broke the strikeout record against them. They were not in a forgiving mood, but we beat them anyhow, 5–1. I pitched a three-hitter, struck out ten and walked only two.

Four days later, I beat the White Sox, 7–1, and four days after that, I beat the Tigers again, 8–1, with an eight-hitter. After three starts, I had three wins, three complete games, three runs allowed, 15 hits, seven walks and 32 strikeouts, and my teammates had scored 20 runs for me. Maybe this was going to be our year.

It continued that way through April, May and June, right up to the All-Star Game on July 11 at Yankee Stadium. By then I was 12–3 with 115 strikeouts. This was my second All-Star Game and this time I got to play. But there was something about All-Star Games that stirred up trouble for me during my career.

Joe McCarthy was the American League manager because the Yankees won the pennant the year before—of course. When McCarthy called me into the game, I didn't know whether to feel good about it or not. It was the sixth inning. There was one out, and the National League had the bases loaded after Tommy Bridges of Detroit got himself into trouble and was struggling to hold onto a 3–1 lead.

I looked down at the batter, Arky Vaughan, Pittsburgh's shortstop, who was definitely not the hitter you'd pick to pitch against with the bases loaded. He was the league's batting champion only four years earlier with .385. He'd been in the majors six years and his lowest average was .314. He played 14 years and hit over .300 in 12 of them, ending with a .318 average for his career.

Arky was typical of the good hitters of that day. He was a valuable baseball commodity—a shortstop who can hit. He didn't grip the bat way down at the end and swing for the fences. He was a singles and doubles hitter, good enough to belong to the exclusive 2,000-hit club with 2,103. If it hadn't been for the war, he would have had 2,500.

He moved the ball around, hitting to the opposite field, left field in his case as a left-handed hitter. He never hit 20 home runs in any season, but he led the National League in triples three times, showing he had both speed and power, and he hit 30 or more doubles seven times. He hit the ball where it was pitched and punched to the opposite field if it was on the outside part of the plate, not trying to pull every pitch regardless of its location, the mistake that too many of today's hitters make.

You could think of a lot of others you'd rather face than Arky Vaughan, but this was an All-Star Game—everybody was a good hitter. So I straightened up and threw my first pitch—a fast ball. Vaughan took a cut and sent a ground ball to Joe Gordon at second, who shoveled it over to our shortstop, Joe Cronin of the Red Sox, for the force-out at second. Cronin relayed the ball to first for the out to complete the double play and end the inning, on one pitch.

McCarthy left me in to pitch the seventh inning, and the eighth and ninth. I pitched three and two thirds innings and gave up only one hit. The National Leaguers were crying foul because McCarthy violated the unwritten rule that no pitcher is allowed to pitch more than three innings. McCarthy didn't respond, not even after the complaints grew louder when I struck out two of the National League's biggest hitters, Johnny Mize and Stan Hack, to end the game.

Being named to two All-Star teams was nice, but something else that's special to a pitcher is a no-hit game. I came close in 1937, and in '38 I came close again—twice.

I pitched two one-hitters. Bobby Doerr of the Red Sox broke up the first one with a clean single in Boston, and Earl Averill, who was traded by the Indians to the Tigers on June 14 for a pitcher, Harry Eisenstat, came back to haunt us 13 days later with a single in the sixth. Neither game was close—we beat Boston, 11–0, at Fenway Park and the Tigers, 5–0, in Cleveland. In the two games, I had a total of 23 strikeouts and 11 walks—still too many.

There was something else special about that one-hitter against the Tigers. It was the first night game played at Municipal Stadium in Cleveland. There were 55,305 fans on hand, the largest crowd in the major leagues so far that year, to see this novelty in one of the first cities to introduce night baseball.

Averill's single was a clean hit to left center, and Earl got it on his first trip back to Cleveland after his trade. Greenberg and one of their other good hitters, Barney McCoskey, struck out three times each, and a fast ball I threw to Greenberg with a 1–1 count in the ninth was the fastest pitch I'd ever thrown. Hemsley said the same thing, and so did Greenberg.

There were different reactions to this new thing called night baseball. Some of the players said they liked day games better, but others disagreed. One of the popcorn vendors said he preferred night games because sales were higher. he made $5.00 that night compared to an average of $1.50 for day games.

A rather heavy gentleman said he liked day games better, and his logic was hard to challenge. A Cleveland paper said he weighed 250 pounds and couldn't fit into one seat, so he preferred day games with their smaller crowds so he could sprawl across two seats.

It figured that Averill was the one who thwarted my third close call in my quest for a no-hitter. Earl was one of those batters blessed with that rare combination of talent for hitting the ball far and often. Usually the culprit in breaking up a no-hitter is a singles man, someone who makes contact often and hits for average instead of distance.

Earl did both. He made the Hall of Fame with a .318 average over 13 seasons, and he was always a long ball threat with over 20 home runs in five seasons and more than 100 runs batted in nine times.

The big swingers, with two exceptions, never gave me as much trouble as the singles hitters, because they aren't as consistent as those who hit for higher averages. Guys like Doerr, Tommy Henrich, Taft Wright, Roy Cullenbine and Stan Spence gave me more trouble than most of the long-ball hitters. I was able to handle those big boys most of the time—Jimmie Foxx, Hank Greenberg, Rudy York, Bob Johnson and Zeke Bonura.

The only two long-ball hitters who gave me trouble consistently also gave a few other pitchers trouble—Ted Williams and Joe DiMaggio. Who was better? Williams was the greatest hitter I ever saw, followed closely by Rogers Hornsby, but DiMaggio was the greatest all-around player.

A lot of today's starting pitchers don't have the problem that we did in facing those big guns because of the emphasis today on relief pitching. That gets the starters off the hook in the late innings in many cases and spares them the challenge of facing the other team's best hitters in the eighth or ninth inning with the ball game on the line. Most of today's pitchers don't have the stamina for the late innings, and the importance attached to relief pitching is one reason. The other reason is the fault of the pitchers themselves—pacing.

Most don't pace themselves any more. They know the manager is willing, sometimes more than he should be, to bring in a pitcher from the bullpen in the late innings, so the starter doesn't have to pace himself. He keeps throwing hard from his first pitch of the game to his last, regardless of the situation or the hitter facing him.

Until 20 years ago, pitchers were smarter than that, and so were their managers. We used to let up when we could. Today's pitchers work every hitter they face the same way. We used to let up against the weaker hitters in the batting order unless the other team had men on base. It makes no sense at all to throw as hard to the number nine hitter with two outs and nobody on base as you do when you're battling the cleanup hitter with runners on second and third.

We didn't have the designated hitter in the American League in those years so all of the pitchers hit, or at least they came to bat. We certainly didn't worry about throwing fast balls at 95 miles an hour to the pitcher if we weren't in a jam. We saved that kind of velocity and effort for Williams, DiMaggio and company. We'd pace ourselves by letting the bottom third of the order hit the ball, remembering that we had seven guys behind us and one in front who could catch it.

Pitchers in the American League today don't have the luxury at the bottom of the opposing batting order that we had. Facing the other pitcher usually meant you could pick up an easy out, and you could pace yourself while doing it, unless the game was in the late innings and the opposing manager was sending up a pinch hitter.

Today that hitter in the number nine spot in the American League is always a legitimate everyday player, never the pitcher. He obviously isn't among the team's best hitters or he wouldn't be hitting ninth, but he's certainly a better hitter than most of the pitchers.

If we had a big lead in those days, we'd pace ourselves then too, not worrying about how many strikeouts we had or what our earned run average might be if we pitched a shutout. We even had enough stamina to pitch an inning or so in relief between starts once in a while. I made 86 appearances as a relief pitcher and even managed to pick up six wins for my team and 21 saves. Walter Johnson relieved 136 times, but Tom Seaver, pitching in a different era, made only seven. You can do what Johnson and I did, and others too, if you pace yourself—and if you're willing to put your concern for your personal statistics in the background and concentrate instead on the two most important stats of them all—the number of games your team has won and lost.

It was a decisive year for two guys named Lou, both of them future members of the Baseball Hall of Fame. Lou Gehrig, tragically, had to retire after slowing down noticeably from what turned out to be the effects of ALS—amyotrophic lateral sclerosis—known forever afterwards simply as "Lou Gehrig's disease." For Lou Boudreau, it was a happier time, his first real action as a major leaguer after playing part of one game at third base in 1938. Boudreau came to us as a college All-American in two sports, basketball and baseball, at the University of Illinois. Now he was making the grade in '39 as a 21-year-old shortstop.

His arrival was a stroke of great fortune for us. He became one of our brightest stars, our on-field leader and later even our manager. Lou and I were destined to figure in exciting times and a World Series controversy, and to become lifelong friends in the process. At the beginning, though, he was a handsome, dark-haired college kid who looked as much like a matinee idol as he did a future baseball star.

Lou did something in '39 that became a habit with him. He hit 15 doubles. That's not a whole lot, but in only 225 times at bat, it projects to more than 30 over a full season. The next year, with the benefit of a full year, he hit 46. Seven times he hit 30 or more doubles. Lou was one of those aggressive batters who was thinking two bases every time he got a hit to the outfield.

The arrival of one Lou and the forced retirement of another reflected a certain significance, although I was too young to notice it at the time. There was a changing of the guard underway in the American League. New names were cropping up as the leaders among hitters and pitchers.

Joe DiMaggio led the league in hitting with a .381 average although he was still only 24 years old. Ted Williams performed the unheard of feat of leading the league in runs batted in as a rookie with 145. I led the league in six pitching departments and along the way I reached that magic level of success for a pitcher—I became a 20-game winner for the first time. I had 246 strikeouts while also finishing first in wins, fewest hits per nine innings, most innings pitched, complete games and most strikeouts per nine innings.

Joe was 24. Ted was 21. I was 20.

Something else significant happened that year. In one of my poorer performances, I was defeated by the Yankees in Cleveland, 11–8, on September 1. I lasted only four innings and gave up seven runs on ten hits and a walk. But that wasn't the worst news of the day. Hitler's troops invaded Poland. World War II began.

There was no telling what was going to happen to any of us, including three men in their early 20s named DiMaggio, Williams and Feller.

CHAPTER SEVEN

The Story of a No-Hitter and a Revolt

Here's a trivia question that pops up on quiz shows and sports talk shows every now and then:

> Q. Name the only time that every player on a team had the same batting average before a particular game, and had the same average after the game.

> A. April 16, 1940, when the Chicago White Sox lost a no-hit game on the opening day of the season. Every Chicago player had a batting average of .000 before and after the game.

After those three near misses, I finally made it onto the roster of those who have pitched a no-hit game, fewer than 200 in the game's history since 1901, when the American League was established and organized baseball was formed with two leagues.

No one could have been expecting it on the basis of my previous game. Against the Giants in my final exhibition game before the season opened, I was shellacked for ten runs and 15 hits in five innings. But that goes back to the question of a pitcher pacing himself. I knew it was only a tune-up. I wasn't going to beat my brains out in that game and then have the White Sox beat them out on opening day, when the game counted.

It was a cold, damp day in Chicago, and a raw wind was blowing in off Lake Michigan. Mom, Dad and Marguerite were there. So were the Commissioner, Judge Landis, and American League president Will Harridge.

Mom had reason to keep her fingers crossed that day, and the possibility that her son would pitch a no-hitter had nothing to do with it. The family sat in that same ballpark the year before when I beat the White Sox on a six-hitter for my sixth win against only one loss by mid-May. I got them the best seats in the house, between home plate and first base.

I went the full nine innings that day, but Mom didn't. Chicago's third baseman, Marv Owen, sliced a line drive foul that shot straight in my family's direction like a guided missile on target and hit Mom in the face. She had to be helped from the ballpark and was hospitalized for two weeks with two black eyes and an ugly collection of cuts and bruises.

The whole experience was upsetting enough as it was, but one more thing made it even worse—it was Mother's Day.

So when Mom tested her luck on the following opening day, she was rewarded by seeing her son pitch a no-hitter, with no foul balls hit her way. The combination of low temperatures and the Chicago wind made for an extremely uncomfortable afternoon to watch a baseball game, or to play one. The only people in the whole ballpark who were warm were the pitchers and catchers.

It looked like anything but a budding no-hitter when the White Sox loaded the bases in the second inning, but that was from my walks, not their hits. I worked my way out of that jam and then settled into a routine that held the Sox quiet into the ninth inning. Meanwhile, in the fourth, we took the lead, with a little help from my friends. My roommate, Jeff Heath, singled, and my friend behind the plate, Rollie Hemsley, tripled to the wall in right center field. It turned out to be the only run of the game.

The suspense grew in the late innings. The crowd knew I was making another strong bid for my first no-hitter. The team knew it and was going out of its way to avoid any mention of the subject, in keeping with one of baseball's many superstitions. I never felt that way, though, about that one or any of the game's other superstitions. My teammates didn't have to bother avoiding the subject. I knew full well I had a no-hitter going, and so does every other pitcher in that situation. If he tells the reporters after the game that he wasn't aware of it, don't you believe him.

In the ninth, the tension was compounded by the presence at the plate of Luke Appling, the White Sox Hall of Fame shortstop. Luke was "Ol' Aches and Pains" because he was always complaining of various hurts, but it never seemed to bother him when it came to playing some of the best defense of any shortstop in the majors or hitting .388 to lead the league, which he did four years before.

There was one other thing that Luke did better than anyone else in the sport—hit foul balls. He was a master, the best I've ever seen, at flicking his bat to foul off a pitch while he waited for the one he wanted. It didn't make any difference if he had two strikes either. He was so good at it and so confident in doing it that he just stood up there and took a poke at every pitch, with no concern that he might miss it and strike out.

He came up to bat with two outs and the bases empty in the ninth inning, determined to break up my no-hitter. Then he went into his act. The same guy who once fouled off 18 straight pitches just to use up a lot of baseballs because he was mad at management about his contract started doing the same thing to me. He knew what inning it was, that I had to be running out of gas pretty soon. I was a hard thrower, and by the ninth inning, hard throwers sometimes are tiring.

Appling worked the count to two balls and two strikes and then started waving that magic wand. He fouled off the next four or five pitches. We might still be there if a counter strategy hadn't occurred to me. I wasn't going to keep throwing and play into his hand, so I threw the next two pitches outside the strike zone. That got rid of Appling with a walk. I already had issued four walks, so another one wasn't going to make any difference anyhow.

It was an intentional walk, but nobody else knew it.

That brought up Taft Wright, one of the good hitters in the league and one I had trouble with from time to time because he was such a good contact hitter. Wright hit a sharp ground ball to the left side of our second baseman, Ray Mack, who was able to knock it down before it got through to right field. He picked it up quickly with his bare hand, regained his feet and threw to first for the last out of the game. I had my no-hitter.

That game produced the wildest welcome home you ever saw for just our first win of the season. Seven thousand fans greeted our train when we rolled into Union Terminal in Cleveland, which exceeded the station's biggest crowd by 2,000 people. There was a public address announcer, a uniformed band under the direction of one of the city's best known conductors, Manny Landers. The mayor, Harold Burton, was there, and so was Cleveland's baseball immortal, Tris Speaker. When the team left the train station, we had a motorcycle escort.

One fan would have given anything to be there. Paul Hauschulz was eight years old, and like so many other American kids that age, he was a big baseball fan. Specifically, he was a big Indians fan. He had a good reason for not being at the welcome home ceremony. He was a patient at St. Luke's Hospital with streptococcus, mastoid problems and spinal meningitis. He'd been infectious for a month, despite eight blood transfusions.

There was a story about Paul in the paper that said he showed some improvement after my no-hitter, so I decided to see if I could help him improve even more. I put two baseballs in my pockets, one signed by the whole team and the other with Paul's name on it from me.

He was shocked to see me when his nurses escorted me into his room. We had a nice chat for 15 minutes, even though he was too thrilled to say much, and then I left.

The nice thing is that Paul left, too. He went home that afternoon.

The only thing more eventful than Cleveland's 1940 baseball season was the war in Europe. Even the presidential campaign wasn't as exciting, with President Roosevelt defeating Wendell Willkie, even after some people said no President had ever served more than two terms and that should remain the limit.

While FDR was having no trouble winning a third four-year term in Washington, Oscar Vitt was having a lot of trouble surviving one three-year term in Cleveland. Things were rocking along well enough for me individually—I was 13–5 by the All-Star break, pitched two innings against the National league and had my fourth one-hitter, against the A's. I was making $40,000 and was building a brick house for my parents and Marguerite on the farm—with indoor plumbing for the first time in our lives.

With the team, though, things were different—too different.

It started when we hit a slump during our second swing through the East, and when Mel Harder and Al Milnar got hit especially hard in Boston, things reached the boiling point. Vitt had some harsh things to say to them, and coming after all the other harsh things he'd said to everybody else, we'd had enough.

Vitt made a habit of climbing all over his men when they made a mistake, of speaking with dripping sarcasm to the reporters about his players. When he was talking to our pitchers he said our hitters were killing us, and vice versa. He kept the team in turmoil, and his moves during games were something we disagreed with often and so did the writers. He called us "cry babies" in the newspapers. It didn't help that his wife advised him in his managerial decisions by consulting the stars for signs about who should pitch the next day. Vitt put a ball under your hat in your locker if you were going to pitch that day, depending on his own feelings and what the stars said.

On the train back to Cleveland from Boston after Harder and Milnar got chewed out, the players held a secret meeting, away from the reporters. We decided it was showdown time. We wanted a meeting with the owner, Alva Bradley, immediately. Twelve of us were picked to represent the team. Harder was selected to head the delegation.

We met with Bradley in his office on the morning of June 13, and we didn't pull any punches. We told him that if he wanted us to win the American League pennant, he had to fire Vitt, and the sooner the better. Our demands were especially timely because the Yankees were struggling and ready to be taken.

We did not threaten to walk out, but we made it plain that the situation was a mess and that no team would ever be able to win under the conditions which existed. Harder and Hal Trosky did most of the talking, and I backed them up from time to time during the course of the meeting, and so did the rest of the group.

Bradley heard us out and acknowledged the validity of our case while not necessarily agreeing with every specific complaint that we presented. At the end of the meeting he said he could not fire Vitt because mid-June was too early for such an action. He made it plain we'd have to tough it out as best we could.

That's exactly what we did. We were not about to give up our hopes of winning the pennant, so we decided to go around Vitt. We worked with his coaches, mostly with his number two man, Johnny Bassler. We were doing what people in a lot of organizations with management problems do: ignore the top guy and work with the second in command. We used our own set of signals, worked our own strategy during games and ignored the head man as much as we could.

Things didn't have to be any more strained than they were, even with Vitt acting like Commander Queeg in *The Caine Mutiny*, so we agreed to keep the meeting secret from the press. We couldn't keep the tension and controversy secret because Vitt himself was always out there telling the world, but the players had it within their power to keep the meeting itself under wraps. We were confident that Bradley would keep the lid on things too, because it was in his best interests to do so. But somebody talked. One of the players leaked the story to the reporters and things blew sky high. We had a pretty good idea of who the Deep Throat was, and we suspected the guilty party wanted Vitt's job for himself, and we didn't mean Lou Boudreau, who became the Indians' player-manager two years later. Lou would never do such a thing, and he was so new as a rookie that we did not include him in our meetings. Ray Mack was excused for the same reason. There was no reason to involve rookies in this mess, and they wouldn't have any influence with Bradley anyhow.

The stool pigeon went to the reporters while we were still on the train, early enough so they could file their stories en route. The story was in the Cleveland papers the next morning even before we met with Bradley.

The writers were fully aware of our problems and sympathetic toward us, but there's only one way that kind of a story comes out in the first days of such a controversy. The fans in cities all over the league jumped on us, calling us "The Boo Hoo Boys." They threw fruit at us from the stands, called us every name they could think of, and the writers in their cities printed some of the most abusive articles you could imagine. They didn't limit their throwing to the ballpark either. At the Michigan Central train station in Detroit, we were pelted with eggs and tomatoes and even stones.

We knew why the fans felt the way they did, but we also knew they were wrong. The whole affair was a good-faith effort on our part to correct a critical problem that was damaging the team. Many of those same fans would have done the same thing in their jobs and gone to their bosses if they encountered a situation in their company that we had in ours.

It was more professional and businesslike than today, when players sue owners and owners challenge players' integrity, and the poor fans have to endure the whole sorry spectacle. This was a straightforward attempt to meet a management problem head-on, talk it through and see what could be done about it, with every effort on our part to keep the matter confidential.

Our brazen move worked. We started to win and even took over first place from the Tigers and built up a six-game lead. Then we cooled off and started beating ourselves. The result was that we came back to the Tigers and Yankees and found ourselves in a neck-and-neck race as we headed into the stretch drive.

I won my 25th game in Philadelphia on September 15 on a two-hit shutout with no walks, finally reaching the number of wins Dad predicted for me two years before. I came back on two days of rest and defeated the Washington Senators in Cleveland on a five hitter, 2–1. Vitt was catching some criticism for pitching me too much, but I agreed with him in this case. If you're in a fight for the pennant and you have a pitcher who is young and led the league the year before in victories, why not work him as often as his young arm will stand it in the final weeks? He knew I'd tell him if I were hurting, but he also knew I had a history of being able to pitch on a workhorse schedule without being hurt by it. I had already led the league in the number of innings pitched the previous two years, and I did it again that year and two other times, so Vitt obviously knew what he was doing on that decision.

I made nine appearances over 27 days in September, including four nine-inning performances, and seven innings and eight innings in two other games. For September, I pitched a total of 54 innings, a rate of 324 innings for a full season.

But it wasn't enough. It all came down to September 27 and a head-to-head game against the Tigers in Cleveland. I had beaten them four days earlier in Detroit, 10–5, on an eight-hitter, but this one was due to turn out the wrong way. I pitched a three-hitter but lost, 2–0.

Detroit's manager, Del Baker, gambled in that series and won. The final weekend of the season started with the Tigers needing to win only one of the three games against us. Baker had a strong pitching staff with Schoolboy Rowe, Buck Newsom, Tommy Bridges and Dizzy Trout, but he turned instead to a rookie named Floyd Giebell, who pitched only two games that year. He was a 6'2" righthander who had bounced around organized baseball for a while and was almost 31 years old while still trying to make it in the big leagues.

Giebell was a "give-up" choice by Baker, whose reasoning was that the Tigers could lose that first game to the Indians and me and still have all those other talented pitchers ready to win on either Saturday or Sunday and clinch the American League pennant.

Baker got away with it. Rudy York hit a home run against me with Charlie Gehringer on base and the Tigers were the champions. My teammates were hitting the ball well, but it was one of those days when every long fly was caught, and every hard grounder with a man on first was turned into a double play.

Fate seemed to have a hand in things that day, even on York's home run. It was a long fly ball down the line in left. At the moment he hit it, there was a strong wind blowing across the field, from left field to right and it helped to keep the ball fair by a foot as it sailed over the wall. Rudy did not hit the ball well, and I don't want to take anything away from him, but if he had hit a line drive to that area, it might have been caught.

We might never have scored a run anyhow, so it's of no real difference, but it makes for one of those intriguing "what-if" questions. What if that wind hadn't come up at that moment and York's fly ball had been caught?

It was a great moment for the Tigers, to win the pennant in such a sizzling, prolonged battle. It was a great moment for Floyd Giebell, too. In fact, it was his greatest. He never really made it. He was gone after the next season.

But he had his moment in the sun on that Friday afternoon in Cleveland. He never won another game in the majors.

It was another season of contradictions for the Indians. We finished only one game behind the Tigers, a game ahead of the Yankees. Our pitchers led the league in shutouts and with the best earned run average, but we allowed more runs than any other team. We had the best fielding average in the league and we made the fewest errors. Our statistics on offense may have been the most telling of all. Five of the seven other teams scored more runs than we did and hit more home runs.

I led both leagues in wins with 27, and I finished first in strikeouts, complete games, fewest hits per nine innings, number of innings pitched, number of games pitched, most strikeouts per nine innings and complete games.

That much was satisfying, but there was a void in our lives as a team. We still hadn't won the pennant. People were beginning to say we just didn't have it, that we choked up under the pressure of a pennant race every time we got close to one. We had to live that down, but there's only one way to do that—win.

Oscar Vitt learned the harsh realities of managing in the major leagues in 1940. The players were overcoming the strange, almost bizarre, situation and winning without him. And the fans knew it. They got on him early in the season and stayed on him. You can't fool the fans, and Vitt was finding that out the hard way.

The Cleveland fans were no exception in those years. They could be as hard on you as the fans in any other city. Walter Johnson experienced their wrath five years earlier. Besides being one of the top four or five pitchers in the history of our sport, if not THE top, Walter was also one of the all-time decent human beings, a man loved as much as he was admired—and by everyone everywhere. In Washington, he was considered a living saint, but the people in Washington weren't the only ones who felt that way. The whole American League did.

When he managed the Indians and they didn't win, the fans who loved him so much in Cleveland really let him have it. This was while I was still a kid on the farm, so I didn't witness it firsthand, but there were stories in the papers about Johnson being hit with lemons by his own Cleveland fans and booed by hundreds of them when he came out of the dressing room and tried to step into a car. Once he had to ask for police escort from the ballpark. Eventually thousands of those formerly admiring fans signed circulars to get him fired.

Oscar Vitt was going through the same thing. Believe me, if Walter Johnson can get that kind of treatment, so can anyone else. Vitt showed he had a good side from time to time, like when he gave me the day off after I beat the Tigers and asked me to take his son to the Indy 500 auto race. But he kept inviting trouble with his conduct and comments.

After the season, Bradley said to us, "I told Oscar when I hired him that he talked too much and it would get him in trouble. Evidently he never listened because he continued talking."

When we lost the pennant in Cleveland on that last weekend of the season, Oscar cleaned out his locker, shook hands all around and walked out the dressing room door.

He never came back.

The 1940 season was also the last in the major leagues for one of the true characters of the game, Zeke Bonura, the six-foot, 200-pound first baseman for the Chicago White Sox and the Washington Senators. That was a big athlete in those years before ball players began pumping iron and some went wrong and started using steroids. Zeke had the natural power that went with his measurements. He was in the majors for seven seasons until being sent back to the minors and then joining the Army as America braced itself for World War II.

Zeke made his presence felt in those seven seasons, and not just because he hit more than 20 home runs three times and had a .307 lifetime batting average. It was his own level of social sophistication and complete honesty that made him so popular—like the time in Washington when Shirley Povich of the *Post* asked him on the last day of the season where he would be spending the off-season.

Zeke had come to the Senators that year—1938—from the White Sox. He told Povich, "I'm going home. As soon as this game is over, I'm going to point my car straight toward Chicago."

Povich was confused. "Chicago? I thought you lived in New Orleans."

"I do," Bonura said. "And from Chicago I knew every inch of the way."

Then there was the time that a waiter in a restaurant told him the apple pie he wanted for dessert was served à la carte. Zeke said that would be fine.

When the waiter brought the pie, Zeke said, "Hey! Where's the ice cream?"

CHAPTER EIGHT
After 1941, Baseball, Like the World, Was Never the Same

You could finish carving four presidents out of the rock on the side of Mount Rushmore, which a man named Gutzon Borglum did. You could produce what some critics consider the greatest movie ever filmed, *Citizen Kane*, which Orson Welles did. You could lead both major leagues in pitching for the second straight year, which I did. You could even become the first American President to be inaugurated for a third term, which Franklin D. Roosevelt did.

But to millions of Americans, the two biggest stories this side of the war in Europe in 1941 were Joe DiMaggio and Ted Williams. That's when Joe accomplished what remains the most famous streak in history of all sports, and Ted learned to lay off the high fast ball and achieved baseball's last .400 batting average.

Both of them managed to do something that may never be achieved again. Pete Rose, George Brett and others have taken a run at Joe's superb performance in hitting in 56 games in a row and at Ted's incredible .406 batting average, but even those great hitters couldn't do what Joe and Ted did.

Even corked bats and other devices haven't helped. Corked bats are just a way for the player to get more "bat speed" and thus more power, but there's a simpler way—have the manufacturer make a lighter bat for you. It's all psychological anyhow. In our years as players, the hitters used to make their bats rougher by pounding brads into "the sweet spot" around the barrel end, or have their bats made with knots on the hitting surface, or they'd shave the wood with a razor or a knife, or rub it down with a bone so the bat itself would get a better "grip" on the ball at the moment of contact.

Then they'd treat the wood so it looked like a new bat and no one would be wise. But it really doesn't make that much difference, and there's always a minus to go along with the plus. The flat bats, for example, enabled the batter to hit more balls into fair territory, but you might also pop up a pitch instead of just foul tipping it back to the screen.

In case you're wondering what effect aluminum bats will have on hitting performances when they are introduced into the majors, don't worry about it. That will never happen. Aluminum bats may be fine for the Little Leagues because they last forever and hold down your equipment expenses, the same reason they appeal to high school and college athletic directors. But they'll never be used at the major league level. They would make a mockery out of hitting and of every record in the book. José Canseco might hit 1,000 home runs with an aluminum bat.

You can argue that the influence of aluminum bats is reflected in professional baseball, even if they aren't used there. I see it in spring training when I'm working with the Indians' pitchers, especially the younger ones. When a kid comes into pro ball after pitching in college, you can see his reluctance to come inside to the hitter. He's afraid the hitter will be able to pull the ball for a home run, the way you can with a thick-handle aluminum bat that won't break.

In the majors, that's not the case. The bats are wooden, with thin handles so the hitter can whip them around in a hurry and hit home runs with the increased bat speed coming from the lighter handle. But those bats break, an everyday occurrence today that you never saw until a few years ago.

Aluminum bats do pitchers, especially those in college, a real disservice in making them reluctant to throw inside to the hitter. Every pitcher who ever lived simply must be willing to do that. If he doesn't, the hitter will crowd the plate on every pitch and be able to kill you by pulling everything, getting his full strength into his swing.

To counter that, the pitcher has to move that hitter off the plate with some well-placed fast balls, high and inside. This tells the hitter in the process that the pitcher is just as entitled to that plate. If you can't do that, or you're unwilling to, because you pitched against hitters using aluminum bats, or for any other reason, you'll never make it in the majors.

Doctored baseballs are about as overrated as doctored bats. Burleigh Grimes was one of the greatest spitball pitchers in baseball back when that pitch was legal. He threw it maybe only one pitch out of ten, but he went to his mouth with his glove and fingers on every pitch. The batter psyched himself out by worrying that the next pitch was always going to be a spitter.

When I shook off my catcher because I wanted to throw a different pitch than the one he was signaling for, I never did it with a flick of my glove or a shake of my head. I just stared at my catcher and he knew to signal for another pitch. Any time I flicked my glove or shook my head, it was just a decoy to fool the batter into thinking that something was going on when it wasn't. The batter has only one guess, but the pitcher has more than one pitch. All the stuff about scuffed balls is just so much psych, whether Phil Niekro has an emery board or a file big enough to saw his way out of Leavenworth.

Joe and Ted didn't need any of that hocus-pocus to do what they did in 1941. They had the simplest but surest formula of all going for them—talent and hard work. I can testify to the greatness of those two men throughout their careers, especially in 1941.

My first game against DiMag during his streak came on June 2, when he had hit safely in 18 games. We beat the Yankees in Cleveland, 7–5. Joe hit a single and a double off me.

But neither of us was the biggest sports story that day. Lou Gehrig died in New York on the same day at the age of 37. He was both one of the most ferocious hitters and nicest guys I ever had the honor of playing with or against.

From the time I saw him in Des Moines when I was nine, until he took himself out of the lineup after his unbelievable endurance streak of playing in 2,130 straight games over almost 14 years, Lou was as mean with his bat as he was gentle in his manner. He hit .340 over his 17 seasons, drove in 100 runs 13 straight years and set the American League record with 184 RBIs. But those are merely numbers. They don't even begin to give you the full measure of the man.

One of today's players, Cal Ripken of the Orioles, could break Gehrig's record of that many consecutive games if he goes to 1995 without missing one. That shows how unbelievable Lou's streak is.

Here's Ripken winning respect everywhere for playing in more than 1,200 straight games, and he still has to play six more seasons without missing a game before he equals what Lou did.

I faced Joe D. again 12 days later and he got another double off me at Yankee Stadium when the Yanks beat me, 4–1. So he hit .500 against me during his streak, with three hits in six times up.

I especially remember the game in New York because by then Joe's streak was a month long and it was attracting all that national attention. In fact, any trip to New York in those years was a memorable one. The town was alive with fun and excitement.

On that weekend, *Citizen Kane* was playing at the Palace. Greta Garbo's movie *Streets of Sorrow* was showing at the Fifth Avenue Playhouse. *One Night in Lisbon* was at the Paramount, plus Milton Berle on stage and music by Vincent Lopez and his orchestra. At the Capitol, William Powell and Myrna Loy, one of America's favorite movie couples, were appearing in *Love Crazy*.

But movies weren't the only things going on in New York. The Yankees were always keeping things exciting in the Big Apple, and DiMag's streak was adding to it. When they beat me in Yankee Stadium on that Sunday, June 14, there were 44,161 people there. As if all that weren't enough, three nights later Joe Louis and Billy Conn were meeting at the Polo Grounds for the heavyweight championship. *The New York Times* headline said the fight, their first, was expected to be a "keen contest."

I got to see that classic, in the front row with one of the Cleveland writers, Franklin Lewis. We took the train from Philadelphia, where we were playing a series with the A's, and saw one of history's most memorable fights.

I saw DiMag hit in his 56th straight game. I was in our dugout in Cleveland as we played the Yankees on July 16 in the first of a three-game series. I had good reason to be paying even more attention than everybody else, and that's saying something. Joe's streak was Page One news all over the country and on the radio, in those days before television. They even wrote a song about him that year—"Joltin' Joe DiMaggio"—because of the tremendous amount of press he had been receiving since starting his streak two months and one day before.

The reason for my extra attention was that I was scheduled to pitch in the third game of the series. Joe Krakauskas, a tall left-hander, was pitching for us when DiMaggio got a single, his third hit of the night and his 91st hit in 56 straight games going all the way back to May 5.

His streak was still alive, and if Al Smith didn't stop him the next day, guess who was going to be given the job of trying to stop THE streak.

More than 67,000 fans came down to Lake Erie and filed into Municipal Stadium on the night of July 17 to see if DiMag could keep his celebrated streak alive. It was the largest crowd for a night game in major league history at that time. When Joe D. came to bat in the first inning, I was paying even closer attention than the day before.

He hit the second pitch from Smith and sent a hard ground ball down the third base line near the bag. It should have been a single or even a double, but Ken Keltner was using his head as well as his ability. He always played DiMaggio close to the line, and with Joe and Ted Williams swinging the hottest bats in baseball and getting around so quickly on every pitch, Ken was playing him deep at third as well as close to the line. When that hot smash came his way, he was in perfect position, but only if he made a perfect play. He did. He came up with a backhand stab, regained his feet in foul territory and threw a strike across the diamond to Oscar Grimes at first base.

Smith walked Joe in the fourth inning, but in the seventh inning history repeated itself. Joe D. hit another smash down the line at third, and Ken did what today we would call an instant replay of his stop in the first inning and threw him out again.

We thought DiMag had seen his last chance, but fate seemed to be stepping in. The Yankees got some base runners in the seventh, and in the eighth they loaded the bases and Joe's spot in the batting order came up again.

This time he was facing a right-hander, Jim Bagby. The count went to one ball and one strike, and then Joe hit another scorcher on the ground. This one was headed toward shortstop Lou Boudreau, our young infielder. It looked as if he would make the play, but the ball took a vicious hop at the last second and almost tore Lou's head off. With a less versatile player it would have been a hit, and Joe would have reached 57 straight games.

But Lou never was just an average infielder. He had the coordination and quickness to stay right with that hop, snare it and make a quick throw to Ray Mack, who was covering second. Ray turned a quick pivot and relayed the ball to Grimes at first. Instead of making his historic streak one game longer, Joe had only a double play to show for his trip to the plate, and one with the bases loaded that ended the inning.

But Joe DiMaggio, ever graceful in both action and reaction, didn't kick the bag at first base or argue with the umpire, and if we had been using batting helmets in those days, he wouldn't have sailed his back to the dugout like a frisbee. Instead, he simply trotted to the edge of the grass, where the infielders and outfielders used to drop their gloves on their way to the dugout after an inning on defense. He picked his up and continued trotting out to center field, like the thoroughbred he was.

After the game, Joe told John Drebinger of *The New York Times*, "That play Ken made on me in the first inning, when he went behind third for a backhand stop of that hard smash, was a beautiful piece of work. When they take them away from you like that, there's nothing a fellow can do about it. Anyway, it's all over now."

That's what a champion sounds like after he's been stopped.

I faced the Yankees and Joe the next afternoon in a Ladies' Day game. It was windy and drizzling, but that didn't stop Joe. He got a single off me again, plus another double—when the wind blew his fly ball in the sixth inning from medium center field all the way back into the edge of the infield grass while outfielders and infielders tried to surround it from every direction.

DiMaggio didn't get many hits like that in his career—he always seemed to hit the ball harder than anyone else—and even when he did hit what we called a "Texas Leaguer," he seemed to make them count. In this case, his double scored Tommy Henrich from first base with two outs in the sixth and gave New York its only run. I won my 19th game of the season against only four losses with another 2–1 win over the Yanks.

If it hadn't been for Keltner and Boudreau the night before, I might be in the history books today as the pitcher who stopped DiMag, or the one who gave up the last hit in Joe DiMaggio's streak. As it is, Joe started a new streak of 17 straight games.

The end of his 56-game streak might have cost Joe more than people knew. The rumor was that Heinz food products was prepared to offer him a million dollars if he could match its 57 varieties with hits in 57 straight games.

Ted Williams seemed to be doing it all that year, even in the All-Star Game in Detroit. He hit a three-run homer with two outs in the bottom of the ninth to bring us from behind and give us a 7–5 victory over the National League. I started the game against Whitlow Wyatt of the Brooklyn Dodgers, who led the National League that year with 22 wins. We each pitched three shutout innings, but Ted made a winning pitcher out of Eddie Smith of the White Sox in what many people still call the greatest All-Star Game ever played.

The National League was winning, 5–3, when the American League came up in the home ninth, and Arky Vaughan was the star of the game with two home runs, each with a man on base. As I sat in the dugout, it became apparent that the show wasn't over.

Claude Passeau of the Cubs, the pitcher with the Des Moines Demons of the Western League whom Cy Slapnicka was scouting when he came across me, was on the mound for the National League. He got the first man, Frankie Hayes, on a pop-up, something that's crucial in the late innings. You always want to get that first man out. If he gets on, the whole complexion of the inning changes. The team can steal, pull the hit-and-run or bunt—or you might throw a wild pitch or the catcher might let one get by him for a passed ball. The pitcher *must* get the first hitter out in the late innings of a close game.

Having done that, Passeau proceeded to get into trouble anyhow. Keltner, pinchhitting for our pitcher of the moment, Eddie Smith of the White Sox, singled off the glove of Eddie Miller at short. Joe Gordon, the Yankee second baseman who was to help the Indians so much seven years later, singled to right. Now Passeau was in serious trouble because the potentially tying run was coming to the plate, a situation to be avoided at all cost.

But that was the situation nevertheless, and the hitter who represented the tying run was an outstanding one, Cecil Travis, the shortstop for the Washington Senators. Travis was an exceptional hitter who is the only player I ever heard of who hit .359 and still missed the batting championship by 47 points. It happened that same season, when Williams hit .406. Travis' career became a victim of World War II just a few years later. After hitting at least .302 in eight of his nine seasons, including that .359 in '41 and other years of .335 and .344, he went into the service like most of us, developed frozen feet in the Battle of the Bulge, and was never the same after the war.

But Passeau knew how good Travis was in '41. He pitched him carefully because he didn't want the tying run to get on base. Too carefully, however. He walked him. Bases loaded, one out, American League still trailing by two runs.

Now DiMaggio comes up. His hitting streak at this point is 48 straight games, and he's already had a single in the All-Star Game. Joe sent another one of his rocket shots on the ground to Miller at short, a tailor-made double play ball. Miller stayed with the hot shot, fielded it cleanly and shoveled it over to Billy Herman at second for the force out.

But Travis, one of the unselfish team players, came in hard to the bag in an attempt to break up the double play. It worked. His hard slide was just enough to make Herman throw off balance to first. The throw was wide and pulled Frank McCormick off the bag, and DiMaggio was safe. No double play. Keltner scores. We're still alive, with two on and two out, and Ted Williams coming to bat.

Ted hit Passeau's first pitch over the fence—foul. He took two pitches for balls. Then he jumped all over the 2–1 pitch and hit it almost all the way out of Briggs Stadium for a three-run homer and an All-Star finish. The ball hit the top of the third deck.

While Ted was terrorizing pitchers in the second half of the season, I faced him three times. I "held" him to a .333 performance, three hits in nine trips, all in one game. I was also able to get him to keep the ball in the park, in a year when he hit 37 home runs and led the league. All three of those hits were singles.

There was a lot of talk around baseball that year about just how fast my pitches really were. Radar guns were a generation away, but Lew Fonseca came up with a way not only of testing my speed but illustrating it in a dramatic exhibition.

Lew was producing instructional films for major league baseball, and his credentials were impressive. He was a major league player himself for 12 years, the American League batting champion in 1929 with a .369 average. For his career he hit .316. He got an idea to test the speed of my fast ball and capture it on film. He wanted it to be man against machine, me against a guy on a motorcycle. I was to throw at a standard shooting target, the kind with a bull's-eye.

We conducted the test on a hot day on a street along Lake Michigan in Chicago's Lincoln park. I was in street clothes. Lew wanted me to take my windup with the film rolling and release the ball at the same split second that the man on the Harley Davidson went roaring by. But there was a fraction of a second difference. The motorcycle had a ten-foot jump on my pitch.

As the test turned out, it didn't make any difference. The baseball beat the motorcycle to the target anyway. The cycle was going 86 miles an hour when the driver blew past me, but the baseball won by three feet. The pitch was calculated at 104 miles an hour.

It was even sweeter than that. Despite my troubles with control, I threw the ball straight through the middle of the bull's-eye. The whole production took one pitch.

Soupy Campbell was my roommate in 1941, at the Tudor Arms Hotel on 107th Street at Carnegie. Soup was confused in those years with Bruce Campbell, who enjoyed 13 seasons in the American League as one of its better hitters with a .290 career average. Compounding the confusion was the fact that both of them were outfielders.

The confusion ended there. Soup, whose real first name was Clarence, was never mistaken for Bruce when it came to hitting. He played only two years, hit .226 and .250 and never played in the majors again after the 1941 season.

The surprising truth is that the Indians that year weren't nearly as successful as we were the year before under Oscar Vitt. With Roger Peckinpaugh as our manager, we didn't even play .500 ball. Our record was 75–79, 14 fewer wins than in 1940. Instead of finishing in second place only one game behind the pennant winners, we tied for fourth, 26 games back. We couldn't blame Vitt for any of that. Our only consolation was that the Tigers, the defending American League champions, were the ones we tied for fourth.

We had the individual talent, but we still didn't work together as a team the way you must if you want to be champions. Our two young infielders, Lou Boudreau and Ken Keltner, were giving us the tightest left side in the league. Both of them led their positions in fielding, which the Indians also did as a team. Ray Mack made more double plays than anyone else at his position, and so did Keltner.

I was able to lead the majors in wins again with 25, and I led the league in six other departments. I had 260 strikeouts to lead the league for the fourth straight year—but I also led in walks for the third time with 194. Even that was an improvement over 1938, when I walked 208, the highest number in modern baseball, which began in 1901. Nolan Ryan almost caught me twice, though. He had 204 in 1977 and 202 in 1974.

Walks by a power pitcher like Ryan or me are like strikeouts by a power hitter. If you swing hard, it's more difficult to control the bat. If you throw hard, it's more difficult to control the ball. Some hitters and pitchers let those things bother them. Duke Snider, for example, admits that his strikeouts always ate away at him, and he points out today that his 1,200 strikeouts equal "two full seasons of never doing anything except striking out."

But Duke also hit for power with 407 home runs and for average with .295 over his career and is in the Hall of Fame. Reggie Jackson struck out a thousand times more than Duke, and Babe Ruth struck out more than Duke, so Snider doesn't have anything to apologize for.

I was never proud of my walks. They bothered me, but I couldn't let them affect me. And I certainly couldn't change my style of pitching. I was leading both leagues in wins, not losses, so I had to continue pitching the same way while also working hard to hold the walks to a minimum, whatever that might be in my case.

Nolan Ryan and Early Wynn, my teammate for nine years, have more walks for their careers than I do. Wynn is in the Hall of Fame and Ryan will be voted in five minutes after he's eligible, and they never stopped throwing hard either.

One thing that pleased me in '41 was that I led the league again in innings and games pitched. I pitched 343 innings, the third straight year I led the league in that category, and in 44 games, the second year in a row I topped that department.

Those stats have always meant something to me. They show that a pitcher is taking his turn every time in his manager's pitching rotation, that he's willing to work when he's tired or has the flu or some nagging aches or pains or problems at home. A pitcher isn't helping his team enough if he's not out there working hard every fourth or fifth day doing his best to help his teammates win every game he's in. I had my share of controversy in my 18 years as a major leaguer, but nobody ever accused me of saying no when the manager handed me the ball.

If you could point to any one phase of the game to explain the Indians' disappointing season in 1941, it would be our offense—again. We simply were not scoring enough runs. The Yankees scored more runs than any team except Boston—and won the pennant by 17 games over the Red Sox. Of the eight teams in the American League, we were third in runs allowed, but seventh in runs scored.

Looking back on it from the clear view of almost 50 years later, you can see something else about that year. It was the last *original* baseball season. The sport was never again played the way it was from the time two major leagues were organized in 1901 until then.

Night games became more common during the war years that followed because the workers could be at their jobs all day and still be able to go to a game. This was even appreciated by President Roosevelt, who felt baseball was so important to the nation's morale that he rejected recommendations by some to suspend it for the duration.

Television came into our homes after the war, and fans were able to sit in their living rooms and actually see the games instead of just hearing them. A seven-inch Hallicrafter black-and-white screen was a dream come true, and with that dream came the enormous influence of television over sports scheduling because of its financial potential, and not just for baseball.

We started flying instead of traveling by train. That change took with it the closeness that teammates developed during those all-nighters from Boston to St. Louis and so many other points on the major league map, playing poker, pinochle and gin rummy, reading, thinking about the next game, talking about our families and swapping baseball yarns.

Baseball was integrated. The number of teams in the majors jumped from 16 to 26 and may go to 32 soon. Baseball headed west, all the way, jumping from St. Louis to Kansas City and then to California and even north to Canada. The season was extended from 154 games to 162, and there are playoffs now before the World Series—which brings in even more TV money. With the longer schedule and playoffs before the Series, we have the possibility of baseball, loved for its fresh air and summer sunshine, playing a World Series between Toronto and Montreal in the snow in Canada in late October.

The courts established free agency. Players can move from one team to another, something not possible under the old "reserve clause" in our contracts. They bound a player to the same team even after his contract expired. Now players not only can change teams, they can sign for more than one year, both of which were unheard of in my time.

Those changes all have been profound and lasting. Others have been cosmetic, but today the under-40 fans wouldn't know baseball without them—exploding scoreboards, names on your back, numbers on your front, gloves when you're at bat as well as in the field, and baseball not just under the lights but under roofs too, and on artificial grass.

After 1941, baseball, like the world, was never the same.

CHAPTER NINE
War and Peace

It was a clear, cold, early winter Sunday afternoon as I drove along from Van Meter to Chicago. I was due there later in the day to meet at the Palmer House with Cy Slapnicka and Roger Peckinpaugh. Slap and I needed to agree on my contract for 1942—my negotiations with the Indians seldom took more than five minutes—and Peck was coming along from Cleveland with Slap to talk about the coming season.

It was always helpful to get this business out of the way early so I could concentrate on getting ready for the new season, so I was glad we were meeting at an early date, December 7.

I was driving my new car, a 1941 Buick Century. I was able to afford some extras now, so I got the two biggest luxuries on cars in those days—a radio and a heater. They ran the cost of the car up over $1,000, but they were worth the extra expense. Air conditioned cars were unheard of, and tape decks, stereo speakers, electric windows, cruise control and adjustable steering wheels were not even gleams in Detroit's eye. But a radio and a heater were the very latest "accessories."

As I drove on Route 6 across the Mississippi River at Davenport in the Quad Cities area along the Iowa-Illinois line, I only half listened to the radio—my mind was more on the meeting. Suddenly the announcer interrupted the program with a bulletin about the attack on Pearl Harbor.

Like everyone else alive that afternoon, my life changed drastically in that one shock. As I drove on, fighting to keep my mind on the road,

I knew that the purpose of our meeting had just changed. Now I had to tell Slap and Peck that I was going to enlist in the Navy immediately. I wasn't going to be on the team for 1942, and maybe never again. We never know what the future holds, but on that Sunday we knew even less. One thing we did know: We were losing and losing big.

The United States declared war on "the Axis"—Japan, Germany and Italy—the next day. The next day, I joined the Navy, the first professional athlete in the country to enlist after Pearl Harbor.

A lot of people thought I was crazy. They said I could wait until I was drafted and get in another season or two in the meantime. I had 107 wins at age 22, the most victories in Major League history for a pitcher that age. Why enlist? Why not keep playing ball as long as you can, winning more money and making what we considered big bucks? In fact, if I didn't want to, I didn't have to go at all. I had a deferment from the draft.

The military draft had been started by FDR the year before as we began to prepare seriously for what was inevitable. If you were draft age, physically fit, not needed by your family and not engaged in an "essential occupation" as part of "the war effort," you were classified 1-A. If that was your classification and you were my age, you could kiss everybody goodbye because you were gone. You were going to be wearing a uniform soon, and not a baseball one.

But I was exempt, classified 3-C because of Dad's terminal illness, which was getting worse by the month. I was the sole support of my family. I didn't have to go to war at all.

That wasn't the way most young men felt, though. World War II has been called "America's last popular war," and I think that's true. We were outraged about Pearl Harbor and what Hitler was doing in Europe. We didn't just fight to protect ourselves. We wanted to take those guys on and beat the living hell out of them, and I wanted to be a part of that.

Gene Tunney, the ex-heavyweight boxing champion who defeated Jack Dempsey for the title, was in charge of the Navy's physical fitness program, and he recruited me because I was one of the first athletes to follow a vigorous, year-round conditioning program. So I left my family and my six-figure income and became a chief petty officer at $80 a month and all the "chow" I could eat.

Helping Tunney in his program was fine, but it didn't take me long to know I wanted more action than that. It may seem hard to imagine half a century later, but that's the way young people thought in those days. There was a world war, the second in 25 years, and most able-bodied young men wanted to be in on the fighting so they could feel they were doing their part. The women felt the same way, either enlisting in the service too, or working in jobs that were essential to the war effort and helping even more in spare-time volunteer positions.

Everyone wanted to help. That's the way we were.

After six months of working for Tunney in his physical fitness program, which kept us in fighting trim, I volunteered for gunnery school, and the Navy apparently took my desire for action seriously. Following six months of training, I was made chief of an anti-aircraft gun crew of 24 men on the *U.S.S. Alabama*. Destination: The North Atlantic.

The *Alabama* hadn't been in the Navy as long as I had. She was commissioned in August 1942, and I joined her crew the next month. She was a 35,000-ton battleship and carried a crew of 2,900 men, six times the population of Van Meter.

She joined the fleet in early 1943, spending the spring and summer protecting the supply routes of the Allies in the North Atlantic and engaging in operations with the British Fleet. Then we were assigned to the South Pacific to protect the supply routes there and to help provide naval support for the invasions as the Army and Marines began to recapture the islands overrun by the Japanese in 1942.

One of the hit songs of the war was a wistful number called "When the Lights Go on Again All Over the World." By the time that happened, we had been in combat more than two years and had steamed 175,000 miles, crossing the Arctic Circle six times and the Equator 24. The ship was awarded eight battle stars for the eight invasions we fought in.

Our naval engagements were familiar names in the headlines back home—the Gilbert Islands, Kwajalein Atoll, the Marshalls, Saipan, the Marianas, New Guinea, Tarawa, Guam, the Philippines and Iwo Jima.

One of the worst scares for the men of the *Alabama* didn't involve the combat itself. It was a hurricane. I've been in storms before, but nothing like the one that swept across the South Pacific late in 1943. We were chasing the Japanese fleet, and there seemed like hundreds of our ships on the high seas in hot pursuit when the storm struck.

The hurricane lasted for several days, with winds of 180 miles an hour and gusts up to 210. Three of our destroyers sank because they could not pull alongside the battleships to refuel. They ran out of fuel and couldn't steer their way through the storm. They simply rolled over into the ocean while they were adrift. Planes were blown off the decks of our carriers, and the decks themselves were seriously damaged.

We lost hundreds of men in that storm. Many of them drowned, and others were eaten by sharks. The tide of the war was changing by then. The United States was going to win the war in the Pacific, and in Europe too, but nature was aiding the enemy for those several terrifying days.

In all that combat and the scares and tragedies that always surround you, the saddest part of the war for me came not in combat but back in Iowa. Dad died in January 1943, just before we shipped out to the North Atlantic. He had fought that cancer for six years.

While I was home on emergency leave for the funeral, I took a walk alone out to the wheat field. I looked around Oakview Park and saw it all again—Dad and me building it with our own hands and hearts 11 years before. It seemed so much longer than that. It wasn't really Oakview Park any more. It was becoming a cow pasture again.

But I could still see us out there, playing against the older teams from Des Moines, teaming up with my pals to beat those guys, Mom fixing food for the players to eat between games if there was a doubleheader, and Dad cheering me on in his quiet way, always giving one hundred percent for his boy Bob.

Everything was so different now.

One of the newspaper clippings from home later told me that night baseball was an immediate hit, but there was an early problem. The games began at 9:30 in Cleveland because of concern by the front office about the safety of the players. The business of playing under lights was so new the officials were afraid the ball would be too hard to see until it really got dark, when the lights would be most effective. They didn't want any players getting hurt.

The paper suggested the club move the starting time to 8:30 to help the war workers get home in time to get enough sleep. The paper said, "If the umpires decided that playing conditions were dangerous, they could delay the action until later without annoying the customers." The time was changed to an earlier hour, and now some teams start their games at 7:30, but in those days people were still learning things about night baseball.

Another clipping from home told me just how far the war was reaching in its effect on people. The story described how so many of my teammates on "the home front" were working in wartime occupations if they weren't in the armed forces.

Jim Bagby, Jr., who helped to stop DiMaggio's 56-game hitting streak, was learning to be a draftsman at the Foote-Burt Company on St. Clair Avenue N.E. One of our pitching veterans, Mel Harder, was training for a job at the Ohio Rubber Company in Willoughby. Our second baseman, Ray Mack, and another pitcher, Al Milnar, were working at the Thompson Aircraft Product Company. Ray was a plant layout engineer, and Al was a guard.

Oscar Grimes, our backup first baseman, was a guard too, at Cleveland Welding Company on Berea Road at West 117th Street. Hank Edwards, a rookie outfielder in '41, was working at Republic Steel while awaiting induction into the Army, and Oris Hockett, another outfielder, was a toolmaker at Goodyear Aircraft in Akron.

Some of them worked in those jobs in the off-season and some were there until they were drafted, but everybody seemed to be doing his share.

Those were strange sounding jobs for baseball players, but then baseball itself was strange during the war. I was rotated back to the States early in 1945 and assigned to the Navy's gigantic training center at Great Lakes, Illinois, near Chicago. We were in the last year of the war, and when I came home I could see the difference in major league baseball after four years of manpower shortages caused by the war.

Teams never knew from one year to the next who would be on their roster. Military service was causing chaos with every team. Whereas rosters used to change from one year to the next, now they were changing from one *day* to the next. Players who were 1-A were here today and gone tomorrow, their places filled by the unwanteds of the military draft—4-Fs, kids and old men.

The Washington Senators had a starting pitching staff of four knuckleballers, a 17-year-old third baseman, a 42-year-old pitcher, and another pitcher who had a wooden leg after being shot down over Europe.

The standings changed drastically from one season to the next. The Senators were second in 1943, last in '44, and second again in '45. The Cubs finished 30 games behind the Cardinals in '44 and beat them for the National League pennant the next year. The Tigers did the same thing—20 games back in 1942, only one game behind in '44 and pennant winners in '45.

During a war, not even baseball makes sense. But to the folks on the home front, it was still baseball.

I was discharged in August 1945 at the Navy Pier in Chicago, but there was a bigger story that month in Cleveland and everywhere else: the Japanese surrendered. August 14 was V-J Day, Victory over Japan. There was another story in the papers that attracted attention in Cleveland then, too. "The Quiz Kids," one of the most popular radio shows, was coming to Cleveland for its broadcast.

Since winter, I had been stationed at Great Lakes after being rotated home aboard the *Alabama*. It was a perfect arrangement because I got to play baseball when spring came.

Playing for Great Lakes in the final months of the war was a golden break for me. It allowed me to chip the rust off my pitching arm with other major leaguers like Ken Keltner, Walker Cooper, Denny Galehouse and Pinky Higgins. When my discharge came through, I was rarin' to go. But there were question marks.

Ralph Cannon wrote a thought-provoking article in *Esquire* Magazine—"50 cents at your newsstand"—asking:

CAN THEY COME BACK?

Cannon wondered how many of us would be able to shake off the effects of our wartime absences and become successful players again, and how many might find ourselves unable to perform up to our pre-war standards. Cecil Travis remains the player people mention as the best example of one who made it back from the war but not back to his previous level of excellence.

Those frozen feet from the Battle of the Bulge in Europe in December 1944 slowed Travis down so much that the Senators had to move him from shortstop to third base. He simply did not have the range and quickness to play short, where he had been an All-Star before the war. Then they found out he was even too slow to play third. He never again was a full-time player, and he retired in 1947 at the age of 34. That's what the record book says. The reality is that his career was finished by the war, and his last real season was 1941, when he was 28.

In his article, Cannon wondered if a similar situation might face others. In my case, he wrote, "Feller probably has seen more combat in this war than any other top-ranking American sports celebrity." He wasn't sure I could make it back all the way. People had the same fears about others—DiMaggio and Williams and National Leaguers like Kirby Higbe, Pete Reiser and Johnny Mize.

The happy answer to Cannon's question is that almost all of us were able to pick up our careers at our prewar levels of performance. DiMag, for example, hit 25 home runs in '46, Ted had a .342 batting average, Mize hit .337 for the Giants, Higbe won 17 games for the Dodgers, and I led the American League in wins for my fourth season in a row.

Then people began to wonder how we would have done if the war hadn't come along. Baseball fans filled many an hour in those days with that "what-if" question. Eventually, an analyst in Seattle, Ralph Winnie, sat down at his computer and figured out the answers.

He took our individual stats for the last three years before our military services and our first three years after the war, then averaged them out on a per-season basis and projected them across the war years. This is what he found out:

Ted would have become the all-time runs-batted-in champion with 2,663, which would have been 366 more than the record set by Hank Aaron. DiMaggio would have moved from 28th to third. Williams would be second behind Aaron in home runs with 743 instead of eighth with 521. DiMaggio, Mize and Greenberg all would have had more than 500 home runs, but none of them did.

In pitching, Winnie discovered that Warren Spahn would have had the third highest number of victories instead of fifth. He found that veterans of the First World War suffered the same losses. Grover Cleveland Alexander, who missed 1918 because of World War I, would have won 400 games instead of 373.

In my case, Winnie projected that I would have won 107 more games, finishing with 373 career wins instead of 266, with another 1,070 strikeouts, five no-hitters instead of three and 19 one-hitters instead of 12. He calculated that I would have finished with the sixth most wins in history instead of 28th and the seventh most shutouts instead of 29th.

It may not prove anything, but it made for a lot of talk in the "Hot Stove League" in those days, and still does. There's always the possibility that something else might have happened even if a world war hadn't come along. We could have been injured and missed a full season or slipped on a banana peel, who knows? But this much I do know: I never heard one baseball player who missed time out of his career because of military service complain about it.

Besides, in 1945 all of us were too thrilled about V-J Day to think negative thoughts. We were just glad to come home in one piece and be able to get another chance to do what we loved—play baseball. Elmer Gedeon never had that chance. He was an outfielder with the Washington Senators for a few games just before the war. He was killed in action in France on his birthday in 1944, the only major league baseball player to be killed in the fighting. He was 27.

In recognition of their contributions and in the interest of accuracy, I hope the editors of the *Baseball Encyclopedia* and other publications will start indicating in their records of individual players that those years were missed because of military service. The same should be done in the records of those players who served in World War I, Korea and Vietnam.

Just to show that the man didn't play during certain years could mean anything. Maybe he was injured or in the minors or in the French Foreign Legion. Let's tell the readers that the player missed certain years because he was in the armed forces. That's only fair, and accurate.

The good folks of Cleveland decided to throw a welcome-home party for me. I was jumping right back in without missing a beat, and Lou Boudreau, our player-manager by then, was starting me two nights after my discharge against the Tigers at Municipal Stadium. Over a thousand people were nice enough to show up in the Rainbow Room of the Carter Hotel for a civic ceremony at noon. The size of the crowd floored me, but the real thrill was to see 47,000 people turn out that night to watch me pitch against Detroit. The Indians' telephone operator, Ada Ireland, was so flooded with calls from fans all day long that her switchboard broke down.

Before the game I was given a jeep in ceremonies at home plate. My teammates, knowing of my business activities, gave me an engraved pen and pencil set. Governor Frank Lausche was there, with Cy Young, the winningest pitcher in baseball history, and Cleveland's own Tris Speaker.

Our national feeling of patriotism was just as strong as ever with Americans rejoicing in our victories over Germany, Italy and Japan. The scene is hard to picture in today's terms, but in our world of 1945, it was typical.

There was a march to the flagpole next to the fence in center field for the playing, and singing, of our National Anthem. A group of World War I veterans marched behind Jack Horwitz's band, ahead of Mayor

Burke and me, followed by every member of both teams. One of the Cleveland columnists, touched by the scene as the flag was taken down at day's end, wrote that our wartime enemies "hadn't been able to tear it down."

My opponent that night was one of the hottest pitchers in baseball, Hal Newhouser—"Prince Hal." He won 29 games in '44 and was already a 20-game winner for '45 with a 20-7 record and plenty of time for more with 38 games remaining. I was glad I'd been able to pitch at Great Lakes. It wasn't the major leagues, but it was effective preparation. We played most of the major league teams and lost to only one—the Phillies.

Jimmy Outlaw, another one of my favorite baseball names, stepped into the batter's box as Detroit's leadoff hitter, the first I would face in the majors since I pitched against the Browns three years and 11 months before.

My first pitch was a fast ball for a strike. He worked the count to 3–2, then I struck him out on a curve ball. Those Cleveland fans went crazy. To retire the first man I faced was enough to get them excited, but to do it with a strikeout was exactly what they had come to see.

Pay Seerey won the game for us with a two-run homer, 4–2, and the fans got a bonus in the ninth inning when the game ended the way it started, with Outlaw striking out. I pitched a four-hitter and didn't allow a hit after the third inning. I walked five, but between those Outlaw strikeouts, I fanned ten others including York and Greenberg twice each.

I was back. After all that time away, nothing seemed different. The velocity on my fast ball, an acceptable amount of control, the rhythm and coordination, the feel for the game at its critical points, everything seemed just as natural as ever.

The next time out, I beat the White Sox, 8–2, on an eight-hitter. My control problem was back, too. I had more walks than strikeouts, seven to six, plus a wild pitch.

I was able to continue taking my turn in Boudreau's rotation, still with no ill effects. I pitched 6⅓ innings without a decision in Detroit and lost a 2–1 game to the Red Sox in Fenway Park. In 12 days, I had made four starts and pitched 32⅓ innings.

My morale jumped even higher with a nine-inning 10–3 win, a five-hitter, over New York at Yankee Stadium. I beat one of the Yankee greats, Corporal Spud Chandler, before a crowd of 72,152, the largest attendance at a major league game in six years. Snuffy Stirnweiss,

New York's second baseman, ended the game by striking out. After it was over, he told the writers I was the fastest pitcher he had ever faced.

That was helpful for me to know, and not for ego reasons. I needed some evaluations of what I looked like after my absence, and an experienced player like Snuffy was a good judge. He led the league in hitting the year before, so I was entirely willing to accept his qualifications as a judge. If he thought I looked so fast, that told me what I needed to know.

Other things were also getting back to normal. The War Production Board in Washington announced that automobile factories could start making cars again. There hadn't been a car produced in the United States for four years because the manufacturers were turning out bombers, fighters, tanks and warships. Being able to look forward to new cars in 1946 made us feel like dancing in the streets all over again.

There was other great "peace news" instead of all the depressing war news of the previous four years. The Labor Department ordered girls 16 and 17 years old out of the war plants, where they had been allowed to work because of the manpower shortage, and back to school. Book and magazine publishers could make their publications as thick as they wanted—the paper shortage was over, too.

Penicillin, the new "miracle drug" that was produced during the war and saved so many lives in the fighting, was made available to civilians on September 1. And the greatest news of all on the home front was in those headlines which shouted:

RATIONING ENDS

No more stamps needed along with your money when you bought food or gasoline or other essentials. The government issued books of stamps during the war to accompany each purchase, with the number of stamps in each book based on the number of people in your family.

Now all of that was over. We could enjoy life again—new cars, buying a roast without counting ration stamps, and enjoying a baseball game without any bulletins over the public address system about military attacks or invasions.

Everything was going to be just like before. Or was it?

CHAPTER TEN
1946: The First Postwar Baseball Season

The 1945 season in the American League had a storybook finish, and we had no way of knowing it was a glimpse into the future, especially for the Indians.

The Detroit Tigers and Washington Senators battled each other all season long. They were still headed for a dead heat when the Senators ended their season a week early because their owner, Clark Griffith, didn't dream his team would be a pennant contender after finishing dead last the year before. He had rented Griffith Stadium to the Washington Redskins, as he did every year, but he agreed to an early date for their opener.

With a week left in the season for every other team in the league, the Senators finished their games. Now they were forced to sit and wait while the Tigers could decide things for themselves, with the Senators unable to do anything but check the American League standings every day in the paper.

The two teams were headed for the first tie in baseball history. Their representatives traveled to Chicago for a toss of a coin to see who would be the home team in case a playoff game became necessary. The Tigers won the toss.

On the last day of the season, Detroit was playing a doubleheader against St. Louis. If the Browns won both games, the Tigers and Senators would finish tied. Going into the ninth inning of the first game, the Browns were leading. At Griffith Stadium, the Senators, following the game on radio, began piling into taxi cabs with their luggage for the trip to Union Station and the train ride to Detroit.

Suddenly the clubhouse manager, Frankie Baxter, hurried out the clubhouse door, waving his arms frantically at the cabs and hollering, "Never mind! It's all over! Greenberg just hit a grand slam!"

Hank had also been discharged from the service before the season ended because of a long hitch in uniform and won the American League pennant for the Tigers with that home run. He played two more years and hit 69 more home runs and was elected to the Hall of Fame, but that was his last grand slam.

The press and the fans and all the rest of us followed that neck-and-neck race extra closely because we were fascinated that two teams could play 154 games each and still be dead even six months later. It was a million-to-one shot being played out. It hadn't happened in the whole 44-year history of the majors. Then when it didn't happen after all, we knew we might never see a pennant race again that would come so close to finishing in a tie and making a playoff game necessary.

But it did happen—the next year. The Cardinals and Dodgers tied for the National League pennant, and the Cards won a best-of-three playoff, two games to none.

Only two years after that, the American League season ended in a tie. And we were in it.

The events which led to what happened in 1948 were set in motion in 1946. Boudreau was approaching his peak, Keltner was still at his, and I was winning consistently enough to help. We also were about to acquire several talented players like Early Wynn, Bob Lemon, Eddie Robinson and Joe Gordon.

Another historic event helped point us toward good things. Jackie Robinson was signed by the Brooklyn Dodgers and broke the color barrier as the first black man to play major league baseball. The Dodgers signed him in 1946 to play minor league ball for their Montreal team in the International League. He promptly led the league in hitting.

When Jackie broke in, he helped the Cleveland Indians as much as he did the Brooklyn Dodgers. Now other teams could sign black players too, and without all the heat and abuse felt by the Dodgers. The integration of baseball by Brooklyn made it easier for the Indians to do something else that the historians seem to have forgotten. Just as the Dodgers integrated the National League, the Indians integrated the American League, and in the same season.

Jackie's rookie year in the majors was 1947, the same season that Larry Doby, a talented 23-year-old black kid, started playing for us, as a second baseman. Then came Satchel Paige, one of the legends of baseball even then and one of the top ten pitchers in the history of our sport in my opinion. Doby and Paige became instrumental in our 1948 experience.

The man who made these things happen was himself new on the major league scene as we entered the second half of the 1940s, and our first full year of peace. He was Bill Veeck, and baseball, especially in Cleveland, wasn't going to be the same for a long time. All of us had a time trying to keep up with Veeck and his goings-on.

Veeck, who bought the team in 1946 with a syndicate of investors, was baseball's Barnum Bill. Veeck took the doors off his office because he said his door was always open to everyone anyhow, so why have one? He sat with the fans in the general admission seats and the bleachers during the games and asked them what they thought the Indians should do to keep improving. He loved the members of the press, and vice versa. He wasn't afraid to do some old-fashioned wheeling-and-dealing to acquire the good players needed to win, and he never stopped trying to improve the entertainment value of the product he offered.

He hired one of baseball's premier attractions, comedian Jackie Price, to entertain the growing crowds before games. As the pre-game fans sat there buying Veeck's hot dogs and cold drinks and peanuts, Jackie kept them entertained with his show-biz routine—hanging upside down from the batting cage by his spikes and spraying line drives to every part of the outfield, holding three balls in his throwing hand at home plate and firing a strike to each base all in one throw, and catching fly balls from behind the wheel of a jeep while motoring across the outfield grass.

Even when Jackie failed, he succeeded—like the times in Denver and Mexico City when he was performing for the "barnstorming" teams I organized to play all over the country right after the World

Series each October. Once in Denver and again in Mexico City, his jeep went crashing through the outfield fence. The fans thought he narrowly escaped death during his daring feat by jumping out of the jeep just in time.

What they didn't know was that Jackie held the steering wheel at a set position with a coat hanger. But when he wanted the jeep to take off, he just kicked the hanger off the wheel while catching the last fly ball in his routine. The jeep appeared to be out of control, heading for the fence and certain disaster.

He got a standing ovation every time.

Veeck was a sound baseball man and an energetic, creative promoter, and he had good common sense. He kept the reporters informed, and he kept the fans happy while he built a winner.

While Veeck was building a good show and a good team in his first year in town, the writers and announcers were making Cleveland Strikeout City in 1946. The team never really got hot and seemed destined for another so-so season, but I was fortunate enough to have a strong first half. The writers were wondering if I would become the first pitcher since Dizzy Dean to win 30 games. I had 15 wins by the All-Star break.

My victory pace cooled off, as it has for every pitcher who has pursued that goal, except Denny McLain in 1968, but one pace that didn't slow down was my strikeout rate. I had 190 Ks by All-Star time, enough to lead the league for the whole season in many years, and I still had half the season to go. My fast ball and my slider were blowing them away, and in the first half I had ten games in which I struck out at least ten hitters. I decided that if the Indians couldn't go for the pennant, maybe I could go for the record.

Clark Griffith, an old pitcher himself, decided to make some money off that fast ball of mine. He announced that I would throw some pitches through a special photoelectric measuring device at home plate so my fast ball could be clocked in those days before radar guns. Griff wasn't called "The Old Fox" for nothing. He announced the test a week before the Indians came to Washington, and he had a large crowd in his ball park the night of the test.

There was only one thing he didn't do: He didn't ask me to do it. He never contacted me at all. I was on the rubbing table in the clubhouse getting ready to warm up. Our trainer was stretching my pitching arm

Barnstorming with Satchel Paige in 1946.

Landing at San Diego on his 1946 barnstorming tour. Jeff Heath is on Feller's right, Charlie Keller (in jacket and sweater) is behind Bob, Dutch Leonard (in hat) is behind Charlie, 1946 American League batting champion Mickey Vernon (dark shirt and striped tie) is next to Dutch, and Rollie Hemsley is at top of stairs in front of player with hat.

Another barnstorming partner, entertainer Jackie Price.

Firing one by Johnny Outlaw to break the American League strikeout record in 1946.

The first game of the 1948 World Series. Cleveland's Lou Boudreau clearly tagged Phil Masi before he reached second, but Umpire Bill Stewart called Masi safe. John Lindsay's camera called him out.

Facing Joe DiMaggio at Yankee Stadium...

. . . and Ted Williams at Fenway Park.

The prized Bob Feller trading card.

The grip on the Bob Feller fast ball at the start of his windup (left) and at the point of release. (Look Magazine)

Bob Feller in his prime. (National Baseball Library, Cooperstown, NY)

Babe Ruth leans on Bob Feller's bat, wearing Yankee pin stripes for the last time, as he says goodbye at Yankee Stadium in April 1948, four months before his death. (Associated Press)

At the premiere of *The Babe Ruth Story* in 1948 with Charles Bickford and William Bendix.

and legs when Mr. Griffith came in. He told me it was about time to get out there and start throwing smoke.

I told him as soon as he paid me for it I would. I asked him for $1,000 and settled for $700 before leaving the clubhouse to do it.

I said, "I shouldn't be doing it at all, Mr. Griffith, because you didn't even have the manners to ask me. But you're a good man and you've been good for baseball, so I'll do it for the seven hundred."

I was beginning to develop something of a militant attitude on the question of owners making extra money through their players without paying them anything extra for their roles. I was starting to elevate the subject from a question to an issue, a cause which I continued to fight for as the American League's player representative a few years later.

Mr. Griffith knew even better than I did that his big payday wasn't coming just from the higher-than-usual ticket sales. He knew all those fans were going to buy hot dogs and score cards and everything else so his bonus was coming from several different sources of revenue—but the man making it all possible wasn't going to get a dime or even a bag of peanuts.

He did something far more important than just paying me, and he realized it as much as I did. He was acknowledging the validity of the argument that players are entitled to something extra when they use their baseball skills for exhibitions beyond their normal jobs.

Players have always made free personal appearances for their teams to promote ticket sales and have done other things to help the front office's marketing campaigns, but this was different. A player was being asked to be a performer, displaying his professional skills to help another team make money, always exposing himself to the risk of injury in the process, and for a zero share of the proceeds. It was like telling Fred Astaire he'd be doing his dance routines before the game, with a lot of publicity for a whole week before, and the owner was going to make a lot of money, but he wasn't going to give Astaire anything.

You can imagine what Fred Astaire would have said about that. Well, I was saying the same thing.

For my 700 bucks, I threw several balls through an opening in that photoelectric machine, and 31,000 fans watched almost in silence as they awaited the announcement of the speeds recorded by the machine, which came from the Aberdeen Proving Grounds in Maryland where it was used to test the speed of projectiles. My highest average speed, which is what the "Jugs" machines of today measure, was 107 miles an hour. The highest speed while crossing the plate, which the 1946 machine measured, was 98.6. That was also my body temperature when I calmed down after my showdown with Mr. Griffith.

In contrast to Mr. Griffith's reluctance to pay me, there was Jorge Pasquel, who was all too willing to pay anybody—any U.S. major leaguer. Jorge and his brothers were wealthy importers-exporters in Mexico who wanted in the worst way to bring big league baseball to their country.

They openly courted us, and offered DiMag, Ted and me $120,000 a season for three years, with the whole $360,000 each up front. All of us said no thanks.

The Pasquels recruited a few of our colleagues, though—Mickey Owen, Sal Maglie, Max Lanier and Junior Stephens. I was familiar with baseball in Mexico. I barnstormed there with my team the following season, playing in Tampico, Vera Cruz, Mexico City, Guadalajara, Monterey and other cities. We drew good crowds, had some fun and were paid fairly, although curve ball pitchers had one complaint—in that thin air curve balls didn't break as sharply, especially in Mexico City, which is 7,700 feet above sea level. But the fast balls were even faster.

The pressure the Pasquels put on all major league players in '46 to jump to Mexico and give up their American careers was enormous, and the wonder is that more players didn't yield to the big bucks. Although almost all of us turned down the offers, we gained something important from the experience. Those overtures from south of the border helped to pave the way for a pension plan for retired players, something that didn't exist until 1947.

I don't know about Joe D. and Ted, but I had special reasons for rejecting the Mexican offer—I wanted a championship for the Indians, and the major league strikeout record for myself.

I guess another reason the writers were following me so closely was that I got their attention early that year, with my second no-hit, no-run game. This one was extra sweet because it came against my rivals, the Yankees, and in their ballpark. It happened on April 30, and even though it was a Tuesday afternoon, there were 37,144 fans on hand.

The win improved my lifetime record against the Yankees to 16 wins and 14 losses, and it gave me a total of two no-hitters and six one-hitters, but it was just as much hard work as ever, and just as much drama.

It was like my first no-hitter, when my catcher, Rollie Hemsley, tripled in the only run of the game. This time my catcher, Frankie Hayes, did the same thing. He hit a home run off Bill Bevens. In the Yankee ninth, the tension reached a level indicative of a no-hit game.

Snuffy Stirnweiss bunted down the first base line, trying anything he could to break up the no-hitter, which is exactly what every player should do in that situation. It looked like a routine chance for Les Fleming, but the ball rolled right through his legs. The public address announcer told the crowd that the official scorer ruled the play was an error and not a hit. At that time there was no hit-error sign in Yankee Stadium. They put one up the next day. I was told later that this was the first time in the 23-year history of Yankee Stadium that such an announcement had been made.

Boudreau asked for time out and then came to the mound to make sure I wasn't upset at the error. It put the potential tying run on base and brought what could be the winning run to the plate. We were faced with losing not only the no-hitter but the game too.

Tommy Henrich sacrificed Stirnweiss to second, bringing up—who else?—Joe DiMaggio. The fans were screaming and clapping and yelling for their hero to do what he did best—break up the ball game and send all the New York fans home happy. He had grounded back to me on a 3–2 pitch in the first inning, popped up in the fourth and flied to center in the sixth. He was due. The whole team was—the Yanks had hit only two balls out of the infield all day.

I threw DiMaggio my best fast ball on a 3–2 count, and he hit a grounder to Boudreau's left. Lou threw him out at first as Stirnweiss moved to third. Now the tying run was only 90 feet away. Any mistake now could tie the game. I reminded myself to concentrate on the hitter, Charlie Keller. The whole crowd was standing, rooting for me.

I threw my 133rd pitch of the game, an overhand curve ball, that Keller bounced to Ray Mack. It was a high-hopper, and in another case of history repeating itself, Ray threw him out. I had my second no-hitter, plus a roar of congratulations from the New York fans.

They must have liked what they saw, even though their team lost. We went back to New York two months later and 50,000 fans showed up for another afternoon game, on a Saturday. That one was harder physically than the no-hitter. It was a hot, humid June day, and I needed salt tablets and whiffs of ammonia to stagger home on a five hitter, 2–1.

Those low-hit, high-strikeout games were putting people in the American League's ballparks. In our next series after that Saturday crowd in New York, we drew 34,000, a capacity crowd, for a Wednesday afternoon game in Fenway Park. I was able to beat the Red Sox and my old teammate, Jim Bagby, but I wasn't any mystery to Ted Williams.

He and DiMag were having those good years on their return from the war, and Williams let me know that afternoon that he was picking up right were he left off after hitting .406 in 1941. He nailed me for a home run and two singles. The only time I got him out all day was on a low line drive to Pat Seerey.

Part of Ted's philosophy of hitting is, "When you make contact, things start to happen." He made more than his share of contact that day, and something happened every time.

Maybe without intending to, he was also applying the hitting philosophy of someone else. Woodie Held, who broke in as a Yankee himself eight years later and then played six seasons with the Indians, had the simplest and shortest philosophy on hitting I ever heard:

"Always swing hard, in case you happen to hit the ball."

Ted has said that the increased use of the slider after World War II was one reason that batting averages never reached their prewar heights. If so, I guess I'm one of the culprits.

I began to work on a slider in 1941 and perfected it at Great Lakes in '45. By the start of the '46 season, I had enough confidence to throw it often and in different situations, including tight spots like a full count or late in the game with men on base.

The slider is one of baseball's most effective pitches, especially when the pitcher mixes it in with his others instead of throwing it too often.

It can be especially effective for a fast ball pitcher because it comes up to the plate looking like a fast ball. It has less speed, but not enough for the hitter to detect the slightly reduced speed early in the pitch.

The slider darts sharply just before it reaches the plate, away from a right-handed hitter when thrown by a right-handed pitcher. It doesn't break much—four to six inches—but because it breaks so late, the hitter has trouble catching up with it.

I didn't invent the slider—I merely popularized it. The pitch has been around since Christy Mathewson's time. It's used even more today because now more kinds of pitches are being thrown. But as good as the slider is, it is effective only if you can mix it in with a good fast ball. The same is true of a curve ball.

All hitters will eventually catch up with a pitcher who does not throw a good fast ball, especially if he does not have outstanding control. They can adjust to a breaking pitch, but not to an overpowering fast ball. Curve balls, sliders, fork balls, split-fingered fast balls—whatever they are and whatever you call them—are all fine and effective if varied so the hitter doesn't know what to expect.

There's one, simple truth, though, that overrides all others when it comes to pitching: a good fast ball with control can take you from the Little Leagues to Cooperstown.

As the strikeouts continued to mount in '46, I stayed with the pitch that brought me there. I had two or three different kinds of curve balls and a lot of confidence in each of them. I was never afraid to throw my curve when I was behind in the count, 2 and 0 or 3 and 1, or even late in the game in a pressure situation.

The curve made my fast ball more effective because the hitters couldn't time my every pitch, and it also gave me that one additional fringe benefit that a curve ball brings with it: enlarging the strike zone for the pitcher. When you have a good curve ball, it makes your strike zone larger because the hitters swing at pitches that are outside.

But the fast ball was my bread-and-butter pitch. As long as the hitters kept missing it, I was going to keep throwing it. On August 13, in a night game at home against the Tigers, I recorded my 262nd strikeout, breaking my career high of 261 in 1940. I reached 261 in $320^1/_3$ innings, but I reached 262 in only $260^2/_3$ innings.

Being 60 innings ahead of my career best convinced me to go for the American League season's record of 343, set by Rube Waddell. The team wasn't going anywhere anyhow. We finished in the second division, 18 games below .500 in sixth place. Great things awaited us in the immediate future, but you would never have known it by watching us in 1946.

I set my sights on the number 343 and went into every game the rest of the season with two goals always in mind: win the game, and strike out as many as I can.

I wasn't really striking out staggering numbers in each game, but I was achieving what I've always preached about pitching—consistency. I went two months, from the last week of July until the last week of

September, without reaching double figures in strikeouts for 19 games, and I never struck out more than ten men in a game after June. But the consistency was there—nine, seven, five, four, seven, six, seven—all the way into the last week of the season.

In my next to last game of the season, in Detroit against my old strikeout favorites, the Tigers, I tied Waddell at 343 in a game we won, 9–8. I pitched only five innings, so Boudreau gave me the ball to start our last game, only two days later, still in Detroit. I was going for more than just the strikeout record by this time. I was also trying for my 26th win. My opponent was another familiar face, Hal Newhouser, who was going for his 27th. If I beat him, we would tie for the most wins in the league.

As I worked my way through the Detroit batting order for the first time, I remained tied with Waddell, stuck on 343. The first eight hitters managed to avoid the K in the score book. They were choking up on the bat to help themselves make contact. Nobody wanted to go into the record book as the strikeout victim who would become the answer to a trivia question.

But then came Newhouser. I struck him out. The record was mine.

Now each strikeout was the new American League record. I managed to pick up three more through the eighth inning. In the ninth, I got Jimmy Bloodworth on strikeouts, number 348. I also had my 26th win, 4–1, on a six-hitter. I wasn't tied with Waddell any more, but I was with Newhouser. That was good enough for me.

There was confusion over whether I had broken the strikeout record after all. It turned out that the records of Waddell's time were less than 100 percent accurate, and some sources showed that Waddell had 349 strikeouts in '04. Time has solved the puzzle because Nolan Ryan and Sandy Koufax have both passed Waddell and me in strikeouts for one season.

The record for my first year back from the war showed I tied for the league lead in wins, broke the record for strikeouts in a season, and led the league in five other departments—shutouts, innings pitched, games started, games pitched and complete games. I was always as proud of my number of innings, complete games and games started as I was of my other stats. Those figures show that you're helping your team. They prove you're out there on the mound working in a lot of games, available every time you're needed, allowing the bullpen a rest during the hot and heavy part of the schedule in the second half of the season, and giving your club what every winning team needs—a "stopper" who can go out and have a reasonable chance of winning a game for your team every fourth day.

I had some icing on the cake that year. The All-Star Game was resumed after a one-year suspension because of the war. I was the starting pitcher and the winner in the All-Star Game in Fenway Park. I pitched three shutout innings, and the American League won in a romp, 12–0. That was the game when Ted Williams did "the impossible" against Rip Sewell's "blooper" pitch. The pitch used to float up to the plate and supposedly nobody could hit it for a home run, but Ted did. He supplied all the power himself. For the day, he had two homers, four hits and five runs batted in.

My individual numbers were fine, but what were we going to do about our team? I had been with the Indians for eight seasons, and we hadn't won a thing. We knew conditions were changing. The war was over, Cleveland had a new owner in Bill Veeck, baseball had a new commissioner in Happy Chandler, and one player in the minor leagues had a new color—black.

What did these changes hold for the Indians?

All of us would learn the answers in time, but I couldn't worry about them at the moment. As soon as the season ended, I had to start another one—that now-gone special time of the season in cities and towns all over America when the major leaguers came to town and the local folks got their only view of us in those days before television.

Even the name sounded like fun—"barnstorming."

CHAPTER ELEVEN

Barnstorming Just for the Fun of It

Barnstorming baseball was baseball in its purest sense. There wasn't any pennant race or World Series involved, no pressure, no heated rivalries producing charges and counter-charges, no tension-filled controversies. It was just baseball for the fun of it, played in the heartland of America in Rockwell-like scenes where the folks wanted to see what major league players looked like and watch us play and talk to us and have fun around us.

Barnstorming didn't start with baseball. The early aviators did it before us, and one of the origins of the word comes from the use of barns as hangars for their planes. It was as much fun for the players as it was for the townfolk, and the fact that they got some extra money didn't hurt either. The old "Negro leagues" made it a full-time occupation for the black players through the 1920s and '30s, and the show went on until integration took the good black players out of the barnstorming business and into the majors. Television brought major league players into the living rooms of every small town and farm in America. The fans didn't need to go see us on our barnstorming tours any more. They could stay home and see us.

Barnstorming was baseball at its best—innocent and fun, in towns big and small.

But it was a business, too, one that I entered with enthusiasm just before the war while playing on other barnstorming teams before forming my own. After the war, barnstorming hit its peak, and I was there to enjoy it and take advantage of the opportunity—and help others do the same.

I formed my own Bob Feller's All-Stars during the '46 season. In between starts for the Indians, I was adding to AT&T's dividends with long distance phone bills that they must have loved, making arrangements in towns all over the country and calling players around both leagues, and in the Negro leagues, to recruit them for my teams.

By the time the major league season was over, it was clear that we had produced a first-class business operation that was going to be highly successful. It would bring baseball and fun to every town where we played—and cause some objections and controversy in the majors.

I had put together a full roster of players whose combined annual salaries in the majors exceeded two million dollars. The owners of the teams didn't like that. They said they were concerned about their players getting hurt while barnstorming. Then they really objected when they found out how we were traveling. We were going to fly.

That was unheard of for professional sports teams. They took trains. They said I was exposing their athletes to even greater dangers. But I chartered two DC-3s for a month from Flying Tigers Air Lines. We had "Bob Feller's All-Stars" painted on the side and took off to play 35 games in 27 days. We were the only baseball teams traveling by air. No other barnstorming tours were doing it yet, and the major league teams hadn't started flying either. We were pioneering the practice of a professional sports team traveling that way. Today it's hard to imagine teams going any other way.

That was the first autumn when barnstorming teams of major league players were allowed to play for more than ten days. That's because Commissioner Happy Chandler agreed to let me barnstorm for 30 days after I conducted an instructional school for returning veterans before spring training. Major and minor leaguers attended, and Chandler said he appreciated it so much, knowing that I wasn't going to make any money from the project—in fact, I spent $2,500. He agreed to let us play for a month after the season instead of the traditional limit of ten days. Then, to return the favor even more, we played an exhibition game in Chandler's home town of Versailles, Kentucky.

For that whole month, it was Bob Feller's All-Stars versus Satchel Paige's All-Stars. I paid Satch and his players and all of mine, plus my airplane crews, a trainer, a physician, a secretary, a lawyer, a publicity man and an advance man. We ran everything first class, staying in the best hotels, flying in those DC-3s when they were the best in the air, and I was paying first-class salaries ranging from $1,700 for the month to $6,000.

I pitched in every game but two, working from two to five innings each time. The only two games I missed conflicted with a contract I had made to appear at a milk convention in Atlantic City. We were playing in California at that point of the tour, so I flew all night from Sacramento, made my appearance in Atlantic City, and flew all night again to rejoin our tour in California.

The players' share of the World Series that year was the smallest since 1918, with each member of the losing Red Sox getting $2,052.03, so barnstorming for such good wages was even more attractive than usual to the players. I'm convinced that the success of our tour and the money the players made were two of the reasons their percentage of World Series earnings was increased by the owners shortly after that.

Some of the owners objected to what I was doing so much they paid their stars not to barnstorm with me. Tom Yawkey, the owner of the Red Sox, paid Ted Williams $10,000 to stay home so he wouldn't get hurt playing in a game or killed in a plane crash. Yawkey's counterpart in Detroit, Spike Briggs, paid Hal Newhouser the same amount.

But we had most of the best players from the Negro leagues playing on Satch's team, and we had most of the big stars from the majors on mine—the two league batting champions, Stan Musial and Mickey Vernon, Johnny Sain, Charlie Keller, Dutch Leonard, Johnny Berardino—who is now Dr. Steve Hardy on the TV soap opera, "General Hospital"—my fellow Indians, Rollie Hemsley, Jeff Heath, plus Phil Rizzuto, Eddie Lopat, Bob Lemon and Jim Hegan and my former teammate Frankie Hayes.

The Kansas City Monarchs, one of the top black teams, helped me to form Satch's team. Their general manager, Tom Beard, and their owner, a Mr. Wilkinson, were a big help to me. The manager was Frank Duncan, a catcher.

Then, of course, there was Satch.

No ad agency or writer could have created a character like Satchel Paige. Only the good Lord can be that creative.

Satch and I were friends, teammates and business associates. We were together in one capacity or another for almost my whole pitching career. We were a successful partnership, always aboveboard with each other. We worked hard for each other in our mutual endeavors and at the end of our projects, we were still friends.

"Ol' Satch," as he used to call himself, had his own way of doing things, even when he came to the Indians in 1948 as a 42-year-old rookie. Like the frequent question in baseball: Will the game get rained out? Paige didn't need any weather forecasts or a call from the ball club to tell him the answer. He got the word from a more reliable source—his big toe.

I remember one time, when we were together on the Indians, that he put faith in that toe of his. He was late for a game in New York because his toe told him it was going to rain. In another case, his toe was right about the weather. The game was rained out—but what the toe didn't tell him was that he was late for the team's train to Boston. He was fined, but the story doesn't end there.

I missed that train too, because I went to Penn Station instead of Grand Central after a round of business meetings. I realized my mistake immediately so I grabbed one of New York's yellow cabs and hustled over to Grand Central and dashed onto the platform, just in time to be told by a porter that our train had just left.

But the porter also told me the train on the next track was leaving for New Haven. I could switch to the Indians' train there. That's just what I did. Satch headed for the airport and took a plane, comforted in part by what the people at Grand Central told him—that Feller missed the team's train too.

You can imagine Satch's surprise when we strolled into the Kenmore Hotel in Boston. Satch was waiting for us, and he ran smack in to Lou Bourdreau. Lou said calmly, "That'll cost you a hundred dollars, Satch."

His surprise was even greater when he saw who was standing next to Lou—me.

Satch wanted company for his misery. He asked Boudreau, "What about Feller? He missed the train too."

I put my most innocent look on my face and said, "What are you talking about? I'm right here with the team. I was on that train, wasn't I, Lou?"

"He sure was, Satch. He was sitting right next to me when we pulled into town."

Satch never could figure that one out. He looked at me out of the corner of his eye the rest of the time he played for the Indians.

Satch liked a good time as much as anyone, and he wasn't afraid to pull his share of stunts. Baseball players have some time-honored tricks that the jokesters pull on their teammates, and Satch was always happy to play the clown. He gave many a hotfoot to players sitting on the bench, and he wasn't above nailing a teammate's shoe to the clubhouse wall or putting glue into somebody's glove.

But he was vulnerable too, like the time I tossed an ice cream sandwich to him from the cooler while we rested in the dressing room between games of a doubleheader in Detroit.

I called over to him, "Here, Satch—have an ice cream sandwich."

He thanked me, took his first bite and lost his false teeth. They were stuck in the bar of soap I had slipped into the sandwich after removing the ice cream. When Satch started to take the sandwich out of his mouth after that first delicious bite, his teeth came out too.

Those barnstorming games we pitched against each other in the 1940s helped to get Satch into the Hall of Fame in 1971, after it was integrated by the baseball writers and the folks at Cooperstown.

He told people the games gave him the showcase he needed to display his pitching ability. When Cooperstown was integrated, the case for Satchel Paige had been made in part by what baseball people saw in his outstanding performances against my barnstorming team.

Satch wasn't the only black player who said those tours helped him. Others told people those games gave them a chance to play against the greatest stars in the major leagues, and to show the world that good black players could succeed against good white players.

Playing against black players and having them on my own team was nothing new or special to me. Dad recruited black players for our own Oakview team back on the farm. I was pitching to a black catcher more than ten years before Roy Campanella played for the Booklyn Dodgers, and we had black umpires for those games 30 years before Emmett Ashford became the first one in the majors. Ashford umpired for me in Los Angeles in 1946 and '47 in October exhibition games.

When they opened the doors of the Hall of Fame to Satch and Josh Gibson, who might have hit more home runs than Aaron or Ruth, and "Cool Papa" Bell, the man they said was so fast he could turn the light out and be in bed before the room got dark, it made sense to me.

One thing that didn't make sense, though, was all the criticism I caught because of something I said when Jackie Robinson broke in with the Dodgers. I pitched against Jackie on our '46 barnstorming tour when he was playing for Satch. I got him out three times in a game at Wrigley Field, the Cubs' minor league park in Los Angeles, on a strikeout, a popup and a ground out. When we moved down to San Diego for a game, I struck him out three times on ten pitches.

Paul Zimmerman of the *Los Angeles Times* asked me in L.A. if I thought Jackie would be able to hit major league pitching. I said I wasn't sure, that he might be muscle-bound and unable to hit big league pitching, especially the fastballers in the American League.

Jackie and others didn't like that, and apparently he never forgot it. Before our next game, in San Diego, he told me he wasn't going to play, that he wanted more money.

I told him in the clubhouse, "There are 13,000 fans out there who have paid to see us play ball—all of us—and if you're not out there to lead off when I'm finished my warm-ups, I'm calling Chandler at his home in Kentucky. This is the major leagues, and you don't pull that stuff up here, not right before a game."

Jackie never forgot that, either. Twenty-three years later, on the 100th anniversary of professional baseball, there were special ceremonies in Washington in connection with the All-Star Game. The players selected as the greatest living stars at their positions were honored. I was chosen as the greatest living right-handed pitcher, and Jackie was honored for his historic contributions in breaking the color barrier.

At the press conference promoting the ceremonies, Jackie told 125 reporters that I never wanted to see him in the big leagues and that I had my head in the sand on the subject of blacks in baseball.

It was an unfortunate thing to say, especially when it was wrong and so clearly contradicted by the facts and events covering 25 years. I explained briefly that I did have honest doubts about Jackie's ability to hit big league pitching, specifically the high tight fast ball, after I pitched against him, and I mentioned his stats against me. His batting averages in the World Series also showed he had trouble hitting American League pitching, where the high tight fast ball was much more common.

Those years, 1946 and 1947, were times when we were breaking more ground than we realized—barnstorming for 30 days instead of the usual ten, flying instead of traveling by train, giving black players the exposure that was about to help them make the majors, pressuring the owners to increase the players' share of the World Series money, and lining up support for something that never existed before—a pension for retired players.

But your annual player's contract was your main source of concern, and in 1946 and '47 that was especially true for me. I was capitalizing on my wins and my strikeouts with some rewarding contracts, and I was introducing something that is now commonplace—incentive clauses.

In 1946, I signed a contract that paid me a base salary of $50,000, but I made over $100,000 with incentives and other income such as my barnstorming tour, a new book called *Strikeout Story*, a weekly radio show, a daily newspaper column, personal appearances and endorsement contracts with Wheaties and Wilson Sporting Goods.

My total income increased to $150,000 in 1947. After I signed, Bill Veeck told the reporters that my contract was "the biggest ever in baseball."

Then he added, "Feller now owns everything to the left of first base."

My incentive clauses included provisions for a bonus of a nickel for every paid attendance over 500,000 and bonuses of varying amounts for each win over 15.

The Saturday Evening Post ran a cover story in April of 1947 with a painting of me pitching in a night game at Municipal Stadium. The *Post* said the article was "the inside story of how a once naïve Iowa farm boy, by converting himself into a one-man corporation, has the club owners envying his business acumen—and worrying plenty, too, about what the innovation means to baseball."

The article was written by Burton Hawkins, the respected baseball writer for the *Washington Star*, who had been the advance man for my barnstorming tour the previous fall. I had become baseball's first incorporated athlete, something many athletes do today, and Hawkins wrote, "It's got so that the people supposed to be the top businessmen of baseball, the magnates, have taken to viewing Feller with alarm."

Things were beginning to look up for the Indians in '47. We improved our record to 80–74, and moved up from sixth to fourth place behind the Yankees, Tigers and Red Sox. We got help from newcomers like Eddie Robinson at first base, Joe Gordon at second, Dale Mitchell in left field and Don Black on the mound.

With help from my teammates and my catcher, Jim Hegan, plus the managerial skills of Lou Boudreau while he was also becoming the best all-around shortstop in baseball, I was able to lead the league again in wins for my fifth straight season, plus strikeouts, innings pitched, shutouts and most strikeouts per nine innings.

Even though I finished first in strikeouts, my total was down, from the record 348 of the year before to 196. That was the bad news. The good news was that my walks were down too, 127, my second lowest amount in six seasons.

I was happy about again leading the league in innings pitched, for the fifth straight year. The talk about my pitching too much was louder than ever after my 30-day barnstorming trip the previous October. Concern about throwing too much was a valid question, but people seemed to be forgetting that they were always sounding this alarm and nothing ever happened. Nobody remembered to tell my arm that too many innings are bad for it, so it never bothered me. It still didn't shut up the critics, but I wasn't listening to them. I was listening to my arm. We understood each other.

I almost caught up with Cy Young in my first start of '47. He was the only man to that time who had pitched three no-hitters, and on April 22 of that year, on a frigid afternoon in Cleveland, I came within one hit of matching him. Instead of my third no-hitter, I had my ninth one-hitter.

We beat the St. Louis Browns, 5–0, before 3,629 fully frozen fans. Not only did I have a no-hitter going—I had a perfect game, until Al Zarilla singled to center with one out in the seventh. I walked only one man, catcher Les Moss, in the ninth inning. My strikeout total wasn't exceptional—ten—but on a day that cold, I wasn't counting. And all of us were thankful for the time of the game—one hour and 42 minutes.

Dizzy Dean, who was still a player when he saw me strike out eight Cardinals in three innings the first time I pitched for the Indians, was the St. Louis radio broadcaster. He said, "That there is perhaps the best game I've ever seen."

One of the papers ran a feature story the next day abut "Ol' Diz" and his broadcast. The schoolteachers in St. Louis were demanding his firing because of the way he was fracturing the King's English.

The paper said Dean was calling me by my right name after calling me "Fellows" following that exhibition game in '36, and they quoted him as telling his listeners, "Ah'm so blamed cold Ah'm just thankful Ah don't have false teeth. Mah tongue woulda been bit off by now." They wrote it that way, accent and all.

Maybe the teachers liked that and maybe they didn't, but at least he didn't repeat the one that really offended them and got them in an uproar after an earlier game. That was when Diz told his audience that the runner "shudda slidden home."

When the teachers went into a tizzy about such language, Diz said he didn't think his choice of words was so bad—"Ah could have said 'slud.'"

Four days later, I beat the Tigers on a three-hitter against Hal Newhouser, 6–0, at home before a Ladies' Day and school kids' crowd of 40,000. There wasn't any suspense in this one. George Kell led off the fourth inning with a single, so we didn't have to get all worked up about any no-hitter and it happened again in my following start.

Boston's Johnny Pesky got a hit off me in the first inning, but that was all anybody on the Red Sox got that day. Ted Williams struck out and hit into two double plays, and we beat the Red Sox, 2–0. It was my third straight shutout. After four games, pitching the full nine innings in three and eight innings in another, I had allowed a total of one earned run. And I had two one-hitters in my last three starts, allowing a total of five hits over those three games.

It was by far my best start. I'd be curious to know if anybody has matched it. But I was realistic enough to know that nobody can maintain that kind of a pace. I dropped back into the real world with a 6–3 loss to the Senators in which I lasted only one inning and gave up four runs, the start of a 2-4 streak in my next six starts. That will keep you wearing the same hat size.

The last game of the season was another loss, giving me a 20-11 record, my second loss in ten days to Fred Hutchinson. But at least everybody got to go home early because we were ending the season the way we started it. After opening the year with a game that took only an hour and 42 minutes, we ended in even better time—one hour and 34 minutes.

Yes, we did play games in less than two hours, sometimes less than that, once upon a time.

CHAPTER TWELVE
The Million-to-One Shot?

The Cleveland Indians were not the biggest story of 1948. Harry Truman was, and the Berlin Airlift. President Truman ordered the airlift—Air Force cargo planes flying food and supplies into Berlin around the clock for a year—to save the people there while Russian troops kept them surrounded in something called the "Cold War." The American people rewarded Truman with that stunning victory over Tom Dewey.

Those were the things people were talking about in '48, plus the newest form of home entertainment—television, and its popular shows, Milton Berle's "Texaco Star Theater" and Ed Sullivan's "Toast of the Town."

In the world of baseball, though, we became the big story, with one of the wildest, tensest barn-burners of a season anybody ever saw, the second million-to-one shot—a tie. What could never happen did, for the second time in three seasons. Two teams, the Indians and the Red Sox, played 154 games each and finished dead even. The story of that season remains one of the classics in the history of major league baseball. It was a hair-raising, nail-biting time for everybody in the game, including the fans, but it was even more so for us because we were the ones making history.

Unlike the National League two years before, the climax had even more drama because the American League rules called for only a one-game playoff in case of a tie, not two out of three. It was what we now call "sudden death," ten years before pro football made the term

145

famous in the Giants-Colts playoff. It's different now. You have playoffs every year anyhow, but in 1948 it was only in case of a tie, and in the American League you were going to get only one chance.

Nobody had any particular reason to expect great things from us in 1948. We finished '47 in fourth place behind the Yankees, Tigers and Red Sox, 17 games out of first. You just don't expect a team to close a gap that big in only one season, but we did.

Bill Veeck deserves much of the credit. The moves he began making when he bought the club in '46 were producing surprisingly quick results. Our 1947 record may not sound impressive by itself, but it was one heck of an improvement over '46. In that season, the first postwar year, we finished sixth with only 68 wins and 36 games out of first place. By finishing "only" 17 games behind in '47, we cut that difference by more than half and we won 12 more games—80. If we continued to improve at that pace in '48, we would win 90 or more games, and when you reach the 90 mark you're going to be a contender for the pennant. Our leaders, Veeck in the front office and Lou Boudreau on the field, had us headed in the right direction.

The bold move by Veeck, in signing Larry Doby as the first black player in the American League, was viewed mostly for its historical significance. Doby, a second baseman for the Newark Eagles of the Negro National League the year before, and Jackie Robinson were both rookies in '47. In the same year when Christian Dior introduced his "New Look" in women's fashions by dropping the hemline to the ankles, baseball was introducing a new look of its own.

Veeck, who read three and four books a week on every subject under the sun, had his own sense of history. He knew that signing Doby was significant in that respect. But he had a sense of purpose, too. He also knew that Doby would put people in his ballpark, and, most important of all, he was confident that Doby had star potential, enough that he could make us a pennant winner for the first time in 28 years.

Doby played in only 29 games for us in '47 and didn't give any hints of greatness. He hit only .156, had no home runs and drove in only two runs. He didn't even get to play in the outfield, where he starred beginning the next year. In his rookie season he played in only six games in the field—four as a second baseman, one at short and one at first base. The rest of the time he was a pinch hitter.

Veeck didn't stop with Doby in building for 1948. He signed another black player—my old friend and fellow barnstormer, Satchel Paige. The *Baseball Encyclopedia* shows Satch was 42 years old that year, but

Satch was always evasive on the subject. Whatever his age was—42, 52 or 102—he was still good enough as baseball's senior citizen to win six games and lose only one, with an excellent earned run average of only 2.48 runs for every nine innings. When your team finishes tied, any pitcher who won six of his seven starts has a right to claim he was a major help.

Satch didn't say that, because he wasn't the kind of guy to go around blowing his own horn, but the rest of us knew we owed a lot that year to our 42-year-old rookie.

It was no surprise to us barnstormers. When he became the first black man to pitch in the majors—the date was June 9—he threw two scoreless innings. Only two of his pitches were not strikes. Any of us barnstormers could have predicted it.

Veeck used his imagination and persistence to land another player who helped us too, Johnny Berardino. Johnny was a handsome guy who appeared as a tough kid in the *Our Gang* movie comedies. He always had thoughts of heading for Hollywood and a full-time acting career, and that's what he did eventually after retiring in 1952 following 11 years in the majors. That was when he began calling himself "John" instead of "Johnny" and started on the road that led him to his soap opera career on "General Hospital."

He almost made that move four years earlier than he did, because when the St. Louis Browns traded him to the Washington Senators for Gerry Priddy, Johnny said he wasn't about to play for Washington. He said he'd retire instead and start his career in acting. The deal was made on November 22, 1947, but Berardino said he would refuse to report to the Senators for spring training in '48. It was an ultimatum, and Commissioner Happy Chandler responded by canceling the trade. Berardino then un-retired and was still a member of the Browns.

Priddy joined St. Louis anyhow. The Browns bought him from the Senators for $25,000 on December 8, 16 days after the original deal. Enter Mr. Veeck. Twenty-four hours after the Browns brought Priddy from Washington, Veeck traded one of our outfielders, George "Catfish" Metkovich, to the Browns for Berardino. He sweetened the pot with $50,000 in cash.

Then another complication arose. Catfish had a broken finger. He was returned to us, and the Browns received another $15,000 to make the deal complete.

With all of his wheeling and dealing, Veeck got the wrong man. He should have called Clark Griffith in Washington in the first place and just made a deal for Priddy. Berardino gave us some depth as a steady defensive player who played all four infield positions for us in '48, but his best years with a bat were behind him. He hit only .190 that year and .198 the next and never hit more than .227 for the rest of his career. Priddy, on the other hand, was at his peak. He hit .296 for the Browns in '48 and led the American League's second basemen in putouts, assists, double plays and chances per game.

On the other hand, Veeck wasn't really worrying about second base anyhow. He was looking for bench strength. We already had one of the best second basemen in baseball, Joe Gordon—"Flash." We got him from the Yankees for Allie Reynolds for the '47 season in a trade that helped us immensely in '48. But that deal, despite helping us so much then, carried an intriguing question with it.

Joe was one of the stars of the game when we got him, and Veeck could afford to give up Reynolds, one of the best young fastballers in the majors, because we were rich in pitchers. Joe was one of our most valuable players in 1948 with a .280 average, 32 home runs and 124 runs batted in. He was second in homers behind DiMaggio and fourth in RBIs while teaming up with Boudreau to give us one of the best double play combinations in baseball. As a pitcher I could appreciate our strength up the middle. Gordon and Bourdreau proved all year long that there is truth in the old baseball description: "The double play, a pitcher's best friend."

But Gordon was on the twilight side of a major league career that started 10 years before. His hitting dropped to .251 in 1949 with only 20 home runs, and to .236 in '50 with 19 homers. Then he left the majors.

Reynolds, on the other hand, helped to pitch the Yankees to six world championships with 182 career wins and seven victories in the World Series, the second highest in baseball. The question arises: As much as Gordon helped the Indians in 1948, and he did, would Veeck have been better off holding on to Reynolds?

The question becomes even more intriguing when you review the records of the two teams over that span. From our World Series year of '48 through our other World Series year, 1954, we won 666 games while the Yankees were winning 684. That means they won an average of only three more games a year than we did, 98 wins to 95.

If you take the first five seasons of the 1950s, the Yankees won 493 games while we won 481, still an average of only three more wins a season than we had. Between the two of us we won every pennant in the American League from the time we won in '48 through our other championship season in '54.

If Allie Reynolds had been one of our starting pitchers over that span, would we have won another pennant or two? Instead of the Yankees winning five and the Indians two, would it have been only a 4–3 edge for the Yankees, or maybe even a 4–3 edge for us?

If ever a championship reflected what managers and coaches call "a team effort," 1948 was that season. We seemed to get help from everybody. We led both leagues in hitting as well as fielding. Eddie Robinson, Lou Boudreau and Dale Mitchell led their positions in fielding. So we had the first essential for winning in any sport—a strong defense. The other team can't beat you if it can't score any runs—and we allowed the fewest runs of any team in either league.

We got 32 home runs from Gordon and 31 from Keltner. Doby became a star in his first full season with a .301 average. He wasn't our center fielder at the beginning of the year. Thurman Tucker started there, and Larry moved into that position later. Our left fielder, Dale Mitchell, helped as much at the bat as he did with his glove. The same man who topped the league's left fielders in fielding had a batting average of .336.

The pitchers did their share too. Bob Lemon led the league in innings pitched while becoming a 20-game winner. Bearden gave us two 20-game winners on the same staff, and I was able to contribute with 19. Cleveland was among the leaders in ten of the 12 pitching departments, with Bearden leading the league with the best earned run average. I led the league in strikeouts for the seventh time—also the last.

With all of those outstanding individual performances leading to a team championship, the two men who meant the difference in the end between a championship and the runner-up spot were Lou Boudreau and Gene Bearden.

Boudreau was one of the most talented players in baseball in his time, in addition to being one of the classiest human beings you'd ever want to meet. He was an American League All-Star five times, playing his entire 15-year career on ankles made weak by all the running up and down on hardwood basketball floors in college. That didn't stop him from being one of the game's best performers and greatest leaders. During his career, some of the writers compared him to Honus Wagner as maybe the greatest all-around shortstop of all time.

He led the American League in batting in 1944 with .327 and topped that average by almost 30 points with .355 in '48, but he didn't win the championship. Ted Williams beat him out with .369 while keeping the

Red Sox in the neck-and-neck race with us. Lou was as much of a star on defense as he was with the bat. He set the American League record for shortstops twice—in 1944 and breaking it in 1947—and his 134 double plays in '44 are the fourth highest in history for shortstops.

As for his quality as a person, this will give you an idea: he missed being on the All-Star team in 1946, back in the days when the players did the voting, because he voted for someone else at shortstop instead of for himself.

Bill Veeck had the best comment about that. He said Lou was "the greatest shortstop ever left off the All-Star team."

Gene Bearden was unique. He came from out of nowhere in '48 to become one of baseball's star pitchers. He was with us the year before, but only long enough to have a cup of coffee, and there wasn't anything there to suggest that stardom awaited him the very next year.

But Gene was working on something—a knuckle ball. He started fooling around with it in the minors in 1946 and found the hitters didn't like it, which wasn't news to anybody. No batter likes to hit against a knuckle ball pitcher. The ball has no spin on it and its flight is so unpredictable even the pitcher doesn't know where it's going. It's a "butterfly pitch" that floats up there while bobbing and weaving in every direction imaginable.

Everybody was rooting for Gene to make it. He had been badly wounded in the war in the engine room of the *U.S.S. Helena* in the Pacific. He was a star immediately in 1948, won 20 games and finished second to Jack Kramer of the Red Sox in winning percentage with 20 wins and only seven losses, a percentage of .741.

It was a magic year for Gene, and he helped to make it so for all of us. But it was the only one of its kind for him. A knuckle ball pitcher must throw strikes, much more so than any other kind of a pitcher, because if he puts men on base, it's too easy to steal on him. The knuckle ball comes to the plate slower than other pitches, and it frequently darts away from the catcher, so if you allow base runners too often, they'll kill you with stolen bases and by moving up on passed or dropped balls. You also have to get the first hitter of the inning, for the same reason that every pitcher has to. Allowing the first hitter of the inning to reach base changes the whole complexion of the inning. You have to get that first man out, especially in the late innings. If you're a knuckleballer, it's even more important because of the control risks associated with that pitch.

In '48, Gene mastered that art and threw his knuckler for strikes consistently, but that rookie season was the only time he was able to do it. He dropped to 8–8 the next year while pitching a hundred fewer innings but allowing almost as many walks, only 14 under his '48 total. And line drives that were caught in '48 dropped in for hits in '49. When his control deserted him and he got behind in the count, he had to come in with his fast ball or his curve, both of which were below average.

After his blazing debut with us in 1948, Gene lasted only six more seasons. He was traded to Washington only two years after becoming the rookie sensation of '48, and then was traded to Detroit, St. Louis and Chicago—five teams in seven seasons. He never won more than eight games in a season after '48. But for that one year, he was one of the answers to our prayers.

Bearden and Bob Lemon both had better overall seasons than I did in '48. I started slowly and by midseason I wasn't even a .500 pitcher. I had nine wins and 11 losses. I made two important decisions at that point: I wasn't going to barnstorm, and I *was* going to play in the All-Star Game, if chosen.

With the team having a good first half, I knew we had a legitimate shot at the pennant, but I had to be of more help in the second half. That wasn't going to happen if I had to put together another barnstorming tour. I didn't want to be spending my spare time on the telephone and in meetings, signing 50 players for two teams, renting airplanes, hiring a staff, reserving hotels, renting ballparks and supervising publicity—all while my team was trying to win a pennant.

Barnstorming was on its way out anyhow. Television was already taking on the appearance of an overpowering medium, one that was going to help professional sports immensely both in terms of exposure and revenue. But in the process, television was also going to change things. People in small towns and on America's farms were going to have baseball's biggest stars playing right there in their living rooms. You'd be able to see the game while it was actually being played instead of a week later in the newsreels at the movies.

Bringing barnstorming teams into their towns was going to lose its magical appeal. The 1940s were the last decade for that special slice of Americana. No more fans wearing straw hats and white short-sleeved shirts sitting in open bleachers and yelling good-natured taunts at you. No more circus-like posters in gold and red, or red-white-and-blue, promoting our appearances. No more Dixieland bands in striped jackets, dogs bounding across the outfield during the game, mayors tossing out the first ball and freckle-faced kids in short pants looking up with stars in their eyes asking you, "What's it like to be a *real* baseball player?"

Barnstorming baseball teams touring America's heartland after the World Series are just a distant memory now. But those of us who played that special kind of baseball cherish the memories as much as those fans—and friends—who came out in spots all over America to star-gaze at the "real baseball players" who had come to town.

My All-Star decision involved circumstances that were far less folksy. I missed the '47 game because of an injury to my back. I hurt it in my last start before the game after striking out ten of the first 12 batters against the Philadelphia A's. I was going for 20 that night, which would have been another major league record, but I was throwing so hard by the fourth inning that my left foot slipped and I tore some muscles in my back while pitching to Barney McCoskey. I was named to the All-Star team but had to decline the honor, even though the manager of the American League, Joe Cronin, wanted me to appear anyhow.

He told me I could just show up and have a nice time and get a nice gift. I appreciated the opportunity and what Joe was trying to do for me, but I didn't agree with him. He wanted all the players who had been elected to the team to be there, but I thought I'd be short-changing the fans just to go for the good time of it. So I declined.

That turned out to be one of the most controversial decisions of my career. The fans rained down their abuse on me. I was booed loudly in every city, including Cleveland, and caught flack from the reporters and sportscasters. I would have been a lot better off taking Cronin's advice, but I wasn't going to do it. I was hurt. I couldn't pitch. That would have been betraying my teammates because I would have made the injury worse.

But I wasn't going to be unfair to the fans either by giving them half an All-Star. I paid a heavy price, one that lasted several seasons. I was coming in for criticism anyhow. Any time I lost there were rumblings in the media that I was pitching too much, I was too eager to make money, my business interests were interfering with my baseball.

That sounds funny compared to the outside interests of today's players, but in 1948 it was open season to fire these charges against me if I hit a slump.

When I was elected to the '48 All-Star team, it was for the sixth straight time. But I had misgivings. A guy who isn't even pitching at the .500 level doesn't belong on anybody's all-star team. My election that year was just for old times' sake. Although it was a nice gesture, it was something I didn't deserve. That's always been one of the basic points about athletic competition in my view. You compete to see who's the best, and if you win you deserve whatever goes with the victory. But if someone else performs better than you do, and wins more than you, then he deserves the fruits of the victory, not you.

Still, I wanted to play in '48 because of the intense heat I felt in '47, so I decided to go ahead, even though I knew I didn't really deserve it. But then Bill Veeck complicated things.

Bill had visions of a pennant, the same ones all of us had, and he didn't want two of his starting pitchers—Bob Lemon was picked too—to miss a turn by playing in the All-Star Game. He told me just a few days before the game that I should fake an injury to get out of it, but I told him no. Besides, people would know I wasn't hurt because they had been watching me all season. I was healthy and pitching every fourth day and the whole world knew it. How could I fake an injury even if I wanted to?

Veeck said I could say I hurt myself around the house. "Wrap your finger in a bandage," he said, "and tell the press you cut yourself on a razor blade or got hit with a buzzsaw."

I still said no. But that wasn't the end of it. Without my knowledge, Veeck announced to the press that I had "withdrawn from the game for unknown reasons."

I heard about Veeck's announcement from the press, and when I did I blew a gasket. I didn't need to go through another ordeal like the year before. I started an inch-by-inch search of Cleveland for the owner of the Indians, and I caught up with him by phone in some bar at 2:00 A.M. He apologized to me and said he would issue a retraction because I was demanding one.

Veeck kept his promise and did issue the retraction, but it didn't do any good. The truth never catches up with the lie. The only thing the fans knew was what they had read. They thought I tried to duck the All-Star Game—again. It only aggravated the wounds from the 1947 fiasco. The uproar resumed and lasted through the All-Star break—until I started winning again.

The game was played in St. Louis that year. Walter Masterson, Vic Raschi and Joe Coleman beat the National League. I didn't pitch, and Veeck was happy.

I began to hit my stride after the All-Star break, in late July, and went on a streak where I won ten and lost only three. I was winning and giving the bullpen a rest at the same time. I was beginning to feel like somebody doing his share to help his team win, and I wasn't hearing any boos.

Boudreau was doing that much and more. He was showing us how to win, by doing everything at a level of excellence that other players seldom reach. And he was doing an outstanding job as our manager too, making the right moves in games and handling his pitching schedule—the hardest part of managing—so well that all of us were effective, especially in the second half of the season.

I thought 1948 was Lou's best as a manager. I disagree with those who say the player-manager, something you seldom see any more, could not do as good a job as one who stays in the dugout. The argument is that managers who are also players have too many things to think about. I think playing managers like Boudreau and Frank Robinson and others were better for that very reason. They didn't have all the extra time that bench managers do, when they can think of too many other things to do in the course of a game. That leads to over-managing, which hasn't helped a team yet. Playing managers don't have time to over-manage.

Boudreau's leadership—as player and manager—reached a dramatic peak on August 8. We were playing the Yankees at home in a close game. Lou was out of the lineup with an injury. It was a "must" game for us. It was the kind of a season where every game in the second half of the year seems critical, especially when you're going head-to-head against one of the other contending teams. That was the situation in this game, because the Yankees were in contention all season long with the Red Sox, the A's and us.

The Yankees were leading by two runs when we loaded the bases in the late innings. Bucky Harris went to his bullpen and called in the man they called "Fireman," Joe Page, one of the premier relief pitchers in baseball. Page, who won 14 games the year before—an unusually high number for a relief pitcher—was left-handed, and so was our next hitter, Thurman Tucker. Harris was playing the percentages.

Thurman was having a decent year for us at the plate and was one of the league's better center fielders, so Bucky wanted his ace left-handed reliefer against the left-handed hitter. In the process he was also getting the advantage in a physical mismatch. Page was five inches taller than Thurman and outweighed him by 35 pounds.

But Harris hadn't counted on Boudreau. He knew Lou was hurt and the rest of our pinch hitters that day probably did not strike fear in his heart when he knew Page would be firing bullets at them.

But Lou surprised Bucky and everybody else in the ballpark by limping to the plate and inserting himself as a pinch hitter. This took real guts. Here was the manager putting himself squarely on the spot— late in the season, a crucial game against one of the teams we had to beat, it's the late innings, they have their relief ace on the mound, you're hurt and yet you're willing to take the big risk and pull your hitter and put yourself up there. Anybody who hadn't realized what a great leader Lou Boudreau was, saw it that day.

There was an overflow crowd at the game, and everyone in Municipal Stadium—fans, players, reporters, announcers, hot dog vendors, everybody—leaned forward to watch every second of the unfolding drama.

Page came in with an overhand curve ball, one of his "out" pitches that got the hitter out almost every time. Lou was ready for it. He sent a scorching line drive right through Page's legs into center field. Two runs scored to tie the game. We went on to win, 8–6, and then won the second game too, 2–1. We won two more games than the Yankees that year. If Lou hadn't gotten that hit, the Yanks might have won that game and beaten us in the second game too, so Lou not only helped us to beat out the Yankees by a slim margin—he also prevented history's first tie from becoming a *three*-way tie.

Bob Lemon kept a streak of sorts going for us that year. He pitched a no-hitter, 2–0, against Detroit, the third straight season in which a Cleveland pitcher had thrown a no-hitter. I had mine against the Yankees in '46, and Don Black pitched one for us against the A's in '47.

You always need help in something like a no-hitter, and Bob got it from Dale Mitchell in the same way I got from Ray Mack. In the fourth inning, George Kell hit a drive down the left field line in Briggs Stadium, as Tiger Stadium was called then, 340 feet from the plate. Mitchell streaked over and made the catch and then crashed into the wall.

Kell came close three times that day to ruining Lemon's game. In the first inning, he jammed a shot down the third base line that was foul by no more than six inches. In the seventh, he hit his third line shot of the day, another one to left. But this time Kell made it easy on Mitchell. He hit it right at him.

For Lemon it was only the latest in a series of pitching accomplishments, with more to come. He was becoming a story himself as a long-time minor league infielder who never hit well enough to make it in the bigs and turned to pitching as his ticket to success in the majors. He came up to the Indians in 1941 and '42, but only long enough for a cup of coffee each time. He missed the next three years because of the war (Bob pitched in Hawaii for the U.S. Navy in WWII) and then came back to the Indians in '46. But he hit only .180, so he knew he would have to make a drastic career change or give up any hope of becoming a major league player. He converted his strong third baseman's throwing arm into a pitching arm, appeared in 32 games and won the first four games of his career. The next year he raised his number of wins to 11, and then he hit it big with his 20-win year in '48, his no-hitter and two wins in the World Series.

Bob went on to have one more 20-game season than I did—seven—and 207 career victories. Today he's in the Hall of Fame, because he could throw a curve ball better than he could hit one.

Something else happened in 1948, something that moved all of us in baseball. America's most popular sports hero of the century, Babe Ruth, died. Nobody on the Indians was surprised. He looked so emaciated in April at Yankee Stadium, when Eddie Robinson gave him my bat for support, that we knew he wouldn't be able to last much longer.

We were in Chicago when it happened, but I read every word I could in the papers about the Babe's life and the tributes to him. I suppose the finest tribute of all came from the fans. They always meant more to him than all the VIPs in the world, anyhow. He lay in state in Yankee Stadium, in the main lobby behind the lowest tier of grandstand seats. He was only 150 feet from the home plate that he stepped on so many times. He lay in a mahogany casket, a crucifix at his head and candles around him.

The line to view the Babe was five abreast. The papers said the fans filed by at the rate of hundred a minute. They said the line around Yankee Stadium was six blocks long. More than 50,000 people filed past him the evening he lay there, and the figure was greater the next day.

The Senators were playing the Yankees in New York when Babe died, and I was sorry it wasn't the Indians. If it had been, that line to see Babe would have been at least one person longer.

As sad as we were to lose the Babe, his death wasn't nearly as shocking as the close call we had with one of our own pitchers, Don Black.

Don was in his sixth season with us. He was one of our starting pitchers, and was batting against the St. Louis Browns on September 13 when he simply collapsed right at home plate and fell into unconsciousness. The hush in the ballpark as he lay motionless was greater than you would think possible in a crowd of thousands of people. No one was making a sound. Nothing had hit him—no ball or another player or anything. He hadn't fallen over something. He was just standing there batting one minute, and in a flash he was on the ground and out cold.

He was rushed to St. Vincent Charity Hospital, where the doctors diagnosed his problem as a brain hemorrhage. Even something as important as a pennant race suddenly becomes insignificant. How can this happen to a young and healthy guy only 32 years old, especially a professional athlete in peak physical condition?

Nobody ever knows the answers to questions like that. We knew two other things, though—Don was fighting for his life, still unconscious, for several more days, and while he was struggling so hard, the bills were mounting up in a hurry.

Eleven days after his hemorrhage, the ball club sponsored a "Don Black Night" and raised $40,000 for his family. By that time he was beginning to inch his way back. He still was not allowed to have any visitors, and he lost 20 pounds, down to 165.

Gradually, Don improved to the point where he could listen to our games on the radio as we went down to the finish line against the Red Sox. He was with us in spirit all through those dramatic days of September and early October, but that was all. Don never pitched again. He died 11 years later at his home in one of Cleveland's suburbs, Cuyahoga Falls. He was 42.

All through the final weeks of the season the Indians, Red Sox and Yankees slugged away at each other in our three-way fight. By late September, I was in the middle of my hot streak and able to win some important games for us. When the Don Black game came up, it was September 22 and Lou gave me the ball. I hadn't lost a game in a month, and I was going for my fourth win of September.

On "Don Black Night," everything came together to make it what the press called the biggest game of the year. We were playing the Red Sox, and if we won we would be in a three-way tie. As if that and the Don Black cause didn't add up to enough drama, Joe McCarthy, the ex-

Yankee who had become the Red Sox manager, told the reporters before the game that he was delighted I was pitching for the Indians.

He said his team would "knock his brains out" and said I was "just another pitcher."

I don't know what McCarthy had in mind, but it's a good thing he didn't bet his house payment on his prediction. We went right after the Red Sox and scored three runs in the first inning. That was all I needed. I pitched a three-hitter, neutralized Williams with an 0-for-4 night and beat the Red Sox, 5–2, before 60,405 fans who turned out to root for us and help raise money to pay Don's medical bills.

Late September can be a cold time in Cleveland, and that night was a good example. It was so cold I wore two jackets in the dugout between innings and took an extra three minutes to warm up before the game.

Thurman Tucker, Joe Gordon and Ken Keltner took care of things in that first inning. Tucker walked, stole second and scored on Gordon's single. Then Keltner hit a two-run homer. Everybody ws contributing.

The game gave all three of the leading teams records of 91 wins and 55 losses with eight games to play.

Four days later, Lou came right back with me against the Tigers. After I pitched us into that three-way tie, Lou was giving me the chance in this game to pitch us into first place by ourselves. It worked. Before 58,919 fans in Detroit, we beat the Tigers, 4–1, on a five-hitter. We were in sole possession of first place for the first time in exactly one month, since August 26. We were a full game ahead of both the Red Sox and the Yankees. There were five games to play.

The three teams continued to trade punches into the final weekend of the season. On October 1, two days before the season was supposed to end, we were on top again, but only by one game over the other two. History's first three-way tie was becoming more of a possibility all the time.

The Red Sox silenced all that talk the next day by defeating the Yankees, 5–1, and eliminating them from the race. Now there were only two teams left, and we were one game ahead of the Sox.

On the last day of the season, October 3, Lou gave me a chance to win the pennant for my team. A win over Detroit at home and we'd be the American League champions, the team with a chance to beat the other Boston team, the Braves, in the World Series. We didn't want an all-Boston series.

But it was the kind of a day that pitchers dread, and their managers too. I had nothing when the game started and nothing when I left it two and a third innings later. I gave up five hits and three walks, didn't strike out a man, and was unable to do what I wanted to do most—win the pennant for my team. Instead, we lost to Detroit, 7–1, the Red Sox beat the Yankees again, 10–5, and the American League had its first tie.

I was completing my tenth season as an Indian and had won 175 games for them, but I lost the one I wanted most. As our train rolled on toward Boston and the one-game playoff for the American League pennant, I knew all I could do now was keep my fingers crossed that Gene Bearden could beat the Red Sox in Fenway Park, never an easy job for a left-hander.

Since striking out Leo Durocher in 1936, I had achieved every goal a pitcher could hope for except one, to play in the World Series. I wanted that chance. All of us did—especially Bearden, Boudreau and Keltner.

CHAPTER THIRTEEN
Bittersweet

Lou Boudreau's imprint was all over that playoff game. He led our batting attack with two home runs and two singles, scored three runs, and made five assists and three putouts without an error. He took command of the game immediately by hitting a home run in the first inning and never let up, and yet something he did as a manager instead of as a player was just as important, maybe more so—he picked Gene Bearden as his starting pitcher.

The decision was a stroke of genius, and shock to all. Gene had pitched only two days before and shut out the Tigers in our next to last game of the regular season. Bob Lemon, more rested and having a 20-win year too, was the logical choice, but Lou thought Gene's knuckle ball would be effective against the Red Sox.

Boston led both leagues in scoring that year, with four players—Johnny Pesky, Vernon Stephens, Dom DiMaggio and Ted Williams—scoring more than 100 runs each. A knuckle ball might be just what the doctor ordered—the Cleveland doctor.

Bearden responded with a magnificent performance, one that people still remember and for good reason. Only 48 hours after shutting out the Tigers in a crucial game, here he was starting the most crucial game of all, and in baseball's most notorious burying ground for left-handed pitchers, Fenway Park, with its Green Monster wall rising ominously in left field barely 300 feet from home plate.

Gene pitched a five-hitter, went the distance and held the first five batters in the Boston lineup—DiMaggio, Pesky, Williams, Stephens and Bobby Doerr—to four hits in 20 at-bats. When you hold those five to a combined .200 average, you have a good chance of winning.

Keltner equalled Lou's batting performance with a single, double, home run and three runs batted in, plus six chances in the field without an error. Larry Doby contributed with two doubles.

The 1948 American League pennant was ours, 8–3, and back in Cleveland our fans went nuts. The headlines in the papers told the story. After we got back there for the third game of the World Series, I got caught up on my newspaper reading and was able to enjoy the headlines from our playoff victory—

CITY IN A FRENZY AT PENNANT NEWS

TRIBE WINS, OUR TOWN "BLOWS ITS TOP"

HARD-WON VICTORY SENDS CITY WACKY

Those were the headlines we had been trying to write for six months. Maybe the editors thought they wrote them, but the players on the Indians knew better. The editors might have been the ones with the pencil and paper, but those headlines were written on the playing fields of the American League for the previous six months, and we were the ones who wrote them.

A reporter asked one of our coaches, Bill McKechnie, who had managed four pennant winners and two World Series champions, if he was used to all this.

Bill told him, "It never gets old, son. It never gets old."

The nicest headline of all was the one that read:

DON BLACK, UP FIRST TIME,
HAS OWN QUIET CELEBRATION

The article said our missing teammate was getting better, but only slowly. He didn't remember anything about his collapse or the night Veeck held for him. His headaches, so severe for a week after his hemorrhage, were letting up, but he had a long way to go. He had been following us over the last few days of the season, after he started to come around, and was able to listen to our games on the radio as long as he didn't let himself get too excited.

It was good to read that Don was thinking of us, because the feeling was mutual. We had a party at the Kenmore Hotel in Boston the night of our playoff victory for the pennant, and the night was still young when Lou and his wife walked up to the microphone in front of all of his players, our team officials and some VIP friends. Lou said:

"I offer a toast to a guy who right now is in the hospital—Don Black."

Tears were coming down his cheeks.

While the people in Cleveland were in a frenzy, the Braves' fans in Boston were in the same condition. The former mayor, John Fitzgerald, "Honey Fitz," was at Braves Field for the first game. He hadn't missed a World Series game by the Braves or the Red Sox for 43 years and he wasn't going to miss one now. His grandson, John Kennedy, would just have to wait a few days for any more help from Honey Fitz in the campaign to get reelected to the House of Representatives.

They even set up 100 television sets on the Boston Common, and 10,000 fans got to watch the first World Series game ever televised, on sets donated by the Gillette Safety Razor Company. *The Boston Post* called it "a vast and unique experiment" and distributed free score-cards. Each RCA set had a "shadow box" around the screen to maintain contrast in the picture in daylight. Each set had anywhere from 20 to 40 fans in front of it. The paper said, "The action on the baseball field was clearly visible..."

Bob Hope was writing a column in one of the Cleveland papers and he said TV had an effect on the players. Hope wrote, "Even Joe Gordon got camera wise, turning clear around once to field a ground ball on his good side."

Tickets were being scalped for the outrageous price of 50 dollars. You could buy 30 boy's plaid shirts for that much at Gorin's in Boston. The store had an ad in the *Post* that day offering the shirts for $1.69, and men's all-wool sweaters for $3.94. You could even buy a man's suit in Boston for less than the 50 bucks the scalpers at Fenway were demanding. The suits cost only $39.75.

The 40,135 fans in Braves Field and the 10,000 more in front of those 100 TV sets on the Boston Common got to see one of the memorable World Series games after the former Secretary of State, Jimmy Byrnes, threw out the first ball. Lou named me as the starting pitcher. My opponent was Johnny Sain, the owner of the most wins in either league that year with 24.

If the Cleveland fans were thrilled because their team was in the World Series for the first time since 1920, the Braves' fans had even more reason to be excited. Their team hadn't been in it since 1914 when "the miracle Braves" came from last place on July 4th to win the National League pennant.

The '48 Braves were a sound team, with Tommy Holmes, Alvin Dark, Bob Elliott, Earl Torgeson and Eddie Stanky. They won the pennant by six-and-a-half games and led their league in team batting average, hits and doubles, but their pitching couldn't match ours. They had Sain, Warren Spahn, Bill Voiselle and Vern Bickford, but Spahn and Said were their two most reliable starters, giving birth to the slogan that their pitching rotation was "Spahn and Sain and two days of rain."

When the game started, I was as ready as I've ever been in my life. This was what all of us wanted, that we had worked for, and what I had been dreaming about since I was a boy on the farm in Van Meter. I couldn't blow this chance. Missing out on a chance to win in the World Series isn't like messing something up during the season. There's always a next season, but you never know if there's another World Series in your future. You have to go out and do the job right now.

I was 29 years old. Only three days before, I failed to win the pennant for my team and missed winning 20 games for the first time in six seasons. I was coming off a double-barreled disappointment, but I couldn't let that bother me now. This was the chance of a lifetime for all of us. Others had done the job for us in the playoff victory. Now it was my turn, and my responsibility, to be equal to the challenge and do my share as a member of the Cleveland Indians. Maybe that sounds trite, but if you're a professional athlete in a team sport you'd better feel that way or else you're going to be a loser—in more ways than one.

From the start, I felt up to it. I retired the first 11 Braves hitters before walking Earl Torgeson in the fourth inning. I didn't allow a hit until the fifth, when Marv Rickert got to me for a single. That irritated me. Rickert wouldn't even have been in there if my old roomie, Jeff Heath, hadn't broken his ankle sliding into home in one of the last games of the season. Veeck had sold Jeff to the Braves over the winter, and the poor guy suffered the worst kind of luck. He hit .319 for the Braves with 20 home runs, and then that happened. He watched the World Series in a cast and retired the next year after 14 seasons. He was denied the opportunity that he deserved, to play in the World Series.

After Rickert's hit, I got the next nine batters. Through seven innings, I had a shutout and a one-hitter going. But Sain was doing almost as well. He had a shutout too, a four-hitter, and no Cleveland player had been able to get past second base. By the time the Braves came up in the bottom half of the eighth inning, Sain and I had posted 15 zeroes on the scoreboard at Braves Field.

Then I did exactly what a pitcher is not supposed to do in that situation. I walked the first hitter in the inning. I lost their catcher, Bill Salkeld, on a 3–2 count. The Braves' manager, Billy Southworth, immediately sent in their other catcher, Phil Masi, as a pinch runner for Salkeld. Then he had his center fielder, Mike McCormick, lay down a sacrifice bunt, advancing Masi to second base.

Lou asked for time out and came to the mound. He told me to walk the next hitter, Eddie Stanky, to set up a double play with Sain, the next man at bat. I thought that was a mistake, and I told Lou so. I told him Stanky wasn't a good hitter, and I was confident I would get him out. He wasn't hitting in the number eight spot in the order because he was a threat. I thought Lou was showing a .247 hitter more respect than he deserved.

But Boudreau knew what Branch Rickey said about Stanky: "He can't hit, he can't throw, he can't run and he can't field—all he can do is win games." His reputation was that he was one of those players who don't have great individual skills but always seem to find a way to beat you. That's what Lou was afraid of.

There was another factor in his thinking. Not everyone liked Stanky. He was a peppery little guy with a grating voice, and he played so hard that some thought he played a little too hard. National Leaguers told me he'd stand behind second base and wave his arms to distract the hitter, and that he once got thrown out of a game before it even started. No wonder they called him "The Brat."

I made one more plea to Lou. "I can get Stanky," I said. "He hasn't hit one past the mound all day. Besides, he has a bad wrist and a bad leg."

Boudreau wouldn't change his mind, and he gave me his final reason. He said, "I don't want to give this little so-and-so a chance to beat us."

So I walked Stanky intentionally, setting up the possibility of a double play with the pitcher coming up. Only Sain didn't hit into a double play. He went out all right, but on a routine fly ball to short right field. That brought up one of the best hitters in the National League, the Braves' leadoff man, Tommy Holmes, a .325 hitter that season, the third highest average in the National League.

But Boudreau wasn't finished with his strategic moves. When I looked back to check Masi as he led off second, Lou flashed the sign to me for the pickoff play by putting his glove over his knee so the fingers extended below the knee. Infielders often fold their gloves and rest them on the left thigh until just before the pitcher releases the next pitch.

It was a surprise play that we had been practicing for five years. We used it successfully several times that season. We had it down pat.

I was even more familiar with the plan than the rest of our pitchers because my old scout, Cy Slapnicka, taught me his move to second during some of my first practices with the Indians. He'd loosen his necktie and roll up the sleeves of his white dress shirt and come onto the field in street clothes and show me how to do it. I'm sure Lou hadn't forgotten that.

Up in the press box, Tris Speaker told the reporters, "They'll pick him off." In the Braves dugout, Nelson Potter, a pitcher who joined the team during the season after ten years in our league, yelled out to the field, "They've got a great play at second base! If he gets six feet off there, they'll get him!"

As I turned my head back to face the hitter, I knew what Lou was doing. He had flashed a different sign—a raised heel—to Larry Doby in center field. I counted to myself...one...two...three...throw! Boudreau was taking off as I was starting my count. At the same time, Doby was breaking toward second from the outfield to back up in case of a wild throw. If the throw was wild, Boudreau's job was to become tangled up with the runner so he couldn't take third while Doby was retrieving the ball. The shortstop had to be careful, though, not to get called for interference, which would enable the runner to advance to third base anyhow.

I whirled and threw a perfect strike to the bag at second. Under the timing of our play, it was the pitcher's job to throw to the bag, not to the shortstop. It was the shortstop's responsibility to get there. He did.

We caught Masi napping. Unfortunately, we caught the umpire, Bill Stewart of the National League, doing the same thing. Lou put the tag on Masi as he slid back into the bag. Neither the Braves nor Stewart knew we had that play in our book, so nobody was looking for it.

Lou tagged Masi out by two feet. It wasn't even close. Everybody in the ballpark saw he was out—except one, the umpire. We hadn't just picked off Masi. We had picked off Stewart too.

Stewart gave the safe sign. On the next pitch, Holmes swung late and hit a line drive just inside the bag at third. Keltner made a dive for it, but the ball was hit too hard and made it into the outfield. Masi scored easily and the Braves won the first game of the Series, 1–0.

I became only the tenth pitcher in World Series history to throw a two-hitter, and I became the first to do it over nine innings and lose. Mort Cooper pitched a two-hitter for seven innings in the '44 Series for the Cards when the Browns beat him, 2–1. I threw only 85 pitches, and Sain and I got the game over in an hour and 42 minutes.

Lou told me later that he couldn't alert the National League umpires to the play because Southworth was in the room during the pre-Series meeting of the managers with the Commissioner. Lou said he should have pulled them aside after the meeting but he didn't and they didn't know to be looking for it in a situation like that.

It might not have made any difference. With the way Sain was pitching, we might never have scored a run even if we played until dawn. But Masi was out. The pictures in the paper the next day left no doubt. You don't like to say you lost a game, whether it's the World Series or any other kind of a game, because of the umpires or the weather or the condition of the playing field. Good athletes and good teams don't let those factors beat them. We lost mainly because we couldn't score two runs, but that call at second base gave the Braves the run they needed.

Now I get asked about instant replay and whether that would have made a difference on that call. It might have, because that's one of the situations where instant replay might work in baseball.

I'm all for replays in baseball, but only in certain situations where the play did not continue after the decision in question. With men on base, for example, you'd have no way of knowing where the runners should be if the umpire rules that an outfielder caught a ball and the replay camera shows he trapped it.

If the umpire calls the runner out at home for the third out and the camera shows he's safe, where do you put the runners now? They're out warming up for the next inning when the replay shows the umpire was wrong.

But on some plays replay would work. It could decide whether a ball went over the fence fair or foul. With nobody on, it could decide plays at first base. Even in some cases with runners on base, replay would work if the play involved was for the third out, but not when you have to figure out whether this guy scores or goes back to third, or whether the runner on first would have made it to third on a shot down the line.

As for replays on balls and strikes, I'm opposed to it. If you want to go that way, you could even use radar or laser beams or photoelectric cells and replace the home plate umpire altogether. But who wants to do that?

In this case, though, our pickoff—or *attempted* pickoff—has endured through 40 years as one of the most controversial plays in World Series history. And there's this much about it: I get asked about that play everywhere I go, and I have never had even one person tell me that Masi was safe.

Ten years later, Bill Stewart told me he blew the call.

In fact, both decisions were controversial—Stewart's and Boudreau's. Dutch Reuther, a veteran baseball man and a respected scout in those years, told a reporter after the game, "Not in a million years do I put Stanky on. A nickel hitter and I give him a base on balls in the World Series? You aren't kidding me, are you?"

On the other side, my boyhood idol, Rogers Hornsby, an experienced manager for 13 years who led the Cardinals to the World Series championship in 1926, agreed with Lou. Joe Williams of the Associated Press asked him if he would have walked Stanky and Hornsby said, "Positively. Only one down. You put a guy on first base. You set up a double play. Positively."

There's a P.S. to that famous play, but most people seem to have forgotten about it. As a matter of fact, there are two of them. We pulled the play again in the first inning of the next game and it worked. Bob Lemon picked off Earl Torgeson, even after Southworth warned him. Bill Grieve made the call. Torgeson did us a great favor. Lemon was struggling. The Braves had already scored a run and had two on and only one out. They were headed for a big inning and could have gone ahead in the Series, two games to none.

We had that play down so precisely that we pulled it twice in the same game in a spring training exhibition against the Cubs. Charlie Grimm was their manager and he ran out onto the field, grabbed his runner by both shoulders and screamed, "If you so much as move one foot off the base from now on, I'll personally chop it off."

Lou claims that our pickoff play even cost the Braves a pivotal run in the last game of that Series. Stanky was on second base in the third inning, and he stayed so close to that bag he could get only to third on a single to the outfield by Holmes. Then Alvin Dark lined into a double play to end the inning. Even when you don't get the out, the play can be effective, and that was one example. Lou said that in addition to working for outs, the play saved us 18 to 20 runs that year by intimidating runners into staying too close to second base and not being able to score on a hit to the outfield.

Things began breaking our way in the World Series with the pickoff play in the first inning of the second game. We scored our first run of the Series in the fourth, and naturally Lou was the one who got us going. He doubled to right, scored the tying run on Gordon's single to left. One out later, Doby scored Gordon and we had a lead for the first time.

Lemon worked out of trouble several times with help from double plays, and we picked up insurance runs on Lou's single in the fifth and Bob Kennedy's hit in the ninth. We tied the Series at one win each with a 4–1 victory over a future Hall of Famer, Warren Spahn.

Then it was time to return to Cleveland, and to Bearden.

We moved to Cleveland for the third, fourth and fifth games, to an atmosphere I hadn't seen before, not even when Dad and I went to St. Louis for the World Series in 1934. Cleveland was going bonkers.

When we won the pennant, some 150,000 fans poured into the downtown streets. A woman was hit by a falling street lamp. Forty-five drunks were arrested. Ninety tons of confetti and other paper had to be cleaned off the streets. But the atmosphere during the Series was even crazier.

The transit system added a hundred buses, streetcars and trackless trolleys. Thirty other buses were assigned to special routes and 50 more were placed on standby. Some of the major roads were closed to all but Series traffic before and after the games.

Some 20,000 fans stood in 22 lines in a drizzle for the few tickets left. A truck driver named Jim Banyard, 24 years old, waited in line for five hours to buy a bleacher seat that cost a dollar. He came prepared with a homemade oilcloth tent, four sandwiches, five boiled eggs, a banana, an apple, a piece of pie, a quart of milk, an alarm clock, two candles and a radio.

Six big-screen TV "receivers" were installed in the Central Armory for fans to see the games free, donated by the Philco, Stromberg-Carlson and Hammon companies. Downtown parking was raised all the way to $2.00.

Bearden was sensational all over again. All he did was pitch a five-hit shutout and we picked up our second victory, 2–0. Gene even scored our first run. He doubled to right and scored later on a wild throw by Dark. Jim Hegan singled in Keltner in the next inning and the scoring for the game was finished.

Bearden was almost unhittable. He retired 16 of the last 18 batters he faced, and by the end of the game the Braves had scored only two runs in 26 innings and none in the last 17. Bearden struck out four, didn't walk a man and even had a single to add to his double, all of this in front of 70,306 screaming fans. This was a rookie?

But Bearden made a few enemies in Cleveland that day despite his performance. The Hotel Atherton installed a TV set in its bar for the first time, gave free scorecards to the customers and offered a ballpark menu of hot dogs, soft drinks and peanuts. But Gene messed up their hopes for a big day. He threw only 84 pitches. The game was over in an hour and 36 minutes.

In the fourth game, on a Saturday afternoon, our fans set a record for the largest crowd to see a World Series game—81,897. The sizes of our crowds were becoming famous. We broke the major league attendance record with 2.6 million admissions. People flocked to Veeck's giveaways during the season—chickens, new cars, free trips—and to see a championship team. Now we had the World Series attendance record too.

People all over the state were involved in our drive to become world champions. At Ohio Stadium in Columbus, where Ohio State was playing Iowa in a Big Ten football game, university officials lifted the ban against radios.

Steve Gromek, well rested, was our pitcher in the fourth game. His opponent was the man who beat us in the first game, Johnny Sain. Sain didn't shut us out this time, not even for one inning. Dale Mitchell singled to lead off our half of the first, and Boudreau—who else?—doubled him home. Doby hit a home run over the right field fence in the third and we had a 2–0 lead. The Braves ran their scoreless streak to 23 innings, or Gromek did it for them, before Rickert broke their dry spell with a homer leading off the seventh.

Bill Stewart had an uncomfortable time of it in this game. He called Lou out at third trying for a triple and the fans really got on him. By this point they were gunning for him, after his call against us on the pickoff attempt in the first game and also calling Dark safe at first base in the second game.

When he called Lou out at third, he was completing a tour of the infield. He had ruled against us in controversial plays at first, second and third. The Cleveland management didn't take any chances after the fourth game. Stewart was given an escort from the field, just in case.

But that was all the Braves could do. We won the game, 2–1, and headed into the fifth game needing only one win to become champions. And I was going to pitch.

Our fans broke their one-day-old attendance record with a Sunday afternoon crowd of 86,288. My opponent was Nelson Potter. Southworth was saving Spahn for the sixth game and keeping his fingers crossed that Potter could get him there.

It was another one of those days when a pitcher just doesn't have his good stuff. I was escaping from jams most of the game, but not often enough. Bob Elliott, Boston's hard-hitting third baseman, nailed me for two home runs in the early innings and we were behind, 4–1, after only three innings.

Then our offense, with only eight runs in 37 innings, came to life with four runs in the fourth to take the lead, 5–4, thanks mainly to a three-run homer by Jim Hegan.

Now we had the lead, and only five innings stood between us and the World Series championship. I could guarantee it simply by shutting out the Braves over those final innings.

I went into the fifth inning with that attitude. I set the Braves down 1-2-3 and struck out Rickert to start the sixth. But then the Braves started scoring again. Salkeld reached me for a homer to tie the game in the sixth, and in the seventh all hell broke loose. Holmes singled, Dark sacrificed, Torgeson singled Holmes in to give the Braves the lead, 6–5.

Lou lifted me at that point. Ed Klieman came in, faced three hitters and didn't get any of them. Russ Christopher followed him and gave up two more singles, and by the time it was all over, the Braves had an 11–5 lead and the game.

There was one nice part about that game. Satch got to pitch. He faced Spahn and Tommy Holmes and got them both.

It was an agonizing disappointment for me. To come so close in the opener and then have this happen in the fifth game was a crushing letdown. I wanted so badly to win, especially after not having my good stuff on the last day of the season against the Tigers. Now all I could do was try to keep my head up and root for Bearden in the sixth game— and hope for another chance either in this Series or somewhere down the road.

But let me tell you—it was hard. People have played baseball with more ability and more success than I did, but nobody has ever played it with more competitive zeal. I had that fire in my belly every time I went out there, and when it was a crucial game, that fire burned even hotter. I won my share, but to lose that last game of the year, lose the opening game of the World Series on a controversial play and then get knocked out in the seventh inning of what could have been the final game added up to a heavy load.

You can say what you want to about any particular athlete, and people could say what they wanted to about me—whether they loved me or hated me, whether they thought I was a hero for pitching so much or thought I was doing it only for the money, whether they thought I was ducking an All-Star Game or was honestly injured. But whatever you think about any athlete, you have no way of knowing how it feels to go through the highs and lows of the profession.

I had been to the heights and now I was in the depths. Sophie Tucker said, "I've been rich and I've been poor, and rich is better." I was finding out that the sports version of that is, "I have won and I have lost, and winning is better."

That's what we did the next day. Lemon pitched a strong game into the eighth inning, and then Lou called on our Man of the Hour, Bearden, to slam the door on a Braves rally and set them down in the ninth. We won the championship, 4–3, with Boudreau, Gordon, Hegan and Eddie Robinson driving in our runs.

The whole bittersweet World Series ended with extra meaning for me. Bob Kennedy caught a fly ball in left for the last out of the World Series. The man who hit it was Tommy Holmes, who drove in the only run of the first game after the umpire called Phil Masi safe at second.

The people of Cleveland gave us a first-class parade and celebration and 200,000 of them showed up. One of the Cleveland papers ran an article quoting a clinical psychologist at Western Reserve University on why fans go so crazy when their sports teams win championships.

Dr. Marguerite Hertz said, "People have a basic need for self-respect, and a desire to be important. The Indians provided the opportunity for people to satisfy this need...so they do things which in saner moments would appear ridiculous..."

She said the traffic jams, the mob scenes, the ticker tape and the whole carnival spirit represented "a healthy release of animal instincts."

I think a movie made by Republic Pictures must fall into that same category. They came to Cleveland and filmed an entirely forgettable movie called *The Kid From Cleveland*, starring George Brent and Lynn Bari and introducing Rusty Tamblyn.

The poster said it was "the story of a kid, a city and 30 godfathers." Everybody associated with the Indians was in it—Veeck, Hank Greenberg, who was our general manager, Boudreau and all the rest of us, even our trainer, Lefty Weisman. The only legitimate actor in the whole group, including the Hollywood cast, seemed to be Johnny Berardino.

Those "30 godfathers" must have been the only people who ever saw it. At least that's what we hope.

There was a strange twist to things during and after that World Series. After the first game, Tommy Holmes was generous enough to tell reporters, "Bob Feller showed me the greatest curve ball I have ever seen since I started playing baseball."

On the day the World Series ended, October 11, there was an Associated Press story in the papers that George McConnell, 93, had died in Los Angeles. He was the man credited with originating the curve ball 70 years earlier.

Now it was time to visit Van Meter, to enjoy the championship and hope that somewhere in my future there was another chance waiting for me to win a World Series game.

No barnstorming to worry about. All I wanted to do was look after my business interests, get some rest—and enjoy being a champion.

The good folks of Van Meter wouldn't just let me slip back into town for a visit, though. They always went out of their way to be nice to their former neighbor, Bob. This time they held a homecoming ceremony for me, and the mayor, Gilbert Johnson, presented me with a thousand dollars worth of gifts.

The theme of the day told you a lot about Iowa people: "When a Feller needs a friend."

CHAPTER FOURTEEN
It's Déjà Vu All Over Again

While we were enjoying our status as world champions, I received a letter from an actor in Hollywood asking for a favor. It was written in longhand on the stationery of St. John's Hospital in Santa Monica. The date was August 11, 1949.

The actor apologized for bothering me with his letter and said he hoped I would remember him. He said he hated to interrupt me because "I know how busy you are," but he added that the favor would "mean a lot to a little guy out here."

It turns out the actor had injured himself playing baseball in a charity game at the old Hollywood ball park, Gilmore Field. He was beating out a bunt when he collided with the first baseman and "my thigh ended up in four pieces." He spent two months in the hospital and four more months on crutches.

At St. John's, he met a 10-year-old boy whose father came home from World War II four years earlier as a hero. But then the man killed himself and the boy's mother. The boy was in the hospital for a lengthy period receiving psychological treatment when he and the actor met. The actor took an interest in him, and they became even closer when they discovered they both loved baseball.

"He is an ardent fan," the actor wrote to me, "and it seems to be his one real interest. Of course I became head man when I tossed your name around as someone I knew personally."

The boy had a birthday coming up, and the actor asked me if I could send a baseball autographed by the Cleveland players. He added, "You'd contribute a lot toward pulling this little guy out of a dark world he's making for himself."

The actor closed his long letter by saying:

I know this is an imposition, Bob, and I would hesitate to bother you if I didn't believe it could do a lot to really help a nice little kid who can very easily end up going haywire.

Best to you always,

Ronald Reagan
"Dutch"

By that time our old sports announcer from Station WHO in Des Moines, who interviewed me on his radio show while I was still a high school pitcher, had become a successful movie star. I was impressed with the sincerity of his request—how he said he hoped I would remember him, even though he was famous now, and how genuine he was in his interest in the boy's recovery.

I sent Reagan a ball autographed by the whole team. All of us by then were all too familiar with the aftermath of war. There were horror stories in the paper every day for years after, right up to the Korean War, of men cracking up because of the psychological strain of their war memories, or unable to adjust to their lives without a leg or an arm. As tragic as that little boy's experience had been, the papers were full of stories like that coming out of the war. All of us were happy to sign that ball and get it on its way to Reagan and his friend in the hope that it might do some good.

You lose track of people after something like that, so I never knew if the boy was able to return to a normal life, but I think of him every time this story comes up, even though I never met him. I hope he's out there somewhere as a happy and successful 50-year-old man who was helped along the way by a future President of the United States.

Ronald Reagan and I crossed paths from time to time over the years after that letter. Each time, he knew what I was doing, and he was up-to-date on what was going on in baseball, no matter how busy he was in his acting career, as Governor of California or as President.

He invited some of the members of the Baseball Hall of Fame to the White House while he was President, and I got to chat with him for a few minutes. We talked about baseball and Iowa—and about that autographed baseball for the little boy more than 30 years before. I told him I remembered it well and that I even kept the letter over the years.

He couldn't believe it. There wasn't anything in 1949 to believe it was a letter from a future President, but that wasn't why I kept it anyhow. I kept it because of what Ronald Reagan did, taking the time to write out a two-page letter in longhand to help a kid he hardly knew. That seemed to me to be a special act of human kindness, and the memories of deeds like that are worth preserving. That's why I kept the letter.

The President asked me to send him a copy, which I was pleased to do as soon as I got back to Cleveland. After only a few days I got another letter from Reagan, only this one was on White House stationery instead of a hospital's. He told me:

> ...thank you again for sending the baseball more than 30 years ago. I'll confess I'm more than a little overwhelmed that you kept the letter.
>
> I'll sign this one the same way. I remember in '49 I did it in case you didn't remember me. Now I'll do it for "Auld Lang Syne."
>
> Again, thanks and best regards.
>
> Ronald Reagan
> "Dutch"

I knew two other men who were destined to become President. One was General Douglas MacArthur's aide at Fort Myer in Washington in the late 1930s, Major Dwight Eisenhower. Ike was such a big baseball fan that when he went to see the Senators play at Griffith Stadium he'd come out early so he could watch batting practice. We struck up an acquaintance, which was easy to do in those days with the size of the Senators' crowds, and after he became President we had another Griffith Stadium conversation or two.

During the war, I was walking along the beach at Saipan after we had recaptured the island from the Japanese. Walking along a beach was a lot more relaxing than killing or being killed on it, so I used to exercise my legs with long walks whenever we were occupying a beach instead of fighting for it.

On one of those walks a young Navy officer came by. He recognized me and we started talking more about baseball than about the war. He was yet another future President who was knowledgeable about my sport. The young officer was Richard Nixon.

Reagan reversed roles on me during the 1988 presidential campaign. The Republicans asked me to campaign in Ohio for George Bush, so I made an appearance with President Reagan at Baldwin-Wallace College in Berea, a Cleveland suburb. It was my 70th birthday, so instead of my signing a baseball for him, he autographed one for me.

Then he gave me some advice on turning 70. "You know, Bob," he said, "when you turn 70 three things happen. One is you begin to experience short-term memory loss. And I can't remember the other two."

There was a new smash hit on Broadway in 1949, *South Pacific*, with Mary Martin and Ezio Pinza. On the radio we were laughing at "People Are Funny" and "Truth or Consequences", and getting all choked up listening to "This Is Your Life" with Ralph Edwards. On TV, Milton Berle was such a hit that he was being called "the man who owns Tuesday night" and "Mr. Television." America stopped what it was doing every Tuesday night at eight, Eastern time, to tune in "Uncle Miltie."

There was a new personality in the American League that year, too—Casey Stengel. Ol' Case played as an outfielder in the National League for 14 years starting with the Dodgers in 1912 and was a manager without any great degree of success with the Dodgers and Braves for nine seasons in the 1930s and '40s.

Bucky Harris committed the unforgiveable sin of not winning the pennant for the New York Yankees in 1948, so they fired him and hired Stengel. Bucky was too good a manager and too good a man to get treated that way, but the Yankees had no tolerance for anything but the top spot in those years. George Steinbrenner catches a lot of heat these days, but when it came to winning, Del Webb and Dan Topping, the Yankee owners in those years, and George Weiss, their general manager, weren't any more tolerant or civil in their treatment of managers than Steinbrenner is. Don't get me wrong. I like George— socially!

Bucky became their manager in 1947 and won the pennant and the World Series in his first year there. He lost the pennant in '48 on the last weekend of the season when the Red Sox eliminated the Yankees, so—boom!—they fire him.

Bucky had the last laugh, though. He had argued most of the '48 season that he needed pitching help, and he wanted Weiss to bring up from their farm system a kid named Bob Porterfield. They did, but by the time they agreed to move, there was time for Porterfield to win only five games. The argument by Harris was that Porterfield could have been winning games for the Yankees all along if they had made the move sooner.

Bucky didn't have any trouble finding a job. He'd been a manager for 22 years by that time, and his old pal and admirer in Washington, Clark Griffith, hired him again in 1950 for his third term there. In 1951, on the last day when you could make trades in those years—June 15—Griffith and Harris swapped one of their pitchers, Bob Kuzava, to the Yankees for Porterfield and two other pitchers, Fred Sanford and Tom Ferrick. Kuzava was a big, promising left-hander, and Porterfield was still seeing only limited action for New York, so the Yankees thought they had pulled another slick deal on one of the have-nots of the American League, which was their usual attitude.

While Kuzava was winning 23 games in four seasons with the champion Yankees, Porterfield was winning 67 for the lowly second-division Senators. In 1953, while Kuzava was 6–5 for the world champion Yankees, Porterfield led the league for the fifth-place Senators with 22 wins and only 10 losses.

David had whipped Goliath again.

Stengel was treated the same way by the Yankees. After they lost to the Pirates on Bill Mazeroski's dramatic home run in the ninth inning of the last game of the 1960 World Series, Stengel was fired, and so was Weiss, the general manager. One of the official explanations was that they had reached the age of 65, and it was Yankee policy to retire employees at that age. That statement would never hold up today, but in 1960 you could say it and hope people would believe you.

The truth, of course, was that Stengel committed the same sin in 1960 that Harris did in '48—he didn't win it all. Here was a man who managed the Yanks to ten pennants in 12 seasons, and eight World Series championships. But that wasn't good enough, so Ol' Case eventually got the axe too. No wonder the Yankees were the team you loved to hate.

Stengel was an immediate success in '49. His team won the pennant and the World Series in each of Casey's first five years as manager, until we knocked them off in 1954 by winning the most games any American League team has won in a single season—111. And that was when the teams played only 154 games instead of 162 today.

As much as we disliked the Yankees—fans and players alike—they were good for baseball. They packed fans into every ballpark in the American League. The consistently unsuccessful teams like the Browns, Senators and A's paid a lot of their bills with those big crowds that poured through the gates when the Yankees came to town.

The Dodgers and the Indians were just as strong as the Yankees, and the Cardinals and Tigers were consistent winners too, but the Yankees were dominant. Baseball needs another team like that. We don't have that kind of strength and drawing power in teams any more.

Some of the people I respect, like columnist George Will, like to point out that we have a different World Series champion every year and different pennant winners, starting with the introduction of free agency in the 1970s, when players became able to change teams.

That's great, but only to a point. Baseball needs take-charge teams, teams that win every year and draw big crowds in every city, but that's difficult in these times because there are only 17 minor leagues feeding 26 teams today compared to 56 leagues for 16 major league teams in the 1940s.

Baseball usually thrives in cycles, and we need another cycle to bring us enough good players to build a few dominant teams which will generate the big crowds and the consistently strong folllowings which the good teams of the 1940s and '50s did.

Unfortunately, all professional sports want parity. They don't want two or three teams to excel. They want every team to be in the race until the last day of the season, for the TV ratings. In pro football, for example, it's said that Commissioner Tagliabue won't be happy until all 28 teams finish the season 8-and-8.

Stengel came to the Yankees with the reputation of being a clown as a manager, but that was because he didn't have good teams in what we used to call "the other league." He became a character in the National League so he could entertain the fans and writers more than his teams did, but when he joined the Yankees, he knew he would win so he became serious, at least as serious as Casey ever was.

Al Lopez, who ended his playing career with us in 1947 and became our manager in 1951 to begin a managerial career that lasted 17 seasons, said in later years that Stengel actually became a different manager with the Yankees because he knew he was rich in player talent.

"I played for Casey in Brooklyn and Boston," he said, "and he didn't do the things he did in New York. He managed a game much differently with the Yankees and tried some unpredictable strategy because he knew he could get away with it. If something out of the ordinary didn't work, he knew he had the talent among his players to win the game some other way."

If you don't believe that people in athletics are judged mainly by what they've done lately, consider this headline from a Cleveland paper right after we won the World Series:

BOUDREAU MUST REPEAT
IN '49 TO REMAIN IDOL

Well, I'm glad Lou wasn't the type who demanded to be idolized, because we didn't repeat in '49. Casey won the first of those five straight championships with the Yankees that year, and we slipped to third place behind the Yankees and the Red Sox. It was the same three teams, but we switched places with the Yanks while the Red Sox finished second again. We were eight games behind, but imagine how the people in Boston felt. They finished only one game behind, the year after finishing tied with us.

The Yankees won the pennant with consistency that year. They didn't lead the league in one batting department or in fielding either. The Red Sox led in runs, doubles, home runs and team batting average, and we led in fielding.

But the Yankees, although they were not *at* the top in batting or fielding, were *near* it in enough categories to show they were consistent, and they did lead the league in one important category—relief pitching.

That was due to the work of one man, "Fireman" Joe Page, the best relief pitcher in baseball that year. Page accounted for the unbelievable total of 40 wins that year, with 13 victories of his own and 27 saves while pitching in 60 games. Even when Jim Konstanty of the Phillies set a major league record the next year by pitching in 74 games, he had five fewer saves than Page did in '49.

We thought we might pick up some offense in '49 after Bill Veeck traded our first baseman, Eddie Robinson, to the Senators for Mickey Vernon, the batting champion only three years before with a .353 average. But the trade was a wash. Mickey hit .291 and Eddie hit .294 and each hit 18 home runs. But we experienced a sharp drop in the home run department when Boudreau tailed off from 18 homers in 1948 to four, and Keltner, who was injured much of the time, went from 31 to eight. The dropoff in their RBI totals was even sharper. Lou went from 106 to 60, and Ken from 119 to 30. Not even another exceptional year by Larry Doby could offset that kind of a plunge. Larry hit 10 more home runs—24—and had 85 runs batted in, 19 more than in '48.

I didn't contribute the way I was supposed to either. I won only 15 games, my lowest total since my first full year in 1937, and I had only 108 strikeouts, the lowest total for any full season. I also had my lowest number of walks, which would have been grounds for rejoicing if I hadn't dropped off in every other department too. I pitched only 211 innings and wasn't among the league leaders in anything.

It was grounds for a reevaluation, and I did plenty of it as the season wore on. Every athlete gets to that time in his career when his numbers start to drop, and when that happens you start to hear the whispers. You've lost a step in the field, you're not as quick, or you've lost some of the velocity off your fast ball. It may not even be true, but when you reach a certain age—I was going to be 31 in November—if your stats show any dip at all, the whispers begin.

In my case, the whisperers had been waiting in the wings for years anyhow. Some people were always convinced I was pitching too much, and my overwork would bring an early end to my career. That talk was always so much garbage to me and I never gave it five cents worth of credibility, and I think my career proved me right. I went on to pitch another seven seasons, 18 in all, and a total of 3,827 innings. That's more innings than Jim Bunning, Bobo Newsom, Mickey Lolich, Bob Friend, Carl Hubbell, Earl Whitehill, Juan Marichal and a whole pack of others—but in 1949 the talk grew louder.

They were talking about another of our pitchers in '49 too, but only in the most enthusiastic terms. That was Bob Lemon.

The former good-field, no-hit third baseman and center-fielder-turned-pitcher was a 20 game winner for the second straight season with 22 victories and only 10 losses. Over the three seasons from 1948 through 1950, he won 65 games for us. A guy who had to be feeling as good about it as Lemon himself was Al Lopez.

They asked Al in '47 to spend some time with Lemon to help him make the switch to pitching. Lemon had what baseball people call "a live arm," one with strength to throw hard and make the pitch do something, but he needed help.

Lopez told him to concentrate on two pitches—his curve and

sinker—and to work hard at throwing them for strikes. Lemon was learning from Lopez what every pitcher learns early in his career: Pitching is like real estate—the three most important things are location, location and location.

"I could see he needed work with his control," Lopez said later. "I figured if he could get his curve and sinker over for starters, then we could work his other pitches back into his routine later."

Lopez told Lemon during our exhibitions in spring training that year to keep throwing the curve and sinker and not even look to Al behind the plate for any signals. The instruction from Lopez was right on the money, and when Lemon cashed in with three straight 20-win years right after that, you had to think that Lopez, who helped Lemon so much although he had no experience as a coach or manager, was destined for greater things when he started managing.

He was given the best kind of reward for helping Lemon too. When Al led us to those record-breaking 111 wins in 1954, 23 of them came from his former pupil.

Bill Veeck surprised the world by selling the Indians at the end of the 1949 season, only three years after he bought the team. We reached the pinnacle in '48, and Veeck, never one to stand still even at the pinnacle, sold the club to a successful insurance executive named Ellis Ryan. The price was staggering for the time: $2.5 million. Today there must be two dozen players who make that much money in one season.

Hank Greenberg was the general manager for the new club, and one of his first acts was to cut my salary. He told the reporters with a chuckle, "I'm just getting even for all those times Feller struck me out."

The 1950 season was what Yogi Berra calls "déjà vu all over again." We had another highly successful year, winning 92 games—enough to win the pennant in many seasons—but we were still running up against the Yankees and the Red Sox, and now the Tigers were getting into the act.

The race went down to the last weekend again, and New York beat out the Tigers by three games, the Red Sox by four and us by six. We picked up a lot of punch at the corners of our infield with the arrival of Luke Easter at first base, and Al Rosen at third. Easter hit .280 and had 28 home runs, and Rosen did even better than that—.287 and he led the league in homers with 37. Doby had another exceptional season with a .326 average, the fourth best in the league, and Dale Mitchell hit .300 as usual, with a .308 average.

But you could see a certain changing of the guard. Lemon was the dominating member of our pitching staff now instead of me. I improved my win total to 16 and was able to pitch 247 innings, but Lemon was doing it all. His 23 wins led the American League and so did his 288 innings. Early Wynn, who joined us in a trade with the Senators in 1949, won 18 games for us in '50. Mike Garcia, a 14-game winner as a rookie in '49, won 11. A young Bobby Avila was getting more playing time at second base in place of Joe Gordon, and in the most noticeable change of them all, Lou Boudreau wasn't our starting shortstop any more. Ray Boone was, and he was hitting .301. Lou played in only 81 games that year, 13 of them as a pinch hitter. Manager Boudreau was playing Shortstop Boudreau less and less.

Those winds being felt in Municipal Stadium weren't the usual ones blowing in off Lake Erie. These were the winds of change.

In 1950, things were strange all the way around. The United States became involved in another shooting war when the North Korean army came storming across the 38th Parallel on June 25, and invaded South Korea. We were beginning to wonder what the devil was going on—we had just come back from a war five years before, and now we were faced with the risk of having to go marching off again.

Ted Williams, who was one of the few of us who did have to put his military uniform on again, gave the All-Star Game its biggest story, but not the way he did in '41 with his home run in Detroit. This time he broke his elbow crashing into the left field wall at Comiskey Park in Chicago and was out for the rest of the season. It was a devastating blow to the Red Sox. With Williams in there every day for the second half of the season, who knows? Instead of losing the pennant by only four games to the Yankees, the Red Sox might have won it. The Yankees might never have won those five straight pennants and World Series.

Something else happened in that same month. Lou started me in six games, and I went the distance in five of them. The only exception was a game in Detroit when I got knocked out of the box in the first inning. My only loss was a 2–1 game when I pitched a five-hitter but the

Browns beat me. In my last three starts, I beat the Senators, Tigers and White Sox and allowed a total of only four runs.

I wasn't striking people out any more—only seven in that three-game winning streak at the end—but I was winning consistently and going the full nine innings.

I could still hear the whispers. Some people weren't going to be convinced until—and unless—I had another banner year. That, of course, was exactly what they were saying, that I couldn't have another banner year, that I was finished.

I knew better, but in that situation, it doesn't do any good to try to convince people with talk. But when the 1950 season ended with such a strong September for me, there wasn't any doubt at all in my mind about one thing: in 1951, I was going to shut some people up.

CHAPTER FIFTEEN
The Top Again

When we were aboard the *Alabama* during the war, our skipper, Captain F.D. Kirtland, gave us four fundamental rules to follow so we would be prepared for combat:

1. Your guns and ammunition must be in the pink of condition.
2. You must see your enemy first.
3. You must shoot first.
4. You must hit first or you might not get off another shot.

Captain Kirtland obviously knew what he was talking about. We survived eight of the bloodiest invasions of the war in the Pacific without losing one life to enemy action, and we didn't even have a man wounded. We were the only ship in the entire Third Fleet not to suffer one casualty from enemy action, a remarkable achievement in view of all the combat we experienced.

My 1951 baseball season was sort of a peacetime adaptation of the Captain Kirtland code. I was going to be in my best physical condition ever, and I was going to get the upper hand against the "enemy" by getting off to a fast start and maintaining a winning pace all season long. I didn't care what the whisperers were saying. I was headed for a great year, and if they couldn't see it coming too, that was their own tough luck.

Following Captain Kirtland's first rule of preparation, being "in the pink of condition," was no problem in 1951 or any other year. I was always in top shape. In fact, I used to get kidded about it, even ridiculed. I worked out with weights and barbells and did stretching

184

exercises 25 years before they became widespread. I was considered a physical fitness nut because I was always doing something to maintain my peak physical condition so I would have an edge on the competition.

When we were on the road, I did pushups in my hotel room, lifted my dumbbells, did some other calisthenics and aerobic exercises and then topped it off with a nice hot bath. I was improving my condition so I'd be one up on our opponents when we took the field.

My determination to get off to a fast start, building on my strong finish of the year before, paid immediate dividends. I won my first four games, lost to the Red Sox in Fenway and then won six more in a row. By June 18, I had ten wins and only one loss, and I pitched into the ninth inning in all but one of those 11 games. One interesting note was that my trend toward lower strikeout totals was continuing. I had reason to be grateful that I worked hard on developing a good curve ball when I was younger, because by now it had replaced my fast ball as my out pitch. In 97 innings over that span, I had only 42 strikeouts—but I also had two shutouts and an average of fewer than three runs allowed per game.

My "comeback," if a pitcher who wins 16 games the year before needs a comeback, reached its peak on July 1 in a day game in Cleveland. I pitched my third no-hitter. This one wasn't a no-hit, no-run game because it wasn't a shutout. It almost wasn't a no-hitter either.

By that game I actually was making a comeback within a comeback. In May, I had a freak accident in the whirlpool bath at Municipal Stadium. As I was picking up the hose to fill the tub, the hose came loose and I was doused with hot water. I was scalded from my chest to my knees.

Al Lopez was a rookie manager with us that year—Lou Boudreau had moved on to the Red Sox to finish out his playing career—and Lopez and his pitching coach, Mel Harder, were counting me out for the next several weeks. The next day, I showed up at the ballpark, put on my uniform and was ready for another game.

Lopez and Harder were so convinced that I would miss several weeks that they did everything but order me to go back home. The team was off to a winning start, and I was doing my share. This was no time to give in to something like scalded skin unless you were incapacitated, and I wasn't. Maybe it hurt like the devil, but so do a lot of other things. I wanted to pitch, so I was at the ballpark. To me it was that simple.

I made our next road trip, missed only one turn and then came back to pitch the first game of a Sunday doubleheader against the White Sox in Chicago. I went the distance and beat the Sox on an eight-hitter, 11–2, with plenty of hitting help from my teammates.

Lopez asked me several times during the game if I wanted to come out. Our trainer, Wally Bock, got about half sick pulling the cotton wrapping off my raw flesh after the game, and I noticed that not a whole lot of my teammates felt like watching the fun.

My burns kept on healing and we kept on winning. Then came the no-hitter against Detroit. It was in the first game of a doubleheader at home. We had a 1–0 lead going into the Tigers' fourth when Ray Boone, taking Boudreau's place at shortstop, bobbled Johnny Lipon's ground ball for an error. Lipon stole second, and then I compounded things by making a wild throw on a pickoff play and Lipon took third. George Kell scored him on a fly ball.

Luke Easter, whose ground ball in the first inning scored Dale Mitchell, singled after Sam Chapman's triple in the eighth. We had the lead, 2–1, and I had a no-hitter with the ninth inning coming up.

I got the first two hitters—Charlie Keller, the old Yankee, and Kell— on fly balls. Next at bat was Vic Wertz, our future teammate.

Wertz hit a line drive a mile into the upper deck—foul by ten feet. Wertz and I batted our way to a 3–2 count. I came in with a slider, knee high on the outside corner. Wertz took it for strike three.

We had the win, and I had my third no-hit game, tying Cy Young as the only pitchers to throw three no-hitters from the beginning of the century until then.

We were in another tight pennant race, this time with only two teams involved near the end—the Yankees and us. I was able to keep on contributing, while also silencing the whispers at least for the time being. When the good people of Cleveland, who had already done so many nice things for me, held another "Bob Feller Night" on August 13, I said thank you by beating one of my favorite teams, the Tigers, 2–1, on a seven-hitter. I proved again, to myself as well as to others, that I could win without my big strikeout pitch of earlier years. I didn't strike out a man in this game, but I won my 19th.

Major league baseball was performing something of a public service in 1951 by staging two sizzling pennant races. Over in the National League, the Dodgers and the Giants were going all the way to the wire in their famous tie that was broken when Bobby Thomson hit his "shot heard 'round the world" in their third playoff game to give the Giants the pennant.

Those races couldn't have come at a better time, to give the American public something to get excited about that would take everybody's mind off the war in Korea. Even people who are old enough to remember that year have forgotten how uncertain things were.

It was still touch and go over there. Truman fired MacArthur for continuing to publicly challenge the President's policy. Just before the year started, Truman declared a national emergency to put America on a wartime footing again. The fear was that the Russians were making Korea a stepping stone toward another world war. Bob Considine, a popular columnist of that time, called the action in Korea "World War Two and a Half." The most prestigious newscaster in the world, Edward R. Murrow, flew to Korea to cover the fighting. Truman ordered the military draft to be stepped up, so Selective Service started calling up 80,000 men a month.

We were able to help keep the fun in things for Americans with those two pennant races. We managed to keep the fun in it for ourselves, too. We even got help from a particular fan in Philadelphia.

I always enjoyed playing in New York and Washington because the fans in Yankee Stadium and Griffith Stadium were the fairest in the American League. There was an extra reason for enjoying New York. The Brooklyn fans used to come over and cheer for the visiting teams. The fans in New York and Washington knew their baseball, and they were largely a transient population. They were from all over the country and didn't give you that belligerent, even abusive treatment that fans in other cities sometimes do.

Philadelphia was the worst. The fans there all seemed to have leather lungs and they screamed the most obnoxious comments in the league. One guy was especially abusive. He was so serious about it that he even followed us to New York and gave us his treatment up there too.

I got the clown's number, though. On a trip to Philadelphia, I stopped by a novelty store and bought a set of those teeth that chatter incessantly and stuck them in my pocket. Sure enough, our hero shows up and gets on us without let up through the first few innings. In the fourth or fifth inning, I got a stool out of the clubhouse, sat it on the field next to the dugout near the grandstand railing, put the teeth on the stool and released the hook that held them together.

Those teeth started yackety-yakking and their noise was made even louder on the metal stool. Mr. Loudmouth was only a few rows back, and he saw and heard it all. So did everybody around him, and all of them were as fed up with him as we were.

He got up and left. We laughed him out of the ballpark.

The Yankees managed to beat us again, this time by five games, for their third straight pennant. The Red Sox dropped off a bit and finished 11 games behind in third place.

We were maintaining our standing as one of the top teams in baseball, and our disappointment at losing the pennant the last three years to the Yankees was tempered each time by our awareness that we would be a solid contender for the pennant the next season. The fans in Brooklyn made their slogan, "Wait 'til next year," famous, but the fans in Cleveland—and the players too—felt the same way. We were always confident that we could win the pennant the next season.

We continued to be a strong offensive team. Luke Easter tied for fourth in home runs with 27 and had the fourth highest number of runs batted in with 103, one more than Al Rosen. Larry Doby was second only to Ted Williams in slugging percentage, and Bobby Avila was giving us more speed on the bases by finishing among the leaders in stolen bases.

But the pitching statistics sent a loud warning to the rest of the league: The Indians were developing a dominating pitching staff. We had three 20-game winners on the same team that year—Early Wynn, Mike Garcia and me. Along with Bob Lemon we had pitchers among the leaders in nine of the 12 pitching departments. I led the league in wins with 22 and in winning percentage with .733 on a 22–8 record. Garcia and Wynn tied for third in wins, and Wynn and Lemon were second and third respectively in strikeouts. Wynn was third in fewest hits per nine innings, and he and Lemon were one-two in most innings pitched.

Lou Brissie came to us that year from the Philadelphia A's in a trade for Minnie Minoso and Sam Zoldak and was third among the league's relief pitchers in saves. Mike was fifth in that department even though he also started 30 games.

Wynn was second in complete games and Lemon was tied for fifth, and Brissie and Garcia were second and third in appearances, Lou in 56 and Mike in 47.

Any pitching staff that does all those things is going to keep you in most games, and in most pennant races. We were reaping rewards already from having a savvy former catcher like Al Lopez as our manager and another man with plenty of pitching smarts, Mel Harder, a 200-plus game winner in 20 years with the Indians, as our pitching coach.

All that talent and the good coaching from Lopez and Harder were keeping us hot on the Yankees' heels while also positioning us for our historic performance three years later.

For the record: I pitched just under 250 innings that year—249 $^2/_3$. There was still something left in my arm and my career, and I didn't hear any whispers to the contrary.

I got off to another promising start in 1952, winning three of my first four decisions. My only loss was a 1–0 game against the Browns in St. Louis on April 23, and therein lies a story.

I pitched a one-hitter, the 11th of my career and the first one I lost. but that's not the big story. The real news was that *both* pitchers had one-hitters.

Bob Cain, the victim in my no-hit game the year before, matched me in this one with a one-hitter of his own. It was the first time in major league history that both pitchers threw one-hitters in a game. To the best of my knowledge that feat still has not been duplicated.

I faced only 28 hitters, one over the minimum. Bobby Young tripled off me in the first inning and scored when Rosen threw out Marty Marion on a ground ball. In the late innings, Rosen might have gone to the plate with his throw, but in the first inning, percentage dictates exactly what Al did: Get the out so you can prevent a big inning.

Just to show my versatility, I beat the A's in Philadelphia in my next start on a neat 18-hitter. The final score was 21-9, and I pitched the full nine innings. It sounds unbelievable, but that's baseball. You pitch a one-hitter and lose, and the next time out you get rocked for 18 hits and win.

I've always thought it's not *how* you pitch but *when*—when your team is scoring runs. Roger Clemens came up to me before an Old Timers game in Milwaukee a couple of years ago and asked me what advice I'd give him. I said, "Not much, except this: Never start a game if your team is going to be shut out."

We were in the hunt all the way with the Yankees and again lost only in a photo finish by two games. The rest of the league was nowhere near us. The third place team, the White Sox, finished 14 games behind.

But I won only nine games and lost 13. It was the first losing season of my career, even including my amateur days in Iowa. I didn't know what it was like to have a losing season, and my disappointment was compounded because I was having that kind of a year on a team that was a big winner.

The sands were running through the hourglass at what seemed to be a faster pace now. I was going to be 34 in November, and I knew that even my performance in 1951 didn't mean I could go on winning forever. The whispers started again, and this time I had to agree with them. I wasn't going to kid myself. I was on the other side of the mountain.

I was preparing myself for the inevitable end of my playing career, both financially and professionally, but I wasn't prepared for a losing season on a winning team. That would take some getting used to, but instead of doing that I was going to make sure I didn't have to. I was going to come back with a winning record in 1953 and let other pitchers worry about getting used to a losing record.

I stepped up my conditioning program with more of everything—calisthenics, lifting and running. I always did more of that than anybody, but now I had to do still more because my body demanded more if I were going to continue to win.

I've never minded extra work, and I didn't mind it then. It was all part of what athletes call "being willing to pay the price." It's a price, though, that many baseball players have been reluctant to pay. As a group, they are among the worst conditioned of our athletes. They get to play mostly in one small area on defense and run only when they hit the ball or go after a fly ball in the outfield. They do some amount of conditioning in spring training, but once the bell rings for the season to start in early April, many of them simply don't work as hard as they should to maintain a physical peak. They're doing better nowadays than in my time.

It's critical for pitchers to get in as much running as they can, all year long. They should run in the offseason, and during the season they should run sprints in the outfield during batting practice. If they are going to be winning pitchers, their legs must be as strong as their arms because legs do just as much work in the act of pitching a baseball. You propel yourself into your pitch by pushing off your back leg and exploding into the second half of your delivery. Running sprints makes that part of the mechanics of pitching much more effective.

Pitchers of today don't have the one unique advantage that we had when I came up. Most players in those years were from rural areas. We were used to working on a farm, and that meant long hours every day of the week under the hot summer sun. We built up a great amount of endurance, and when it came to pitching we had the stamina to go out there every few days and go the full nine innings most of the time.

You'd never think of it as one of the differences between players then and now, but it's true—pitching hay, which many of us did in those years, helped us in pitching baseballs later.

My power of positive thinking worked. I wasn't through after all. I won 10 games for the Indians in '53, and there is always room in baseball for a pitcher who can win 10 games for you. It was another winning season too, because my record was 10–7. I also showed a far better earned run average, only 3.59 per nine innings compared to 4.74 the year before.

I was glad I had accentuated the positive over the winter and into the start of the season, instead of resigning myself to the effects of old age and accepting that losing record. There is no room in my life for losers, including me and even starting with me.

The guy who had the bittersweet season that year was Al Rosen. He missed the hardest of all achievements for a player—the triple crown—by one percentage point. He led the American League in home runs with 43 and in runs batted in with 145, but he lost the batting championship to Mickey Vernon by one point on the last day of the season. Mickey was back with the Senators after only one year with us, and he hit .337 to Al's .336. It was a sensational season for our third baseman, but if he had hit just one point higher and Vernon one point lower . . .

The outcome of the pennant race was the same. It was the Yankees and the Indians again, and in the same order as before. We won more than 90 games for the fourth straight year—92—but the Yanks won 99 and went on to beat the Dodgers in the World Series again for their fifth straight pennant and World Series championship.

We knew we had lost again, but we also knew that any team able to win more than 90 games four years in a row is a team that can win it all.

We didn't walk away after the 1953 season with our tails between our legs. Just the opposite. We couldn't wait for 1954. We were convinced we were destined to win the pennant. What we didn't know was that we were also destined to make 1954 one for the record book.

CHAPTER SIXTEEN
The Chance That Never Came

In the same summer that Roger Bannister reached one of sports' unreachable goals, the four-minute mile, the Cleveland Indians were writing a little history of our own.

The Yankees won 103 games, far more than needed for a pennant in most years, but they finished eight games behind us because we won 111. It is still the most wins by a team in American League history, and has stood up even through the three decades since baseball expanded the number of teams for the first time and extended its season from 154 games to 162.

Some great hitting was instrumental in our success. Avila led the league with a .341 average, and Doby led in home runs with 32 and runs batted in with 126. Rosen, who won the Most Valuable Player Award for his outstanding year in 1953, hit an even .300 and Al Smith, our left fielder, chipped in with .281. On defense, Jim Hegan led the American League's catchers with a .994 fielding average and Avila had more assists than any other second baseman, 406.

But that's not really what won it for us. The key was our pitching. Of the top five pichers in winning percentage in the league, three of them were Indians—Lemon, Garcia and Art Houtteman. Lemon and Wynn tied for most wins with 23, and Garcia was tied for fourth with 19. Wynn was second in strikeouts, third in fewest hits per nine innings, fourth in earned run average and tops in innings pitched. Garcia won the ERA championship, Lemon tied Bob Porterfield for most complete

An excellent example of Feller's high kick. His forward body motion and pivot created his blazing fast ball that traveled over 100 MPH. (National Baseball Library, Cooperstown, NY)

His fast ball is clocked at 98.6 miles per hour in a test in Washington in 1946.

With a younger member of the Cleveland mound staff at spring training in Tucson in the late 1940s.

Being greeted by Jim Hegan at Municipal Stadium in Cleveland after Feller's third no-hitter, in 1951.

The pitching form of Bob Feller in 1955 on the day of his 12th one-hitter, the most in baseball history. (Associated Press)

An early meeting of the Players' Association in 1956 in Washington, with Feller flanked by attorney Norman Lewis (left) and Robin Roberts. Standing (l-r) are Ernie Johnson, Sam White, Ted Kluszewski, Don Mueller and Sherm Lollar. (Associated Press)

Bob Feller closing out his playing career. (National Baseball Library, Cooperstown, NY)

With President Eisenhower on Opening Day 1957 in Washington.
Note the rain check for a lower box seat: Cost, $2.50.

Discussing baseball and other matters with another
Ohio celebrity, Senator John Glenn.

Bob Feller and Anne
Gilliland on their
wedding day, October 1,
1974.

At an Old Timers Game
in 1980 with Johnny
(Double No-Hit) Vander
Meer.

With former sportcaster "Dutch" Reagan at a 1981 White House luncheon for Hall of Famers. (The White House)

Feller is joined by Bowie Kuhn (left) and Happy Chandler (with cap) in a greeting from then-Vice President George Bush, when Bob was honorary captain of the American League team in the All-Star Game in Cleveland in 1981. (The White House)

With Ted Williams and Tommy Lasorda at one of Ted's dinners for the Jimmy Fund, Boston, 1989.

games and Wynn was only one behind with 20, Garcia tied Virgil Trucks of Chicago with five shutouts, and one of our two rookie relief pitchers, Ray Narleski, was third in saves with 15.

Even Al Lopez would admit that a manager doesn't have to flash too many signals or worry about too many changes in his batting order when his pitchers are that good.

After one month, we were putting on a respectable showing but we weren't running away from the rest of the league. On May 14, after George Strickland's grand slam gave us a 5–2 win over Chuck Stobbs and the Senators, we were 15–10, a game behind the White Sox. Lemon pitched a six-hitter for his fifth win. He hadn't lost a game yet.

That was one of those games that can ignite a team. Strickland was no great shucks of a hitter, and that's putting it mildly. His lifetime average was .224. But when we got two men on in the first inning, Stobbs walked Rudy Regalado intentionally and Strickland hit his homer. Two days later, we took over first place.

Garcia got us there with a one-hitter against the A's. Joe DeMaestri got a single in the fourth inning and that was the whole Philadelphia offense. Rosen hit two home runs and Avila had five hits. We were on a roll—our fifth straight win, 15th in our last 19 games.

I got into the act by beating the Orioles, 14–3, on May 23 in the first game of a doubleheader. It was the first year in Baltimore for the transplanted St. Louis Browns, and the change in uniforms didn't seem to be having any effect. They still looked like the Browns to us. It was one of those wins that feel especially good. This was my first victory of the season, the 250th of my career, and I was able to put the icing on the cake by pitching the full nine innings. I gave up eight hits and walked only one. My first two starts of the season, against the Senators and A's, had been unimpressive, so the win over the Orioles was a great tonic for me.

I lost my next time out, but it was another complete game while we lost to the White Sox. Then I clicked off seven straight wins including five complete games in a row and another win where I came within one out of finishing.

We were winning because we were coordinating everything into a successful combination—hitting, fielding and pitching. But we were winning for another equally important reason, maybe the most important reason of all. We were playing like a team. We had unselfish players, even though they were stars, who put the good of the team ahead of their own wishes and even their own injuries and illnesses.

Al Rosen, Vic Wertz and Hal Newhouser were examples. Rosen was once smacked in the face with a ground ball. Both eyes were swollen shut. The next morning they were still shut. He couldn't see a thing. But he kept ice packs on his face all day long, and finally his eyes opened just enough for him to see.

He played for us that night, the game after he had been injured, and darned if he didn't get four hits.

Wertz came to us on June 1, in a trade with the Orioles for one of our pitchers, Bob Chakales. Wertz became our first baseman and hit .275 while giving us a lot of protection around the bag, but he gave us more than that.

Vic was cut from the same mold as Rosen, and here's what I mean: The following year he fell victim to polio. This was back in those summers when the disease was all you heard about. Patients lived in horrible contraptions called iron lungs, devices that looked terrible but saved the lives of thousands of victims.

Wertz wouldn't let even a monster like polio keep him down. He astounded all of us by coming back the next season. Not only that, he hit 32 home runs and drove in 106 runs.

Newhouser was suffering from arm problems after 15 years with the Tigers. He'd even been treated for a heart condition. In 1953, he considered retirement, but then he decided to hang in there at least one more year and signed with us. He was 7–2 for us and also had seven saves, giving him a hand in 14 of our wins.

When your team is loaded with talent and you have players with attitudes like Rosen, and Wertz and Newhouser, you just know you're going to win.

There were other signs too, little things that tell you something. Dave Philley came up for us in the late innings of a tight game against the A's with Al Smith and Bobby Avila on base. A sacrifice fly will give us the lead. But Philley doesn't just hit a sacrifice fly to score a run. He hit one 400 feet that scored both of them.

How many times have you seen *two* runs score on a sacrifice fly? We won the game, 4–1, because Philley was able and willing to do that little extra something that separate life's winners from the also-rans.

On an eastern swing when we had to play without Rosen or Avila because they were both injured, we went out and won 10 of the 14 games. In one of those games, we beat the Red Sox in Fenway Park, 13–5, and tied an American League record by having nine players who got two or more hits in that game.

We were that kind of a team—if we had to win without our stars, like the league's home run champion and its leading hitter, we would.

Lopez has said that train travel was a big contributor to team attitude. Others have said the same thing, and I agree. We were stuck with each other overnight, all day, sometimes half way across the country from Boston to St. Louis on just one leg of a trip that would last for two weeks. And you took four trips a year to each of the seven other cities in the league. We played each team 22 times, 11 at home and 11 on the road.

If you're on the train for most of those trips, and we were, you'll either become a close-knit team or you'll end up choking each other. Teams in the 1950s, like the Indians and the Brooklyn Dodgers, had a lot of talent, but they had a lot of closeness too. We weren't nine individuals out on that field—we were one team.

By the Fourth of July, our team talent and team attitude had us in first place, 4½ games ahead of the Yankees and 30 games over .500 at 52–22, and it was because of teamwork that day too.

Mike Garcia started that holiday game against the White Sox, but came down with a hemorrhage of the middle finger on his right hand and had to leave the game in the second inning.

Narleski came in and pitched hitless ball through the seventh inning. Garcia hadn't given up a hit either, so we have a combined no-hitter going when Early Wynn, one of our most important starters, comes in as a relief pitcher in the eighth. By this time we're winning, 2–1.

Wynn holds the Sox hitless until there are two outs in the ninth. Then Minnie Minoso singled to center. But Minnie was caught stealing, the game was over and we were where you wanted to be at what used to be the traditional halfway point of the season. That was when they used to say that the team in first place on the Fourth of July is the team that will win the pennant.

Far be it from us to break the tradition. Two days later we took another step toward upholding it by scoring eight runs against the Orioles before they got anybody out. The final score was 11–3.

We thought we might get away with storming our way through the second half of the season, but there was always the Yankees to worry about. We lost four in a row in mid-July to the White Sox in Chicago and our lead shrank to only a half-game by the All-Star break.

We had another curve thrown at us on July 23 when we lost our shortstop, George Strickland, with a broken jaw for six weeks, but we kept on winning and staying a step ahead of the Yankees.

Another one of those plays that make you think this is your year came in August. We were losing to the Orioles, 1–0, and they had Vern Stephens on second and Clint Courtney on first with nobody out in the fourth. Jim Fridley ripped a line drive to Lemon, who threw to Avila at second to double up Stephens. Avila's throw to Wertz trying to nail Clint Courtney for the triple play was late. But Courtney overran the bag. Wertz tagged him coming back. Triple play.

We won the game, 4–1.

By mid-September we weren't letting up. The Army-McCarthy hearings on TV were getting a lot of attention, but we were making the news too. We just kept on winning, and our attitude was that the Yankees were just going to have to catch us. We weren't going to drop back to them with a losing streak. They were going to have to overtake us by winning at an even faster pace than we were, if that was possible.

It may have been possible, but it didn't happen. The Yankees had their last real chance in a Sunday doubleheader against us in Municipal Stadium on September 12. We were in the middle of another hot streak which lasted from September 8 through 20 and brought us another 11 straight wins.

The Yankees ran into our buzz saw right in the middle of that streak. The good people of Cleveland broke their attendance record for one game that day when 86,563 of them came out to cheer for their heroes and hiss and boo against the hated Yankees.

We swept the doubleheader, 4–1 and 3–2, behind Lemon and Wynn. We stretched our lead over the Yanks to 8½ games. The baseball world knew we really won the pennant that day, although the mathematics took a little longer. It didn't make any difference what the math said. Reality said the pennant race was over. The Yankees were never going to catch us—not the way we were playing.

On September 17, we clinched a tie for first place by beating the Tigers in Detroit, 6–3. Avila was healthy and headed for the batting title and that night he hit a grand slam to break a 2–2 tie. It was our eighth straight win, and Lemon's 23rd victory of the season.

Avila was a fascinating study that year. His league-leading average was .341. He was always a good contact hitter with a respectable average who hit .281 over a career of 11 years, but he certainly never hit for an average that high except that year. In fact, he never hit .300 in the five more seasons he played. His best average after winning the batting championship was .272.

That .341 was his "career year," as the writers and announcers say. We didn't know it at the time, but his type of hitter was a vanishing breed, one who was willing to pass up the temptation of home runs— he had only 15 that year—and was perfectly happy to rap out 189 hits to help his team win that way.

Most of today's hitters make the mistake of going for the long ball, trying to match the home run totals of Babe Ruth instead of trying to match the average of Wade Boggs. The truly outstanding hitters, of course, can do both—men like Dave Winfield, Kirby Puckett, Andre Dawson, Don Mattingly and George Brett, Tony Gwynn, Paul Molitor, Joe Carter, Alan Trammell and Cal Ripken.

But how many of the other players in the majors are as talented at hitting as those players? The rest of them would be better off by forgetting their lust for the home run and instead trying to do what Al Smith did for us—and for himself—in 1954. Some of today's players who are hitting .260 might find themselves a whole lot closer to .300, or above it, and discover new opportunities and recognition for themselves and victories for their teams. but they have to take their eyes off the outfield fence first.

We were such a strong team that year we didn't have to worry about dragging matters out either. We went right out the next night and wrapped everything up with a 3–2 victory. The game was played in a downpour, but winning teams win under all conditions, and so did we that night, thanks to a dramatic pinch hit home run into the rain in the seventh inning by Dale Mitchell, followed by another one by Jim Hegan.

Early Wynn pitched us to the championship, and that's exactly what it was—an early win. We won the pennant with ten days to go in the season. It was our 107th victory—and we were going to win some more.

Back in Cleveland, our fans outdid themselves. It was 1948 all over again and then some. Two thousand of them turned out at Union Terminal to scream their welcome, and they followed that two days later with a victory parade from the far East Side to the far West Side, complete with confetti. The parade was 18 miles long.

Still we kept winning. Don Mossi, our other ace rookie reliefer came out of the bullpen long enough to pitch a five-hitter as we beat the White Sox, 3–1, to tie the American League record of 110 wins set by the great New York Yankees team of 1927—"Murderers Row."

Three days later, on September 25, we broke the record, and we did it in championship style. Wynn pitched a no-hit game into the ninth inning and ended with his fourth two-hitter of the year as we defeated Detroit again, 11–1.

We were the American League champions and the record holders too—in a year when the Yankees won more than 100 games for the first time under Casey Stengel.

I felt good about that year for many reasons. The team had performed extremely well. We were building a reputation for excellence that bordered on a tradition. We had a long way to go to match the Yankees in that department, but the record shows that when we started winning in 1947, we swept through the next ten years with a reputation as one of the quality teams in baseball, with numbers to back it up.

My own performance during that historic season was a source of pride to me, too. I won 13 games and lost only three and lowered my earned run average again, to 3.09 per nine innings. I pitched only 140 innings, but as we would say today, they were quality innings. I started 19 games and pitched a complete game in almost half of them—nine.

My walks were down too, and not because I was pitching fewer innings. I was averaging only two-plus walks for every nine innings pitched. In two of my complete games, I walked only two batters, in two others I walked only one, and in one of them I didn't walk anybody—in a shutout against the A's.

At age 35, I had reason to feel good. I was still pitching, still winning and still contributing to my team's success. I picked up my 2,500th strikeout in a game against the Red Sox in June, as well as that 250th win.

By now I had achieved some milestones, but the funny thing about them is that after a few, you don't think that much about any new ones that come your way. You concentrate instead on things of substance, things that may have more meaning than just a number.

In my case that meant only one thing—I wanted to win a World Series game. Lopez had me scheduled to pitch Game Three. This could be my last chance.

The world knows that 1954 wasn't my last chance. That was in 1948.

The Giants, our old spring training partners since I came up in 1936, swept us in four games and I never got to throw a pitch. The Indians used seven different pitchers in those four games. Three of them—

Lemon, Garcia and Narleski—pitched in two games, and one of them—Mossi—pitched three times.

The whole World Series caught us off balance. Clinching the pennant with ten days left may have cost us some of our sharpness in the interim. Willie Mays made his famous catch off Vic Wertz in the ninth inning with the score 2–2 and two men on base. Then Dusty Rhodes hit his routine fly in the tenth inning that was a home run only because we were playing in the Polo Grounds. Lemon loses a heartbreaker, and we drop the opener.

That catch by Mays was a great one, especially coming in a World Series game, but I agree with those, including Lopez, who say it was a long way from being the best. In fact, it wasn't even the best by Willie. I've seen him make better.

From the time Wertz hit it, we knew Mays had it all the way. His hat flew off, which it always did anyhow, and he got an excellent jump on the ball. It was a good pressure play—but he got some help. The wind was blowing in, and the ball came straight down, almost like a pop fly over home plate, even though Wertz hit it 440 feet.

Lopez has been quoted as saying that Willie actually overran the ball and could have caught it a lot easier than he did.

I saw Larry Doby make a better catch than that. He climbed up the fence in Cleveland and hung on the top of it and jackknifed over it as he caught the ball.

Once while I was in New York to rehearse for Dinah Shore's TV show, I saw DiMaggio go back among the monuments in center field in Yankee Stadium to catch a fly ball hit by Hank Greenberg. He caught it with one hand and with his back to the plate despite those stone monuments around him. Bob Lemon, when he was a center fielder, made a sliding catch on the grass racing toward the infield to save a 1–0 win for me in Chicago on Opening Day 1946, and it ranks up there with some of the greatest I've seen.

Three things made that catch by Mays one that people still talk about: it was an excellent catch, it was in the World Series and—never underestimate this reason—it was on national television.

In the second game, Rhodes hit another homer, a more legitimate one this time, we lost again and the wheels were off the wagon.

Lopez said he thinks we would have won that World Series if it had started in Cleveland. I think there's a lot of truth to that.

The ball that Rhodes hit as a pinch hitter in that first game went about 257 feet. If we had been playing that first game in Cleveland, it would have been an easy out. In fact, it would have been an easy out in any other stadium in the major leagues. But the Giants' ballpark got its name from its former use as a polo field. Unfortunately, it got its dimensions from the same source.

Conversely, the ball that Mays caught off the bat of Wertz would have been deep into the seats in most parks because it was hit to center. Just as the dimensions were freakishly short down the right field line where Rhodes hit his fly ball, they were freakishly long in center where the Wertz ball was hit. Center field was almost 500 feet away—483 to be precise. That's a $3.00 cab fare.

You don't always hear about "the home field advantage" in baseball, except when someone is talking about the Minnesota Twins in their domed stadium with all the noise, but it can be as much a part of baseball as it is in football, where you hear the term more often.

The Giants and Yankees always encouraged their left-handed hitters to try to pull the ball down the right field line because of the "short porch" in the Polo Grounds and Yankee Stadium. Certainly the Red Sox have an advantage in Fenway Park with its "Green Monster" in left field, or if they don't, it's their own fault.

The distances to the outfield fences aren't the only home field advantage in baseball. You can create your own. When the White Sox had Chico Carrasquel and Nellie Fox hitting one-two in their lineup, it was common knowledge around the American League that the dirt along the third base line in fair territory was sloped toward the infield so their bunts would stay fair while rolling down the line. A team with a strong set of infielders can cut its grass extra short and reduce the amount of watering so the ground is hard and the grass is short. Their infielders are good enough and quick enough to field the ground balls on such a field, and their own hitters are helped because the infielders on the opposing teams can't move that quickly so the balls get through for hits for the home team.

The opposite is true, too. A team with a weak infield defense can let its grass grow tall and receive extra generous amounts of water so the grass is tall and thick, slowing down the other team's ground balls enough for the home team's infielders to get to them.

Lopez, who was responsible for a great deal of our success because he was a superb handler of pitchers, felt backed against the wall when he found us down, two games to none. He has said that he had to change his schedule and go with Garcia in the third game and come back with Lemon in the fourth.

There were suggestions after we lost the third game that Lopez start me in the fourth, giving Lemon an extra day of rest in the hope that I could beat the Giants. But Al went with Lemon instead, on the old theory that he couldn't save him until tomorrow because there might not be a tomorrow.

That didn't work either. The Giants jumped to a 7–0 lead in the first five innings against Lemon, Newhouser and Narleski. Mossi and Garcia came in later, and that didn't even help. Of our eight starters and relief pitchers, I was the only one who didn't pitch in that whole World Series, while the others gave up 21 runs in four games.

I've never been quite sure why Lopez didn't use me in that series. I had been effective all year long, I pitched 100 more innings than Newhouser and I certainly knew the Giants' hitters. I had been pitching against them for 16 years.

Leo Durocher, the Giants' manager, says he's wondered the same thing. He told me he's asked Al dozens of times why he didn't use me, but Leo says he's never gotten an answer. To the best of my knowledge, Al has never given his reason to anyone.

I've never asked him myself, even though I've seen Al a thousand times since. He's never said anything about it. He could just tell me he thought Lemon had a better chance to win in the fourth game and I would accept that. I wouldn't take it personally. As it is, I still wonder.

I have a hunch, though. I don't think Al felt I could win in the World Series by that time. In those later years of my career, he seemed to think I was doing it with mirrors, and maybe I was, but what difference does it make *how* you're winning as long as you *are* winning?

He didn't seem to be convinced of my ability when we were in spring training that year, and my performance all year still didn't seem to change his mind. Even when I led the league in '51 with 22 wins, he seemed to have trouble believing I could still get people out because I didn't have the blazing fast ball anymore. It almost seemed as if he couldn't wait to take me out if I gave up a couple of hits. He'd almost beat the ball back to the mound.

Durocher had just the opposite assessment. During his team meeting before the World Series, he told the Giants, "Feller is the only guy over there who could give us trouble."

Despite my disappointment, and it was a bitter one, I have never held it against Al. He has always been a respected member of our profession, a gentleman in every way and a good friend. He had his reasons for his decision, I'm sure. I don't blame him for our defeat either. Al couldn't have been too stupid if he managed a team to 111 wins. His players just didn't perform. Lemon and Garcia were never effective, and in a short series, pitching makes the difference. Our team earned run average was 4.84. New York's was only 1.46. The Giants' pitching was great.

Johnny Antonelli was an example of the kind of Series the Giants had. He was 21–7 that year with an average of 2.30 earned runs for every nine innings. In the World Series, he pitched in two games, won one and saved the other and had an ERA of 0.84.

Our hitters didn't do their jobs. The Giants outscored us, 21–9, and outhit us, .254 to .190.

Your manager might be the greatest genius in the history of baseball, but he can't do a thing about numbers like that—and the result that follows.

My diasppointment ran deep. We might win the pennant again in '55 and maybe I'd get another chance then, but it was getting late in the game for me to keep counting on next year. Besides, the Yankees were still the Yankees. They might win it instead of us. One thing we could be fairly sure of—we didn't figure to win 111 games again.

There wasn't any moaning or despair in our locker room after we lost. It all happened too fast for any of that. It was painless at that time—a painless Series. The pain set in later.

As for me, I didn't have any time to feel sorry for myself either. My family came to the fourth game with me. I promised my sons before the game that we'd go fishing after the World Series.

When we got into the car after the game, one of them asked me, "What time do we leave tomorrow?" At times like that, a young son is a good thing for a man to have.

CHAPTER SEVENTEEN
Both an End and a Beginning

As disappointed as I was about not getting to pitch against the Giants, a far more jolting development occurred. Mom told me she wouldn't be able to come to the Series. She was being bothered by pains in her chest. One of our friends in Des Moines, Dr. Dorner, whom we had met in connection with his work at the Mayo Clinic while Dad was there, diagnosed her illness as lung cancer.

It was the cruelest kind of coincidence—cancer again, diagnosed by one of the same doctors. We wanted to be sure, so we sought a second opinion. I flew her to the clinic in Rochester, Minnesota, in my plane, to Dr. Herb Schmidt. The coincidences were becoming almost too much. Dr. Schmidt was another physician we'd met when Dad's cancer was discovered at the clinic almost 20 years before. And while Mom was unable to come to the Series, Dr. Schmidt and his wife did, and they were our house guests.

Now, only a few days later, we were in his office at the clinic dreading what we might hear and hearing what we dreaded. It was the same as in Dad's case. Dr. Schmidt confirmed the diagnosis.

Mom died two months later, on her 60th birthday.

I was involved in battles on several fronts in 1955, beginning with out efforts to repeat as American League champions. I was meeting and negotiating with the owners of all the teams in the American

League as its player representative, and at home I was trying my hardest to cope with a growing health problem involving my wife—all of this while struggling as hard as I knew how to continue my pitching career.

Allie Reynolds of the Yankees retired at the end of the '54 season after 13 years and 182 wins. That created a vacancy in the position of American League Player Representative, the man who represents his fellow player representatives and all the other players in the league in dealings with the owners on problems and issues. I was the Indians' player representative, and the other representatives elected me to the League position.

It wasn't something I needed. I was comfortable financially and prepared for retirement whenever it came, but there were a lot of other guys not that lucky. We had finally gotten a pension plan pushed through in 1947, over the strong objections of some of the owners and through the efforts of Commissioner Happy Chandler, but it still wasn't worth the paper it was printed on because it was underfunded. The owners were paying lip service to their commitment. Besides, one of their main reasons for agreeing to the pension plan was to keep other players from jumping to the Mexican League.

The minimum salary in those years was only $5,000 a season, and there were a lot of players in the majors making that or only a little bit more. Monthly retirement checks were going to be worse than a disappointment when the player became eligible to receive his pension. They were going to be an insult.

Two of the players who led the effort in the 1940s for a pension plan, Dixie Walker and Johnny Murphy, proved to be visionaries. They insisted that money from the television rights, not just radio, be included in the contributions to the plan. They were looking ahead, just as Commissioner Chandler and Larry MacPhail, one of the Yankees' owners, were in supporting the idea of a pension plan.

The owners had a meeting in Atlanta during my term as the league player representative, while Ford Frick was the Commissioner of Baseball. They wanted to divide up the money from the plan and dissolve it. The minute I got wind of what they were up to, I contacted Joe Reichler, the baseball writer for the Associated Press, and leaked the whole story to him. The news went all over the country the next day.

To the surprise of no one who knew the owners, they suddenly had an attack of morality. Instead of abolishing the plan, they approved something some of us had been demanding—a fairer share of the growing amount of television money—and they tripled the amount of their contributions to the plan.

Professional athletes get a lot of heat from the fans and the media because of their salaries, but when you hear about something like that meeting in Atlanta 35 years ago, you realize the players aren't always the villains in the piece. The journeyman baseball player had only an average income for generations, until television money and free agency brought the good life of today. But until the late 1940s, the average player didn't make much more than anybody else, couldn't change jobs because the "reserve clause" in the standard baseball contract bound him to his team for life unless traded, and didn't even have a pension.

On the other hand, the current players don't want to hear about that history or about the guys back then who made the current advantages possible. Their agents and lawyers tell them, "Don't listen to those old goats. Don't worry about the players who made your good life possible by blazing the trail before you came along."

Men like DiMaggio, Williams, Musial and me are doing fine, but there are a lot of players from the early years of the pension plan who contributed more money than they could spare. Some of them aren't even included in the plan. They are the same players who stood up to management in the days when that involved a risk, just to make sure there would be decent salaries and pensions today.

A lot of those men are being cruelly neglected by the players of today, and the owners as well. It shouldn't be happening, but it is. Today's players could be contributing more money to the pension plan to help the former players, but they don't. Too many of the players of today seem to have the attitude of too many owners of yesterday.

Strikes are another part of contemporary baseball, something no one would have dreamed about until today. They're not always the fault of the players, or the owners either. Instead, they are caused more often by the lack of a body composed equally of players and owners that would have the final say in issues like strikes.

Both groups, players and owners, should form such a body and grant this kind of authority to it. The umpires probably should be represented too. The group would be the final arbitrator and both sides would be compelled by their agreement to abide by the ruling of the body. Even the selection of the baseball commissioner would be by vote of this group, so that the commissioner would be serving everyone—not just the owners who appoint him. Under the present arrangement, since Judge Landis became the first more than 60 years ago, the commissioner is an employee of the owners. That won't work, not when there are three groups involved and the commissioner is beholden to one of them.

This subject concerns me because I was one of the players who established the Major League Baseball Players Association in 1954, never dreaming it would become the powerful force it has.

Stan Musial, Robin Roberts, Ralph Kiner, Eddie Yost and represent-atives from all the other teams got together and formed our own organization, building on the pioneering work done after the war by Johnny Murphy, Allie Reynolds, Dom DiMaggio and others. We held our first two annual meetings in New Orleans and Key West in 1955 and '56. We never intended it to become the organization it has, but there's nothing wrong with that. I'm sure the Players Association has done a lot of good for its members over the years and has been on the right side of many of the issues.

But the Association has gone too far. I don't have anything against the organization, but it has gone beyond the reasonable and has become *un*reasonable. Nothing ever pleases that organization anymore. Its leadership has the players mesmerized into thinking the Association is the last word on everything, the same way many of the agents do. As a result, the players have lost control of their own destiny.

There's nothing wrong with having a Players Association. Nor is there anything wrong with having agents. It's the people involved who make the difference. In the case of the Association, those people are always derogatory and belittling everything that doesn't originate with them. The owners have been the same way, but at least they are willing to agree to something once in a while. But not the Players Association.

That's wrong, and it's not even smart. In labor-management rela-tions, you have to show a willingness to talk, to put things on the table for discussion and negotiation. When an association is obstinate and derogatory, it is not serving the best interests of its members. That's the problem with the Players Association today. Its leaders seem to have replaced the negotiating table with a stone wall.

At home in 1955, the problem was of a far different nature. My wife and I had three sons, but over the years what should have been the perfect family life changed into a living nightmare as Virginia (née Winther), whom I married while I was in the Navy, became addicted to barbiturates and amphetamines, and also developed other serious problems. All of it threw me into a financial and emotional battle that lasted even beyond our divorce in the early 1970s all the way to her death in 1981.

It seemed to start after my 1946 season. Things at home went downhill, and with each passing year that hill became steeper. Her use of drugs became worse, and so, naturally, did her performance around the house and as the mother of our three sons. It became an uninterrrupted torture.

Like the members of other families with these same problems, I concealed the situation from public view as well as I could, but it became an open secret in Cleveland. I provided for my sons to the very best of my ability, and I coped with the additional financial burden caused by all the drugs. They don't give that stuff away, and the people who treat you for it aren't free either. I got her the best help I could find, including several stays for her at the Mayo Clinic and other treatment centers.

I hired a live-in maid to make sure my sons got proper care, especially because I had to be out of town so often. I put money aside in insurance investments every year to make sure I was prepared for future expenses including the education of my sons. When the time came for college, the money was there. I made sure of that, even though my wife's addiction cost me several hundred thousand dollars over the rest of her life, a period of 35 years.

Anyone who has been dealt that hand knows that the emotional burden is even worse than the financial one. In my case, that was doubly so because I came from such an ideal family background. Any kind of problem with alcohol or drugs was simply unheard of in my house when I was growing up. Later, of course, I saw people who drank more than they should—some of my teammates and shipmates—and I saw people with serious problems because of it, starting with Rollie Hemsley.

But I had never experienced the problem in my own family. Now here was my own wife getting hooked. People who do that pose a grave danger not only to themselves but to those around them. I fought hard to prevent that. My parents, especially Dad, had devoted their years to building a bright future for their son, in the same way that all decent, right-thinking parents do. I wasn't going to let anyone, not even my wife, destroy my future or that of my sons, even if she seemed determined to destroy her own.

Professional athletes have to work extra hard in the final years of their careers, and the handwriting on the wall is clear. Many athletes have trouble handling that prospect. Even though you are well prepared in every way for that time, whenever it might come, the end of your playing career is still something you have to deal with. When you have problems at home like the ones I was wrestling with, the burden on you is doubled.

That was my life as the 1955 season began. Even during my peak years, I wasn't always pitching under ideal conditions, especially when the Indians were playing at home, but I never mentioned it publicly. You have to play under all conditions, and my wife's addiction and the multiple problems stemming from it were simply some of the conditions I was performing under, so I went ahead and pitched anyhow.

My wife's amphetamines, which are uppers, and her barbiturates, which are downers, were changing her way of living, including her pattern of sleeping. That had serious ramifications for me as a professional athlete. She became a nocturnal person who couldn't sleep before three or four in the morning. She would fiddle around the house or read in bed with the light on.

I pitched on a lot of Sundays because the Indians liked to use me as a drawing card to attract big Sunday afternoon crowds. Those 50,000 and 60,000 fans cheering me on had no idea that any rest I got the night before came only after I isolated myself in another room. It was not an ideal arrangement for someone who supported his family by earning a living as an athlete.

With that experience, you can imagine my attitude on the drug problem in baseball and in society. Drug use might be a physical condition or a character defect, depending on the individual, but I remember what my father used to tell me—"Show me what a man does when he has nothing to do, and I'll tell you what kind of a man he is."

I'm a hard-liner on the subject. I favor mandatory testing if it is accurate. I can understand somebody making that mistake once, but when you do it a second time, I'd have to give that some thought.

When Peter Ueberroth was commissioner, he made a statement that no realistic person could ever believe. He said baseball had solved its drug problem. That might have been good for PR purposes, but no sane person would ever believe for one minute that any sport, or any other profession in America, has solved its drug or alcohol problems.

There's always some good news to help us through the bad, and one of the bright spots in 1955 was my 12th one-hit game. I beat the Red

Sox, who by now might have been starting to take things personally. Four of my one-hitters were against them. In this one, Sammy White, Boston's catcher, lined a single to center field, a real frozen rope. When your no-hitter vanishes on a ball hit that well, you can't blame it on bad luck.

There was symbolism in our performance that day. My one-hitter came in the first game of a doubleheader in Municipal Stadium. A rookie left-hander, Herb Score, won the second game and struck out 16 Boston hitters in seven innings. Cleveland's pitchers made a lot of news that day.

It was more than just news, though. Score was being touted as "the next Bob Feller," and when he struck out 16 on the same day that I pitched a one-hitter, the significance was obvious to everyone: Just as my career is winding down, the Indians come up with another guy capable of throwing smoke and striking out 16 as a rookie.

Herb was destined for greatness, and everyone knew it. He had all the pitches, a big strong body and the kind of attitude that breeds success. He was, as they say, "coachable." He proved the book on him was right too. He won 16 games as a rookie and was even better the next year, a 20-game winner in only his second season. To add to the excitement about him, he led the league in strikeouts in each of his first two years.

It all ended in a flash in May of 1957, however, on that night when Gil McDougald's line drive struck him in the face. Herb has been one of the Indians' broadcasters since then, but if it hadn't been for that line drive, he wouldn't just be in the broadcast booth. He'd be in Cooperstown, too.

The Yankees recaptured the top spot in the American League in 1955, beating us out by three games. We topped 90 wins again with 93, but the Yanks combined slugging and pitching to win the pennant. Mickey Mantle led the league in homers, Whitey Ford tied Lemon for most wins with 18, and Tommy Byrne's 16–5 record gave him the best winning percentage.

New York's pitchers had the best earned run average to go along with all that Yankee power, but Lopez was still working his magic with the Cleveland pitchers and it showed in their strikeouts and saves. They led the league in both departments.

I say *they* because I didn't really feel a part of things that year or the next. Most of my appearances were in relief by this point. I started 11 games in 1955, but I relieved in 14. In '56, the figures were even more telling. I started only four games and relieved in 15, a total of 19 appearances. That's a far cry from the 35 and 40 appearances I made consistently throughout my career.

When you approach the end of your career as an athlete, inconsistency becomes your enemy. On certain days you can still perform well enough to win—maybe not as well as you did in your prime, but still well enough to win. I proved that in my one-hitter. But the problem is being able to do it on a consistent basis, which I proved in my next game. I started against the A's and lasted only an inning and two-thirds. I gave up five runs on five hits and a walk.

My strikeout total for the whole year in 1955 was 25, which I used to be able to get in two games.

As the end of the road came into sharper focus, I continued to prepare myself for the inevitable and to work as hard as I could for the other players in baseball and those to come behind us. I wanted them to be prepared when their time came to face what was just ahead of me.

As the league's player representative, I worked with the other player representatives and we successfully solidified the pension plan by tying it to a share of the broadcast revenues of the All-Star games and the World Series. I became president of the Major League Baseball Players Association and a member of baseball's pension committee.

I wasn't successful in everything I tried. To help insure the futures of former players, I wanted baseball to establish courses in major universities so players could prepare themselves for retirement. They could develop special skills and advance themselves in preparing for a profession beyond baseball. They could learn even basic things that athletes never experience, like how to look for a job, how to perform in a job interview, how to select an investment adviser, how to do what today we call "networking" in your search for a job after baseball.

Athletes just aren't prepared for some of the things that people in "the real world" have been doing all their lives. Such courses could also be available to professional athletes from other sports. I thought the idea made a lot of sense then, and I still think so.

In 1956, we did it again—finished second behind New York. This time it wasn't quite as hard to take because the margin was bigger— eight games. The message to me was clear now. I pitched only two complete games, both of them at the end of the season, and lost them both. I struck out six Red Sox hitters in the first of those starts, the only time all year I struck out more than two. I didn't win a game. It was time to go.

The prospect of retirement wasn't as hard for me to take as it is for most players because I knew I would still be in baseball. I knew I wasn't going to set anymore strikeout records or pitch any more no-hitters. But I had a contract to promote youth baseball for Motorola. I was endorsing Wheaties and the products of Wilson Sporting Goods, two sponsors who had stayed with me through my entire career and even paid me the whole time I was in the Navy.

I knew I would stay busy in addition to my new insurance business. Motorola, in fact, must have set some sort of a record for keeping someone busy. They had me give away a quarter of a million baseballs in my promotion work for them. Later, Grecian Formula signed me for a series of 16 television commercials.

In the 1960s, a chain of fast foods restaurants in the Midwest called Dogs 'N' Suds signed me to make appearances as they opened their new restaurants. They offered a menu of hot dogs and root beer. They had me appear in my baseball uniform for two hours in one store, leave for the airport with an escort, pilot my plane to the next city and make another appearance—all in the same day and all while wearing my baseball uniform, even while I was in the cockpit.

I even had a brief career in broadcasting during the '50s. I was one of the announcers on the Game of the Day on radio in 1957 with John MacLean and Gene Elston. I had a radio show in Cleveland with Pete Franklin, and I was a cable TV announcer in Cleveland.

In 1971, I returned to a combat zone. I headed a group of baseball players including Chuck Dobson, Joe Schultz and Jim Nash who toured Vietnam at the request of the commissioner's office and the USO. We visited the fire bases and the pacification centers, traveled in Huey helicopters, went all over the Mekong Delta and spent our nights in tents listening to the gunfire from the Viet Cong in the jungle next to us.

For over a month, we visited the GIs at their combat posts, talked baseball and cheered them up every way we could. We couldn't grab a gun and help them fight, but at least we could keep them company.

It was almost as if I were barnstorming again. I was also picking up a whole new supply of travel horror stories to go with the rest of my collection. Like the time my luggage was sent to Alaska instead of Cleveland, for reasons still known only to the baggage clerk.

Then there was the time at LaGuardia Airport in New York when the pilot hit the brakes too hard and heated up the area around the wheels. Two tires went flat. After what seemed to be a longer time than necessary, I asked the flight attendant how much longer we'd be.

"Oh, we're almost ready, Mr. Feller," she said. "They're putting the hub caps on now." Either she really thought that airplanes have hub caps, or she felt I was dumb enough to believe her.

But we didn't leave as soon as she expected after all. She made one final check of the cabin door before takeoff, just to make sure it was locked. Only she turned the handle the wrong way. The evacuation chute shot out onto the pavement, and we lost another hour.

We sat on the ground in Denver for an hour once because they needed a new liquor cart—at seven o'clock in the morning. There was a wheel missing from the one we had. Really. I told the attendant, "Look, I'll buy a drink for anyone on board as soon as we get to Salt Lake City." It didn't do any good.

I encountered the most original explanation for sending luggage to the wrong city. I was flying to San Francisco from Chicago, but my luggage was flown to Cleveland.

The clerk's explanation to his superior: "I thought he was going home, and I knew he lived in Cleveland."

A big part of the pain of retirement is the depression that comes from knowing you won't be in baseball any more, but I was still in it. I was doing all this traveling as a representative for my sponsors, but I felt that in an informal way I was also serving as one of baseball's goodwill ambassadors. Helping to promote my sport is something I've always done with enthusiasm because of my belief that it's the best of all sports.

In many cases, retirement is harder on a player's wife than it is on him. He's hanging around the house getting in her way, he's not bringing in the big bucks anymore and he's not getting any of those perks that go with being a professional athlete.

This is going to get a lot worse now with all the fat salaries. You're not retiring from a job paying $35,000 these days. You're losing out on 10 or 20 times that much. When you're an average major league player today, you're making half a million dollars a year, so you're going to delay retirement as long as you can. More players are going to try to hang on forever because they're making so much money.

A half-million bucks a year for the average player is hard to turn your back on, and sometimes it's harder for the wife. With today's salaries there won't be as many graceful retirements.

The natural marriage between baseball and me survived and flourished after I retired as a player and has endured to this day. I still make appearances, receive an average of 25 letters a day and fly well over 100,000 miles a year. In addition to earning a living that way, I manage to stay busy and contribute something to the community by donating my time as the state chairman for the Ohio March of Dimes, a position I've held since the beginning of the 1960s. I served in the Easter Seals campaign and the USO, and I served on the President's Physical Fitness Council during all President Reagan's eight years in office. I try to help the fund-raising efforts of the Boys Clubs of America by making free appearances at four or five of their shows in major markets every year because of my lifelong interest in working with young people.

There have been two memorable moments in this happy life of a baseball ambassador, two special days. One was when I was inducted into the Baseball Hall of Fame. The other was when I married Anne.

The dreams of a farm boy from Iowa came true in 1962 when I was inducted into Cooperstown with Jackie Robinson, Bill McKechnie and Edd Roush, the great outfielder for the Cincinnati Reds and other teams who hit .323 in 18 years in the major leagues.

I was pleased to be up there on the platform with Jackie as Commissioner Bowie Kuhn presided at the ceremonies. I've always been proud of what the black players have said in thanking me for the exposure my barnstorming trips gave them as they were trying to break baseball's color barrier. It was extra meaningful for me to know that I was being inducted into the Hall of Fame with major league baseball's first black player. We were the first two players voted into the Hall in their first year of eligibility since it opened in 1939.

The day was cloudy and threatening, and the fans were keeping their fingers crossed that the afternoon's annual exhibition, this one between the Braves and the Yankees, could be played. Five thousand of them stood on the lawn in front of the Hall for the ceremonies.

I thanked Commissioner Kuhn for the honor, but I pointed out that the plaque, which always lists a player's achievements, was incomplete in my case. It didn't mention that I set the American League record for allowing the most walks in a season—208.

I made sure to thank those who helped me so much—Mom and Dad,

Cy Slapnicka, Steve O'Neill, my teammates and the good people of Cleveland. I paid tribute to those former players who have gone out of their way to pay something back to their communities for the many good things the people in those cities have made possible for them. I've always placed emphasis on giving something back, and I feel so strongly about it that I made sure to mention the subject in my remarks.

I was flattered, and that's putting it mildly, to be enshrined in Cooperstown. There I was, with the greats I worshiped as a kid—Ruth, Gehrig, Hornsby and the rest.

The biggest compliment was to be included with the greatest pitcher of all time in my book—Walter Johnson. He ranks above all the other pitching immortals. In my personal list of the next ten greatest, I would include Grover Cleveland Alexander, Christy Mathewson, Cy Young, Warren Spahn, Lefty Grove, Ted Lyons, Early Wynn, Steve Carlton, Gaylord Perry and Tom Seaver.

There are outstanding pitchers today who may be candidates some day, including my rankings of today's top five—Roger Clemens, Dwight Gooden, Ted Higuera, Frank Viola and Orel Hershiser, in that order. That's how I rate them based on their wins, the teams they play for, complete games, earned run averages and other stats.

Johnson, however, was so great he almost belongs in his own Hall of Fame. Here was a man who spent his entire 21-year career with the Washington Senators. They won two pennants late in his career, but in many seasons they were a seventh or eighth place ball club. He threw his fast ball sidearm and still won 416 games, second only to Cy Young's 511. He was a 30-game winner twice and a 20-game winner in ten other seasons. He led the American League in strikeouts 12 times, had a career average of 2.17 earned runs for every nine innings pitched and had an ERA of 1.89 or lower 11 times.

Now you know why I felt flattered to be in that kind of company. This year, 1990, they are placing a statue of me in full delivery at Cleveland Stadium. This makes me very grateful to the baseball and sports fans not only of Cleveland but of all America.

The Hall of Fame ceremonies were colorful, as they always are with the red, white and blue atmosphere and the beauty of upstate New York, where Washington Irving and James Fenimore Cooper wrote the novels that fascinated me back at Van Meter High.

The good luck that I've been blessed with all through my baseball career held up that day too. The ceremonies were in the morning. In the afternoon, the game was rained out.

As happy as that day was, the day I married the former Anne Gilliland from Ansonia, Connecticut—October 1, 1974—was even more special. It was made possible because of one of the easiest decisions associated with my retirement as a player—choosing to live in Cleveland permanently.

Nobody loves his roots more than I love Iowa, but over the years, Cleveland became by hometown instead of Van Meter. I've always enjoyed the change of seasons in Ohio and the environment of the Great Lakes region, and there is no nicer community on the face of the earth than Gates Mills, where Anne and I were neighbors and members of the same church, St. Christopher's By-The-River.

The basic reason for my decision to stay in Cleveland was—and is— the people there. They've been great to me for 50 years. You can't improve on that, so why move? They've always been honest and aboveboard with me. They were always the strongest supporters you could ask for, and when they were critical of me about something, I probably deserved it. Over the years, I've grown to feel as close to the people of Cleveland as I do to the people of Iowa.

I met Anne through our attendance at St. Christopher's and I was won over by more than her good looks, intelligence and bright personality. I was also attracted by her honesty: She told me she had never seen a major league baseball game.

Meeting her couldn't have come at a better time. I was continuing to pay a heavy price for my first wife's expensive and damaging habits over the years, even though we were divorced when I met Anne.

In the last 15 years of my marriage to Virginia, the first 15 years of my retirement as a player, things continued to career downhill. I was spending so much time and money on her that I lost the insurance business which I started with two partners in 1954. I was still a player then, and the decision to form that partnership was one that I made with happiness and pride. I understood the insurance business and was confident of my ability to succeed, especially with the help of two competent partners, and I was proud of my foresight in taking this action while I was still a player, preparing myself so well for my years after retirement from my pitching career.

But it all went down the drain. My problems came in bottles—those containing my wife's pills. One experience that remains vivid in my memory to this day occurred in 1964 when I had to go to the Olympics in Japan. We lived in Gates Mills and had a lovely house. I remember all too well having to hide my wife's various medicines in different spots around our property just before I left so she wouldn't be able to overdose on them while I was gone.

I called home every few days to tell her where she would find her next doses. It was a real-life version of that scene in *Lost Weekend* when Ray Milland finds the bottle of liquor that had been hidden from him in the chandelier.

That happened only eight years after my retirement from the Indians, and things continued to get worse for seven more years. I was picking up every job I could, and all of them put together weren't enough. Another equally vivid—and equally painful—memory was the time when I had to sell baseball memorabilia and fast. I needed the money in a hurry to pay more bills caused by Virginia's addiction.

I was sorry that she never chose to continue her recovery after coming out of the various treatment programs that I obtained for her. Rollie Hemsley had shown it could be done, and she knew Rollie, but she never stayed with it the way Rollie and others have.

Things continued to unravel for her, and by the time of our divorce, they were starting to unravel for me too. My income never was enough to feed her habit and cover the sizeable expenses of providing for a family of five including three young men—Steve, Marty and Bruce—who needed to be clothed, fed and educated.

That, of course, doesn't even get to the question of making sure my sons were having a good time while they were growing up. I worked on that side of the problem too, and was able to draw on my baseball experience to help put some fun in their lives.

I helped to start the Little League program in Gates Mills and worked with the village fathers in building a field and equipping it the right way, especially with a good backstop. I coached all three of my sons. I made sure to emphasize the right priorities in coaching kids. Fun comes first. If it isn't fun for the kids—and even for yourself— you're a failure as a coach. Second is instruction. You're there to teach. Third is improvement. If the kids aren't getting better, you're not doing your job. Fourth is the chance to win. If you win, fine, but if you don't, that should be fine too at the Little League level.

With all the fun and learning and improving, we still managed to win our share of games, and one of our teams won the Cleveland championship. Obviously the kids learned and improved too, beause two of my sons became good enough that they played baseball for their college teams.

As my wife's addiction worsened, so did the family financial condition. By the time we were divorced, I was deep into my investments, which I thought would last me the rest of my life. But all of those resources in the family nest egg were flying out the window at an alarming speed.

My financial situation became public knowledge so I won't duck the subject here. It was a fact of my life every bit as much as my stikeouts and no-hitters were earlier. If this is to be the Bob Feller story, I have to deal with this chapter of my life again, just as I did when it happened.

There were stories about my problems in the newspapers, but I am happy to say that I eventually paid off all my debts. In the first year or two after our divorce, I didn't know how much longer I could hold out. It didn't even help when we sold the house after the divorce. Virginia and my sons got all the money.

In the middle of all this, Allen Lowe extended the kind of help you get from a good friend. Allen was the manager of the Sheraton Cleveland Hotel, and we had been friends since I came to Cleveland in 1936 and stayed at the Carter Hotel, where he was a bellman.

Allen helped me to get the job of Sports Sales Director of the Sheraton chain, bringing as much sports business to Sheraton hotels as I could. I was responsible for going out and booking large sports events such as the semi-annual meetings of the Major League owners, the annual meetings of the NCAA and sports alumni groups and the road business of football, basketball and baseball teams and leagues.

I stayed in the job for three years, and later held the same position with the Hilton organization, and the money from those two jobs, all of it made possible by Allen's hand of friendship, was a lifesaver for me. Not only that, I got to live at the hotel free, which relieved me of that major expense at a time when my salary was only slightly more than minimal.

Then I met Anne. I assured her I wouldn't hold it against her that she had never seen a mjaor league game. Despite that obvious cultural gap in her life, or maybe because of it, we were married at the Old Stone Church on Public Square in Cleveland in 1974. In addition to having a wonderful wife, I was also able to enjoy the company of Anne's two fine young children, John Morris and Rachel, to whom I've grown close in the years since.

Since then we've built a roomy and comfortable brick and wood home that would fit right into Anne's native Connecticut as well as it fits into its Ohio landscape. We even have four tractors in a barn. Collecting tractors has always been a hobby of mine. I have two that were made in 1929 and one in 1930, plus models and toy crawler tractors of every size and description from Anne. She has always tolerated this hobby of her ex-farm boy and cheerfully adds to my collection on every occasion, and even when there's no occasion.

As for hobbies, Anne has more than one—needlepoint, cross-stitch and creating a Victorian atmosphere by recovering and restoring antique furniture. She stays active in the alumni activities of the University of Connecticut, where she went to college, and even offered to help to correct what she considered a serious problem. We went back for a football game at UConn and saw that the Husky dog, the school's traditional mascot, had been replaced by a student wearing one of those Halloween outfits that are supposed to make the student look like the mascot who's been replaced.

When we got back to Cleveland, Anne sent the school a check to help them buy a real Husky.

I thought the reward for my decision to stay in Cleveland would be continuing to feel the happiness I've always felt there, so when I met Anne it was a bonus. I've had some experiences with bonuses because I was one of the first players to get them included in my contracts, so I know a bonus when I see one. Believe me, meeting Anne was the greatest bonus I ever received.

After we were married, Anne immediately became my partner on my baseball odyssey. One of our most memorable trips was to Japan in 1977, where I was a coach with the Tokyo Yomiuri Giants. We spent three months there while I worked with their pitchers. Not only did Anne and I get to enjoy the country and its people, but we were in the Giants' Stadium on Opening Day when Sadaharu Oh passed Babe Ruth on the all-time home run list by hitting his 715th homer.

The moment was doubly significant for me. I was watching a man break the record of one of the heroes of my youth, and the man doing it was a citizen of the nation we had fought against 25 years before. It was a nice sort of irony for me.

I was always sorry to see anybody break any of Ruth's home run records, whether it was Oh, Hank Aaron or Roger Maris. I loved the Babe as a kid, just as every American boy did. He was a lovable guy, a national hero, an immortal athlete and a superb showman.

You get an idea of his greatness when you look at the *Baseball Encyclopedia* and see that Aaron, who hit 755 home runs—41 more than Ruth—had almost 4,000 more times at bat. Ruth is the all-time leader in home run percentage—the number of home runs per 100 times at bat. Ruth hit 8.5 homers every 100 times up. Aaron hit only 6.5 and is in 12th place on the all-time list. In other words, if Ruth had come to bat as many times as Hank did, he would have hit 1,054 home runs.

The same applies in comparing the single season record set by Ruth in 1927 and broken by Roger Maris in 1961. Babe had 540 times at bat in '27, but Maris, in the first year of the 162-game schedule instead of the traditional 154 games, came to bat 590 times. Using Ruth's 8.5 homers per 100 times at bat, if he'd had those 50 extra times up that Maris did in '61, the Babe would have hit three more homers in 1927 and his record would have been 63 homers instead of 60—and it would still be the record today.

A major part of our odyssey was my annual summer tour of minor league cities. From early in my retirement through the 1989 season, I spent ten weeks every summer making personal appearances all over the country, pitching several innings in each town and appearing on the local radio and TV talk shows and newscasts to promote the event.

I pitch to the local celebrities—either a few players from each of the two teams, politicians, other community leaders or people from the news media. I've appeared in cities of every size and description, in every part of America—big cities like Denver, New Orleans and Phoenix and ones with names like Watertown and Medicine Hat.

I've cut back somewhat on my minor league tour since turning 71, but I still do enough of it to keep me busy playing basball, especially with the Old Timers Games that every major league team puts on each summer. Anne still threatens to write a book of her own called *Laundromats I Have Known and Loved*. She says one of the episodes in it will tell about the time in Glens Falls, New York, when a woman in a laundromat promised her, "We're going to put a sign on machine number five over there saying, 'Bob Feller's baseball shirt was washed here.'"

She can also write about the time in Butte, Montana, where we stayed at the Last Chance Gulch Motel. There wasn't a working clothes dryer available that day, but the clubhouse boy at the ballpark where I was pitching told Anne not to worry—he'd get her clothes dried.

Early in the ball game, while I was giving my pitching exhibition, Anne glanced out toward left field and here was the clubhouse boy draping a load of wash over the fence down the line. She thought that was a bit tacky. Then, to her chagrin, she recognized some of the items hanging over the fence—her nightgown, our underwear and other items in the unmentionable category.

Before she could tell the clubhouse boy about her embarrassment, he called up to her from the field. He knew we had to leave right after the game for our next stop so he hollered out, "Don't worry, Mrs. Feller—they'll all be dry by the top of the ninth."

We made our trip across America for ten weeks every summer. The kids who came out in the early years of my trips were bringing their own kids by the time of my summer campaign in 1989. In some cases the original kids were even bringing grandchildren. The fans would remind each other how many times I'd come to town, and they always asked Anne and me to promise to come back next year.

Thanks to my minor league tour, some trading card shows, Old Timers games and my coaching with the Indians, at the suggestion of Gabe Paul, things eventually returned to a normal, happy life. I became the director of the Indians' speakers bureau, and at the beginnning of the 1980s, I started serving as one of the team's pitching coaches every year in spring training at their camp in Tucson, Arizona. Along the way, things improved enough that Anne was able to quit the job she got early in our marriage, training tellers in a bank. Her income was the difference sometimes in those early days between making it and not making it.

Remaining associated with the Indians in those two capacities did more than just help us financially. It also kept me working in baseball, not just as a former player making appearances, but as a member of the team's front office staff and as a coach on the field during spring training. That has always meant a great deal to me, because regardless of what else I might be doing, I am a baseball man first, last and always, and baseball is where I want to be.

Through continued involvement with my sport over the years, I have found that the people in baseball haven't really changed but the sport has. Baseball is changing in many of the same ways that all sports are, and for the same basic reason. The economic impact of television is continuing to affect all of our professional sports in ways we never imagined, and that's not going to stop. Every baseball team now gets huge sums from network television revenue, and under the new contracts with the commercial networks and the ESPN cable network, each team will receive $14 million a year just in TV money.

Television money will continue to produce changes in our sport, just as it always has. I think the number of teams will be expanded from today's 26 to 32. The number of leagues will grow from the traditional two, the American and National Leagues, to four and be realigned with eight teams in each, a throwback to the original arrangement when each league had eight.

The schedule might get even longer. Playoffs at the end of the season were begun in 1969, to determine the pennant winners, as if playing 162 games doesn't do that. They were started because playoff games meant more nights for television and thus more money from the networks. The length of the playoff series was increased from the best of five games to the best of seven, to get more TV money. So don't rule out the possibility that the baseball season will get even longer. There might even be inter-league play, something long overdue, to create new regional rivalries.

Fifty years from now, and maybe sooner, every team in football and baseball will play in a domed stadium with a moveable or retractable roof like the ones in Toronto and Montreal. Some people say "Never!" I say it's inevitable. It's what the owners want, and their money from television will make domed stadiums affordable housing.

Even though the changes that have taken place and the ones to come make baseball far different than when I was a kid or when I was playing, I still want to be a part of it. Domed stadiums and cable TV and artificial turf may make the game different in some ways, but it's still baseball, the greatest sport in the world.

In the late 1960s, when the world seemed upside-down about so many things, there was a lot of talk about baseball losing its appeal to the American people, that football had replaced it as the national pastime. Well, here we are, 20 years later, and baseball is more popular than ever.

Every year seems to bring a new attendance record for major league baseball, and many teams keep setting their own records. Baseball has just signed a four-year television package totalling $1.47 billion. the average salary or major league players is close to $500,000 a year.

That doesn't sound like a dying sport to me. On the contrary, baseball is booming in popularity, and it manages to put on its best shows when it counts the most—in its league playoffs and the World

Series. The Dodgers' upset victory over the A's in the 1988 World Series, including the heroics by Orel Hershiser and Kirk Gibson, and the dramatic show put on by the Mets and Red Sox in 1986, were some of the best primetime mini-series ever on—not to mention some of the earlier smash hits like the 1976 Series between the Red Sox and the Reds when Carlton Fisk hit his dramatic home run around the foul pole, Reggie Jackson's home run display in 1977, or Tug McGraw jabbing his fist into the air for the Phillies in 1980 and telling the world, "Ya gotta believe!"

In addition to its popularity as part of the American fabric for 150 years, baseball is the truest test of excellence. You have to be the best every day, not just on Sundays. You have to be successful over 162 games, not just 16 like pro football or 82 like pro basketball. And baseball doesn't penalize success and reward failure by giving the championship teams a harder schedule than anyone else the next year, with the losing teams getting an easier shedule, all to keep the TV ratings up. In baseball, everybody plays everybody else in the league, and the same number of times, at home and away.

Football at times has out-marketed baseball, and that was much of the explanation for that talk in the late '60s. But sports will survive or not on their own merits, and both football and baseball have plenty of those, and professional hockey and basketball too.

Baseball, however, remains the one professional sport that makes you meet the sternest tests of excellence with its day-in, day-out challenge to win consistently, and with the fewest number of teams making its playoffs. No wild cards allowed, especially since those "wild card" teams in the NFL playoffs look more like jokers. And none of this business of making almost every team in your sport eligible for the playoffs, like basketball or hockey.

As one subtle marketing technique, pro football always makes sure to include the number in the title of the Super Bowl—using Roman numerals no less, and the media people fall for it. The 1990 NFL championship game was Super Bowl XXIV. That's clever, giving the appearance of a long-established sports event cloaked in ivy, when in fact it's one of the youngest. If baseball felt compelled to do that, this year we'd be playing World Series LXXXVII, continuing an American tradition that began right after the turn of the century, 64 years before "Super Bowl I."

Another reason that baseball is the favorite sport of millions of fans in the United States and even internationally in Canada, the Orient,

Central and South America, Europe and now Russia—and will become a Gold Medal event in the 1992 Summer Olympics—is that it's much like life itself.

Every day is a new opportunity. You can build on yesterday's success or put its failures behind and start all over again. You get to wash the slate clean and start all over again. That's the way life is, with a new game every day, and that's the way baseball is.

I remember the newsreels of Babe Ruth in 1947 when he made his next-to-last appearance at Yankee Stadium. Happy Chandler, the new commissioner, declared Sunday, April 27, "Babe Ruth Day" throughout the major leagues, and they held ceremonies saluting the Babe in every ballpark in both leagues.

Ruth stood at home plate in the camel's hair overcoat and cap that he always wore. His voice was so far gone from the cancer that he could barely whisper a croaky few words to the 60,000 fans.

As painful as it was for him to speak, he used some of the precious few words available to him to talk about the game of baseball. He said it simply but beautifully:

"The only real game in the world, I think, is baseball."

I guess most people look forward to retirement by the time they reach their 70s, but not me. Cutting back on my minor league summer tour is about as far as I'm willing to go in giving in to the passing years. I'm going to keep on pitching in the Old Timers games, appearing at card shows, working with the Indians' pitchers in spring training, and participating in charity events for just as long as the Good Lord lets me.

I got into baseball because I loved it. I still do, so why get out? My Dad told me once, "Pitching baseball is like pitching hay. You just have to stay with it." He said he hoped I would stay in baseball a long time.

I have. Dad would understand. So would the Babe.

Index